CROCK·POT®

·THE ORIGINAL SLOW COOKER·

RECIPE COLLECTION

Publications International, Ltd.

Pictured on the front cover *(clockwise from top left):* Spanish Chicken with Rice *(page 91),* Cherry Delight *(page 310),* Fall-off-the-Bone BBQ Ribs *(page 222),* Cod Fish Stew *(page 149)* and Cajun Pork Sausage and Shrimp Stew *(page 125).*

Pictured on the back cover *(clockwise from top left):* Fresh Berry Compote *(page 10),* Jamaican Quinoa and Sweet Potato Stew *(page 165),* Triple Chocolate Fantasy *(page 290),* Barley and Vegetable Risotto *(page 230),* Basque Chicken with Peppers *(page 88),* Viennese Coffee *(page 31)* and Meatball Grinder *(page 265).*

ISBN: 978-1-68022-916-5

Library of Congress Control Number: 2017936728

Manufactured in China.

8 7 6 5 4 3 2 1

Table of Contents

Slow Cooking 101

Sizes of CROCK-POT® Slow Cookers

Smaller **CROCK-POT®** slow cookers—such as 1- to 3-quart models—are the perfect size for cooking for singles, a couple or empty nesters (and also for serving dips).

While medium-size **CROCK-POT®** slow cookers (those holding somewhere between 3 quarts and 5 quarts) will easily cook enough food at a time to feed a small family. They are also convenient for holiday side dishes or appetizers.

Large **CROCK-POT®** slow cookers are great for large family dinners, holiday entertaining and potluck suppers. A 6- to 7-quart model is ideal if you like to make meals in advance, or have dinner tonight and store leftovers for another day.

Types of CROCK-POT® Slow Cookers

Current **CROCK-POT®** slow cookers come equipped with many different features and benefits, from auto cook programs to oven-safe stoneware to timed programming. Please visit **WWW.CROCK-POT.COM** to find the **CROCK-POT®** slow cooker that best suits your needs.

How you plan to use a **CROCK-POT®** slow cooker may affect the model you choose to purchase. For everyday cooking, choose a size large enough to serve your family. If you plan to use the **CROCK-POT®** slow cooker primarily for entertaining, choose one of the larger sizes. Basic **CROCK-POT®** slow cookers can hold as little as 16 ounces or as much as 7 quarts. The smallest sizes are great for keeping dips warm on a buffet, while the larger sizes can more readily fit large quantities of food and larger roasts.

Cooking, Stirring and Food Safety

CROCK-POT® slow cookers are safe to leave unattended. The outer heating base may get hot as it cooks, but it should not pose a fire hazard. The heating element in the heating base functions at a low wattage and is safe for your countertops.

Your **CROCK-POT**® slow cooker should be filled about one-half to three-fourths full for most recipes unless otherwise instructed. Lean meats such as chicken or pork tenderloin will cook faster than meats with more connective tissue and fat such as beef chuck or pork shoulder. Bone-in meats will take longer than boneless cuts. Typical **CROCK-POT**® slow cooker dishes take approximately 7 to 8 hours to reach the simmer point on LOW and about 3 to 4 hours on HIGH. Once the vegetables and meat start to simmer and braise, their flavors will fully blend and meat will become fall-off-the-bone tender.

According to the U.S. Department of Agriculture, all bacteria are killed at a temperature of 165°F. It's important to follow the recommended cooking times and not to open the lid often, especially early in the cooking process when heat is building up inside the unit. If you need to open the lid to check on your food or are adding additional ingredients, remember to allow additional cooking time if necessary to ensure food is cooked through and tender.

Large **CROCK-POT**® slow cookers, the 6- to 7-quart sizes, may benefit from a quick stir halfway through cook time to help distribute heat and promote even cooking. It's usually unnecessary to stir at all, as even ½ cup liquid will help to distribute heat and the stoneware is the perfect medium for holding food at an even temperature throughout the cooking process.

Oven-Safe Stoneware

All **CROCK-POT**® slow cooker removable stoneware inserts may (without their lids) be used safely in ovens at up to 400°F. In addition, all **CROCK-POT**® slow cookers are microwavable without their lids. If you own another slow cooker brand, please refer to your owner's manual for specific stoneware cooking medium tolerances.

Frozen Food

Frozen food can be successfully cooked in a **CROCK-POT**® slow cooker. However, it will require longer cooking time than the same recipe made with fresh food. It's almost always preferable to thaw frozen food prior to placing it in the **CROCK-POT**® slow cooker. Using an instant-read thermometer is recommended to ensure meat is fully cooked through.

Pasta and Rice

If you are converting a recipe for a **CROCK-POT**® slow cooker that calls for uncooked pasta, first cook the pasta on the stovetop just until slightly tender. Then add the pasta to the **CROCK-POT®** slow cooker. If you are converting a recipe for the **CROCK-POT®** slow cooker that calls for cooked rice, stir in raw rice with the other recipe ingredients plus ¼ cup extra liquid per ¼ cup of raw rice.

Beans

Beans must be softened completely before combining with sugar and/or acidic foods in the **CROCK-POT®** slow cooker. Sugar and acid have a hardening effect on beans and will prevent softening. Fully cooked canned beans may be used as a substitute for dried beans.

Vegetables

Root vegetables often cook more slowly than meat. Cut vegetables accordingly to cook at the same rate as meat—large or small or lean versus marbled—and place near the sides or bottom of the stoneware to facilitate cooking.

Herbs

Fresh herbs add flavor and color when added at the end of the cooking cycle; if added at the beginning, many fresh herbs' flavor will dissipate over long cook times. Ground and/or dried herbs and spices work well in slow cooking and may be added at the beginning of cook time. For dishes with shorter cook times, hearty fresh herbs such as rosemary and thyme hold up well. The flavor power of all herbs and spices can vary greatly depending on their particular strength and shelf life. Use chili powders and garlic powder sparingly, as these can sometimes intensify over the long cook times. Always taste the finished dish and correct seasonings including salt and pepper.

Thickeners

It's not necessary to use more than ½ to 1 cup liquid in most instances since juices in meats and vegetables are retained more in slow cooking than in conventional cooking. Excess liquid can be cooked down and concentrated after slow cooking on the stovetop or by removing meat and vegetables from stoneware, stirring in one of the following thickeners and setting the **CROCK-POT®** slow cooker to HIGH. Cover; cook on HIGH for approximately 15 minutes or until juices are thickened.

FLOUR: All-purpose flour is often used to thicken soups or stews. Stir cold water into the flour in a small bowl until smooth. With the **CROCK-POT®** slow cooker on HIGH, whisk the flour mixture into the liquid in the **CROCK-POT®** slow cooker. Cover; cook on HIGH 15 minutes or until the mixture is thickened.

CORNSTARCH: Cornstarch gives sauces a clear, shiny appearance; it's used most often for sweet dessert sauces and stir-fry sauces. Stir cold water into the cornstarch in a small bowl until the cornstarch dissolves. Quickly stir this mixture into the liquid in the **CROCK-POT®** slow cooker; the sauce will thicken as soon as the liquid simmers. Cornstarch breaks down with too much heat, so never add it at the beginning of the slow cooking process and turn off the heat as soon as the sauce thickens.

ARROWROOT: Arrowroot (or arrowroot flour) comes from the root of a tropical plant that is dried and ground to a powder; it produces a thick, clear sauce. Those who are allergic to wheat often use it in place of flour. Place arrowroot in a small bowl or cup and stir in cold water until the mixture is smooth. Quickly stir this mixture into the liquid in the **CROCK-POT®** slow cooker. Arrowroot thickens below the boiling point, so it even works well in a **CROCK-POT®** slow cooker on LOW. Too much stirring can break down an arrowroot mixture.

TAPIOCA: Tapioca is a starchy substance extracted from the root of the cassava plant. Its greatest advantage is that it withstands long cooking, making it an ideal choice for slow cooking. Add it at the beginning of cooking and you'll get a clear, thickened sauce in the finished dish. Dishes using tapioca as a thickener are best cooked on the LOW setting; tapioca may become stringy when boiled for a long time.

Dairy

Milk, cream and sour cream break down during extended cooking. When possible, add them during the last 15 to 30 minutes of slow cooking, until just heated through. Condensed soups may be substituted for milk and may cook for extended times.

Fish

Fish is delicate and should be stirred into the **CROCK-POT®** slow cooker gently during the last 15 to 30 minutes of cooking time. Cover; cook just until cooked through and serve immediately.

Baked Goods

If you wish to prepare bread, cakes or pudding cakes in a **CROCK-POT®** slow cooker, you may want to purchase a covered, vented metal cake pan accessory for your **CROCK-POT®** slow cooker. You can also use any straight-sided soufflé dish or deep cake pan that will fit into the stoneware of your unit. Baked goods can be prepared directly in the stoneware; however, they can be a little difficult to remove from the insert, so follow the recipe directions carefully.

BREAKFAST & BRUNCH

Orange Cranberry Nut Bread

2 cups all-purpose flour	2 teaspoons dried orange peel
½ cup chopped pecans	⅔ cup boiling water
1 teaspoon baking powder	¾ cup sugar
½ teaspoon baking soda	1 egg, lightly beaten
¼ teaspoon salt	2 tablespoons shortening
1 cup dried cranberries	1 teaspoon vanilla

1. Coat inside of 3-quart **CROCK-POT**® slow cooker with nonstick cooking spray. Combine flour, pecans, baking powder, baking soda and salt in medium bowl.

2. Combine cranberries and orange peel in separate medium bowl; stir in boiling water. Add sugar, egg, shortening and vanilla; stir just until blended. Add flour mixture; stir just until blended.

3. Pour batter into **CROCK-POT**® slow cooker. Cover; cook on HIGH 1 ¼ to 1 ½ hours or until edges begin to brown and toothpick inserted into center comes out clean.

4. Remove stoneware insert from **CROCK-POT**® slow cooker. Cool on wire rack 10 minutes. Remove bread from insert; cool completely on rack.

Makes 1 loaf

Tip: This recipe works best in round **CROCK-POT**® slow cookers.

Note: Not all **CROCK-POT**® slow cookers have removable stoneware. For those that don't, use a prepared casserole, soufflé dish or other high-sided baking dish that fits in the **CROCK-POT**® slow cooker.

Fresh Berry Compote

2 cups fresh blueberries

4 cups fresh sliced strawberries

2 tablespoons orange juice

½ to ¾ cup sugar

4 slices (½ × 1 ½ inches) lemon peel with no white pith

1 whole cinnamon stick *or* ½ teaspoon ground cinnamon

1. Place blueberries in **CROCK-POT**® slow cooker. Cover; cook on HIGH 45 minutes or until blueberries begin to soften.

2. Add strawberries, orange juice, ½ cup sugar, lemon peel and cinnamon stick; stir to blend. Cover; cook on HIGH 1 to 1 ½ hours or until strawberries soften and sugar dissolves. Check for sweetness and add more sugar if necessary, cooking until added sugar dissolves.

3. Remove insert from **CROCK-POT**® slow cooker to heatproof surface and let cool. Serve compote warm or chilled.

Makes 4 servings

Tip: To turn this compote into a fresh fruit topping for cake, ice cream, waffles or pancakes, carefully spoon out fruit, leaving cooking liquid in **CROCK-POT**® slow cooker. Stir ¼ cup cold water into 1 to 2 tablespoons cornstarch in small bowl until smooth; whisk into cooking liquid. Cover; cook on HIGH 10 to 15 minutes or until thickened. Return fruit to sauce; stir to blend.

Oatmeal Crème Brûlée

4 cups boiling water

3 cups quick-cooking oatmeal

½ teaspoon salt

6 egg yolks

½ cup granulated sugar

2 cups whipping cream

1 teaspoon vanilla

¼ cup packed light brown sugar

Fresh berries (optional)

1. Coat inside of **CROCK-POT**® slow cooker with nonstick cooking spray. Pour boiling water into **CROCK-POT**® slow cooker. Stir in oatmeal and salt; cover.

2. Combine egg yolks and granulated sugar in medium bowl; mix well. Heat cream and vanilla in medium saucepan over medium heat until small bubbles begin to form at edge of pan. *Do not boil.* Remove from heat. Whisking constantly, pour ½ cup hot cream into egg yolk mixture in thin stream. Whisk egg mixture back into cream in saucepan, stirring rapidly to blend well. Spoon mixture over oatmeal. *Do not stir.*

3. Turn **CROCK-POT**® slow cooker to LOW. Line lid with two paper towels. Cover; cook on LOW 3 to 3½ hours or until custard is set.

4. Sprinkle brown sugar over surface of custard. Line lid with two clean dry paper towels. Cover; cook on LOW 10 to 15 minutes or until brown sugar melts. Serve with fresh berries, if desired.

Makes 4 to 6 servings

Wake-Up Potato and Sausage Breakfast Casserole

1 pound kielbasa or smoked sausage, diced

1 cup chopped onion

1 cup chopped red bell pepper

1 package (20 ounces) refrigerated Southwestern-style hash browns*

10 eggs

1 cup milk

1 cup (4 ounces) shredded Monterey Jack or sharp Cheddar cheese

*You may substitute O'Brien potatoes and add ½ teaspoon chile pepper.

1. Coat inside of **CROCK-POT®** slow cooker with nonstick cooking spray. Heat large skillet over medium-high heat. Add sausage and onion; cook and stir until sausage is browned. Drain fat. Stir in bell pepper.

2. Place one third of potatoes in **CROCK-POT®** slow cooker. Top with half of sausage mixture. Repeat layers. Spread remaining one third of potatoes evenly on top.

3. Whisk eggs and milk in medium bowl. Pour evenly over potatoes. Cover; cook on LOW 6 to 7 hours.

4. Turn off heat. Sprinkle cheese over casserole; let stand 10 minutes or until cheese is melted.

Makes 8 servings

Tip: To remove casserole from **CROCK-POT®** slow cooker, omit step 4. Run a rubber spatula around the edge of casserole, lifting the bottom slightly. Invert onto a large plate. Place a large serving plate on top and invert again. Sprinkle with cheese and let stand until cheese is melted. To serve, cut into wedges.

Banana Nut Bread

⅓ cup butter, softened

3 mashed bananas

⅔ cup sugar

2 eggs, beaten

2 tablespoons dark corn syrup

1¾ cups all-purpose flour

2 teaspoons baking powder

½ teaspoon salt

¼ teaspoon baking soda

½ cup chopped walnuts

Fresh strawberries (optional)

Sprigs fresh mint (optional)

1. Grease and flour inside of **CROCK-POT**® slow cooker. Beat butter in large bowl with electric mixer at medium speed until fluffy. Gradually beat in bananas, sugar, eggs and corn syrup until smooth.

2. Combine flour, baking powder, salt and baking soda in small bowl; stir to blend. Beat flour mixture into banana mixture. Add walnuts; mix thoroughly. Pour batter into **CROCK-POT**® slow cooker.

3. Cover; cook on HIGH 2 to 3 hours. Cool completely; turn bread out onto large serving platter. Garnish with strawberries and mint.

Makes 1 loaf

Blueberry-Banana Pancakes

2 cups all-purpose flour

⅓ cup sugar

1 tablespoon baking powder

½ teaspoon baking soda

½ teaspoon salt

½ teaspoon ground cinnamon

1¾ cups milk

2 eggs, lightly beaten

¼ cup (½ stick) butter, melted

1 teaspoon vanilla

1 cup fresh blueberries

2 small bananas, sliced

Sugar-free maple syrup (optional)

1. Combine flour, sugar, baking powder, baking soda, salt and cinnamon in large bowl. Combine milk, eggs, butter and vanilla in separate medium bowl. Pour milk mixture into flour mixture; stir until moistened. Gently fold in blueberries until mixed.

2. Coat inside of **CROCK-POT®** slow cooker with nonstick cooking spray. Pour batter into **CROCK-POT®** slow cooker. Cover; cook on HIGH 2 hours or until puffed and toothpick inserted into center comes out clean. Cut evenly into eight wedges; top with sliced bananas and syrup, if desired.

Makes 8 servings

Raisin-Oat Quick Bread

1½ cups all-purpose flour, plus additional
  for dusting

⅔ cup old-fashioned oats

⅓ cup milk

4 teaspoons baking powder

1 teaspoon ground cinnamon

½ teaspoon salt

½ cup packed raisins

1 cup sugar

2 eggs, lightly beaten

½ cup (1 stick) butter, melted,
  plus additional for serving

1 teaspoon vanilla

1. Spray inside of ovenproof glass or ceramic loaf pan that fits inside of **CROCK-POT®** slow cooker with nonstick cooking spray; dust with flour.

2. Combine oats and milk in small bowl; let stand 10 minutes.

3. Meanwhile, combine 1½ cups flour, baking powder, cinnamon and salt in large bowl; stir in raisins. Whisk sugar, eggs, ½ cup melted butter and vanilla in separate medium bowl; stir in oat mixture. Pour sugar mixture into flour mixture; stir just until moistened. Pour into prepared pan. Place in **CROCK-POT®** slow cooker. Cover; cook on HIGH 2½ to 3 hours or until toothpick inserted into center comes out clean.

4. Remove pan from **CROCK-POT®** slow cooker; let cool in pan 10 minutes. Remove bread from pan; cool on wire rack 3 minutes before slicing. Serve with additional butter, if desired.

Makes 1 loaf

Hash Brown and Sausage Breakfast Casserole

4 cups frozen Southern-style hash browns

3 tablespoons butter

1 large onion, chopped

8 ounces (about 2 cups) sliced mushrooms

3 cloves garlic, minced

2 precooked apple chicken sausages, cut into 1-inch slices

1 package (10 ounces) frozen chopped spinach, thawed and squeezed dry

8 eggs

1 cup milk

1 teaspoon salt

¼ teaspoon black pepper

1½ cups (6 ounces) shredded sharp Cheddar cheese, divided

1. Coat inside of **CROCK-POT**® slow cooker with nonstick cooking spray. Place hash browns in **CROCK-POT**® slow cooker.

2. Melt butter in large skillet over medium-high heat. Add onion, mushrooms and garlic; cook 4 to 5 minutes or until onion is just starting to brown, stirring occasionally. Stir in sausage slices; cook 2 minutes. Add spinach; cook 2 minutes or until mushrooms are tender. Stir sausage mixture into **CROCK-POT**® slow cooker with hash browns until combined.

3. Combine eggs, milk, salt and pepper in large bowl; mix well. Pour over hash brown mixture in **CROCK-POT**® slow cooker. Top with 1 cup cheese. Cover; cook on LOW 4 to 4½ hours or on HIGH 1½ to 2 hours or until eggs are set. Top with remaining ½ cup cheese. Cut into wedges to serve.

Makes 6 to 8 servings

Orange Soufflé

6 tablespoons butter, softened and divided	1 tablespoon vanilla
1¼ cups sugar, divided	10 egg whites
Grated peel of 1 orange	1 teaspoon salt
½ cup milk	Whipped cream
6 tablespoons all-purpose flour	Fresh raspberries
8 egg yolks	Sprigs fresh mint
6 tablespoons orange-flavored liqueur	

1. Butter inside of **CROCK-POT**® slow cooker with 2 tablespoons butter. Pour in ⅓ cup sugar; turn to evenly coat bottom and sides of **CROCK-POT**® slow cooker.

2. Combine ⅔ cup sugar and orange peel in food processor or blender; process until orange peel is evenly ground and well combined.

3. Whisk orange sugar, milk and flour in medium saucepan; cook and stir over medium heat until just beginning to thicken. Bring to a boil over high heat; cook and stir 30 seconds. Remove from heat. Let mixture cool slightly; beat in egg yolks, one at a time. Add orange liqueur, remaining 4 tablespoons butter and vanilla to egg yolk mixture; let stand at room temperature 20 minutes to cool.

4. Beat egg whites in clean, dry bowl until foamy. Add salt; beat until soft peaks form. Sprinkle in remaining ¼ cup sugar; beat until stiff peaks form. Fold one quarter of beaten egg whites into cooled batter. Fold in remaining egg whites; gently remove to **CROCK-POT**® slow cooker. Cover; cook on HIGH 1 hour or until soufflé is fully set. Top with whipped cream and raspberries. Garnish with mint.

Makes 10 servings

Maple, Bacon and Raspberry Pancake

5 slices bacon

2 cups pancake mix

1 cup water

½ cup maple syrup, plus additional
    for serving

1 cup fresh raspberries, plus additional
    for garnish

3 tablespoons chopped pecans, toasted*

*To toast pecans, spread in single layer in heavy skillet. Cook and stir over medium heat 1 to 2 minutes or until nuts are lightly browned.

1. Heat large skillet over medium heat. Add bacon; cook and stir until crisp. Remove to paper towel-lined plate using slotted spoon; crumble.

2. Brush inside of 5-quart **CROCK-POT**® slow cooker with 1 to 2 tablespoons bacon fat from skillet. Combine pancake mix, water and ½ cup syrup in large bowl; stir to blend. Pour half of batter into **CROCK-POT**® slow cooker; top with ½ cup raspberries, half of bacon and half of pecans. Pour remaining half of batter over top; sprinkle with remaining ½ cup raspberries, bacon and pecans.

3. Cover; cook on HIGH 1½ to 2 hours or until pancake has risen and is cooked through. Turn off heat. Let stand, uncovered, 10 to 15 minutes. Remove pancake from **CROCK-POT**® slow cooker; cut into eight pieces. Serve with additional syrup and raspberries.

Makes 8 servings

Breakfast Berry Bread Pudding

6 cups cubed bread (¾- to 1-inch cubes)

1 cup raisins

½ cup slivered almonds, toasted*

1¾ cups milk

6 eggs, beaten

1½ cups packed brown sugar

1½ teaspoons ground cinnamon

1 teaspoon vanilla

3 cups sliced fresh strawberries

2 cups fresh blueberries

Sprigs fresh mint (optional)

*To toast almonds, spread in single layer in heavy skillet. Cook and stir over medium heat 1 to 2 minutes or until nuts are lightly browned.

1. Coat inside of **CROCK-POT®** slow cooker with nonstick cooking spray. Add bread, raisins and almonds; toss to combine.

2. Whisk milk, eggs, brown sugar, cinnamon and vanilla in large bowl. Pour egg mixture over bread mixture; toss to coat. Cover; cook on LOW 4 hours or on HIGH 3 hours.

3. Remove stoneware from **CROCK-POT®** slow cooker. Let bread pudding cool until set. Serve with berries. Garnish with mint.

Makes 12 servings

Mediterranean Frittata

Butter, softened

3 tablespoons extra virgin olive oil

1 large onion, chopped

8 ounces (about 2 cups) sliced mushrooms

6 cloves garlic, sliced

1 teaspoon dried basil

1 medium red bell pepper, chopped

1 package (10 ounces) frozen chopped spinach, thawed and squeezed dry

¼ cup sliced kalamata olives

8 eggs, beaten

4 ounces feta cheese, crumbled

½ teaspoon salt

¼ teaspoon black pepper

1. Coat inside lower third of 5- to 6-quart **CROCK-POT**® slow cooker with butter. Heat oil in large skillet over medium-high heat. Add onion, mushrooms, garlic and basil; cook 2 to 3 minutes or until slightly softened, stirring occasionally. Add bell pepper; cook 4 to 5 minutes or until vegetables are tender. Stir in spinach; cook 2 minutes. Stir in olives. Remove to **CROCK-POT**® slow cooker.

2. Combine eggs, cheese, salt and black pepper in large bowl; mix well. Pour over vegetables in **CROCK-POT**® slow cooker. Cover; cook on LOW 2½ to 3 hours or on HIGH 1¼ to 1½ hours or until eggs are set. Cut into wedges to serve.

Makes 4 to 6 servings

Blueberry-Orange French Toast Casserole

½ cup sugar

½ cup milk

2 eggs

4 egg whites

1 tablespoon grated orange peel

½ teaspoon vanilla

6 slices whole wheat bread, cut into 1-inch cubes

1 cup fresh blueberries

Maple syrup (optional)

1. Coat inside of **CROCK-POT**® slow cooker with nonstick cooking spray. Stir sugar and milk in large bowl until sugar is dissolved. Whisk in eggs, egg whites, orange peel and vanilla. Add bread and blueberries; toss to coat.

2. Remove mixture to **CROCK-POT**® slow cooker. Cover; cook on LOW 3 to 4 hours or on HIGH 1½ to 2 hours or until toothpick inserted into center comes out mostly clean.

3. Turn off heat. Let stand 10 minutes. Serve with syrup, if desired.

Makes 6 servings

Oatmeal with Maple-Glazed Apples and Cranberries

3 cups water

2 cups quick-cooking or old-fashioned oats

¼ teaspoon salt

1 teaspoon butter

2 medium red or Golden Delicious apples, unpeeled and cut into ½-inch pieces

¼ teaspoon ground cinnamon

2 tablespoons maple syrup

4 tablespoons dried cranberries

1. Combine water, oats and salt in **CROCK-POT**® slow cooker. Cover; cook on LOW 8 hours.

2. Melt butter in large nonstick skillet over medium heat. Add apples and cinnamon; cook and stir 4 to 5 minutes or until tender. Stir in syrup; heat through.

3. Serve oatmeal with apple mixture and dried cranberries.

Makes 4 servings

SIMMERING SIPS

Chai Tea Cherries 'n' Cream

2 cans (15½ ounces *each*) pitted cherries in pear juice

2 cups water

½ cup orange juice

1 cup sugar

4 cardamom pods

2 whole cinnamon sticks, broken in half

1 teaspoon grated orange peel

¼ ounce coarsely chopped candied ginger

4 whole cloves

2 whole black peppercorns

4 green tea bags

1 container (6 ounces) black cherry yogurt

1 quart vanilla ice cream

Sprigs fresh mint (optional)

1. Drain cherries, reserving juice. Combine reserved cherry juice, water and orange juice in **CROCK-POT®** slow cooker. Add sugar, cardamom pods, cinnamon sticks, orange peel, ginger, cloves and peppercorns; stir to blend. Cover; cook on HIGH 1½ hours.

2. Remove spices with slotted spoon; discard. Stir in tea bags and reserved cherries. Cover; cook on HIGH 30 minutes.

3. Turn off heat. Remove and discard tea bags. Remove cherries from liquid; set aside. Let liquid cool until just warm. Whisk in yogurt until smooth.

4. To serve, divide warm cherries and yogurt sauce among wine or cocktail glasses. Top each serving with ice cream; swirl lightly. Garnish with mint.

Makes 8 servings

Mulled Cran-Apple Punch

1 orange

1 lemon

1 lime

15 whole black peppercorns

10 whole cloves

10 whole allspice

3 whole cinnamon sticks, plus additional for garnish

1 (5-inch) square double-thickness cheesecloth

6 cups apple juice

3 cups cranberry juice

3 tablespoons maple syrup

1. Use vegetable peeler to remove 5 to 6 (2- to 3-inch-long) sections of orange, lemon and lime peel, being careful to avoid white pith. Squeeze juice from orange.

2. Place peels, peppercorns, cloves, allspice and 3 cinnamon sticks in center of cheesecloth. Bring corners together; tie with cotton string or additional strip of cheesecloth.

3. Pour apple juice, cranberry juice, syrup and reserved orange juice into 5-quart **CROCK-POT®** slow cooker; add spice bag. Cover; cook on LOW 5 to 6 hours or on HIGH 2½ to 3 hours. Remove and discard spice bag. Serve with additional cinnamon sticks.

Makes 8 servings

Spiced Citrus Tea

4 tea bags

Peel of 1 orange

4 cups boiling water

2 cans (6 ounces *each*) orange-pineapple juice

3 tablespoons honey

3 whole cinnamon sticks

3 whole star anise

1. Combine tea bags, orange peel and boiling water in **CROCK-POT®** slow cooker; cover and let steep 10 minutes. Remove and discard tea bags and orange peel. Add orange-pineapple juice, honey, cinnamon sticks and star anise; stir to blend.

2. Cover; cook on LOW 3 hours. Remove and discard cinnamon sticks and star anise.

Makes 6 servings

Hot Mulled Cider

½ gallon apple cider

½ cup packed brown sugar

1½ teaspoons balsamic or cider vinegar (optional)

1 teaspoon vanilla

1 whole cinnamon stick

6 whole cloves

½ cup applejack or bourbon (optional)

1. Combine apple cider, brown sugar, vinegar, if desired, vanilla, cinnamon stick and cloves in **CROCK-POT®** slow cooker; stir to blend. Cover; cook on LOW 5 to 6 hours.

2. Remove and discard cinnamon stick and cloves. Stir in applejack just before serving, if desired. Serve warm in mugs.

Makes 16 servings

Mocha Supreme

2 quarts strong brewed coffee

½ cup instant hot chocolate beverage mix

1 whole cinnamon stick, broken in half

1 cup whipping cream

1 tablespoon powdered sugar

1. Combine coffee, hot chocolate mix and cinnamon stick halves in **CROCK-POT**® slow cooker; stir to blend. Cover; cook on HIGH 2 to 2½ hours or until heated through. Remove and discard cinnamon stick halves.

2. Beat cream in medium bowl with electric mixer on high speed until soft peaks form. Add powdered sugar; beat until stiff peaks form. Ladle mocha mixture into mugs; top with whipped cream.

Makes 8 servings

Tip: To whip cream more quickly, chill the beaters and bowl in the freezer for 15 minutes.

Cinnamon Latté

6 cups double-strength brewed coffee*

2 cups half-and-half

1 cup sugar

1 teaspoon vanilla

3 whole cinnamon sticks, plus additional for garnish

Whipped cream (optional)

*Double the amount of coffee grounds normally used to brew coffee. Or substitute 8 teaspoons instant coffee dissolved in 6 cups boiling water.

1. Combine coffee, half-and-half, sugar and vanilla in **CROCK-POT**® slow cooker; stir to blend. Add 3 cinnamon sticks. Cover; cook on HIGH 3 hours.

2. Remove and discard cinnamon sticks. Serve latté in tall coffee mugs. Garnish with additional cinnamon sticks and whipped cream.

Makes 6 to 8 servings

Viennese Coffee

3 cups strong freshly brewed hot coffee

3 tablespoons chocolate syrup

1 teaspoon sugar

⅓ cup whipping cream, plus additional
for topping

¼ cup crème de cacao or Irish cream

Chocolate shavings (optional)

1. Combine coffee, chocolate syrup and sugar in **CROCK·POT**® slow cooker; stir to blend. Cover; cook on LOW 2 to 2½ hours.

2. Stir ⅓ cup cream and crème de cacao into **CROCK·POT**® slow cooker. Cover; cook on LOW 30 minutes or until heated through. Ladle coffee into coffee mugs. Top each serving with additional whipped cream and chocolate shavings, if desired.

Makes 4 servings

Warm and Spicy Fruit Punch

4 whole cinnamon sticks

1 orange

1 (8-inch) square double-thickness cheesecloth

1 teaspoon whole allspice

½ teaspoon whole cloves

7 cups water

1 can (12 ounces) frozen cran-raspberry juice concentrate, thawed

1 can (6 ounces) frozen lemonade concentrate, thawed

2 cans (5½ ounces *each*) apricot nectar

1. Break cinnamon sticks into pieces. Remove strips of orange peel with vegetable peeler or paring knife. Squeeze juice from orange; set juice aside.

2. Rinse cheesecloth; squeeze out water. Wrap cinnamon sticks, orange peel, allspice and cloves in cheesecloth. Tie bag securely with cotton string or additional strip of cheesecloth.

3. Combine reserved orange juice, water, juice concentrates and apricot nectar in **CROCK-POT®** slow cooker; add spice bag. Cover; cook on LOW 5 to 6 hours. Remove and discard spice bag before serving.

Makes about 14 servings

Tip: To keep punch warm during a party, turn your **CROCK-POT®** slow cooker to LOW or WARM.

Infused Mint Mojito

2 cups water

2 cups sugar

2 bunches fresh mint, stems removed, plus additional for garnish

¾ to 1 cup fresh-squeezed lime juice

1 bottle (750 ml) light rum

2 liters club soda

1. Combine water, sugar and 2 bunches mint in **CROCK-POT**® slow cooker; stir to blend. Cover; cook on HIGH 3½ hours.

2. Strain into large pitcher. Stir in lime juice and rum. Cover and refrigerate until cold.

3. To serve, fill tall glasses halfway with fresh ice. Pour ¾ cup mint syrup over ice; top off with club soda to taste. Garnish with additional fresh mint. Serve immediately.

Makes 10 to 12 servings

Warm Honey Lemonade

4½ cups water

2½ cups lemon juice

1 cup orange juice

1 cup honey

¼ cup sugar

Lemon slices (optional)

1. Combine water, lemon juice, orange juice, honey and sugar in **CROCK-POT**® slow cooker; stir to blend.

2. Cover; cook on LOW 2 hours. Whisk well before serving. Garnish with lemon slices.

Makes 9 cups

Mulled Cranberry Tea

2 tea bags

1 cup boiling water

1 bottle (48 ounces) cranberry juice

½ cup dried cranberries

⅓ cup sugar

1 lemon, cut into ¼-inch slices, plus additional for serving

4 whole cinnamon sticks, plus additional for serving

6 whole cloves

1. Place tea bags in **CROCK-POT®** slow cooker. Pour boiling water over tea bags; cover and let steep 5 minutes. Remove and discard tea bags.

2. Stir in cranberry juice, cranberries, sugar, lemon slices, 4 cinnamon sticks and cloves. Cover; cook on LOW 2 to 3 hours or on HIGH 1 to 2 hours.

3. Remove and discard cooked lemon slices, cinnamon sticks and cloves. Serve in warm mugs with additional cinnamon sticks and fresh lemon slices, if desired.

Makes 8 servings

Tip: The flavor and aroma of crushed or ground herbs and spices may lessen during a longer cooking time. So, for slow cooking in your **CROCK-POT®** slow cooker, you may use whole herbs and spices. Be sure to taste and adjust seasonings before serving.

Ginger Pear Cider

8 cups pear juice or cider

¾ cup lemon juice

¼ to ½ cup honey

10 whole cloves

2 whole cinnamon sticks, plus additional for garnish

8 slices fresh ginger

1. Combine pear juice, lemon juice, honey, cloves, 2 cinnamon sticks and ginger in 5-quart **CROCK-POT®** slow cooker; stir to blend.

2. Cover; cook on LOW 5 to 6 hours or on HIGH 2½ to 3 hours. Remove and discard cloves, cinnamon sticks and ginger before serving. Garnish with additional cinnamon sticks.

Makes 8 to 10 servings

Hot Tropics Sipper

4 cups pineapple juice

2 cups apple juice

1 container (about 11 ounces) apricot nectar

½ cup packed dark brown sugar

1 medium orange, thinly sliced, plus additional for garnish

1 medium lemon, thinly sliced, plus additional for garnish

3 whole cinnamon sticks

6 whole cloves

1. Combine pineapple juice, apple juice, nectar, brown sugar, orange slices, lemon slices, cinnamon sticks and cloves in **CROCK-POT®** slow cooker; stir to blend. Cover; cook on HIGH 3½ to 4 hours or until very fragrant.

2. Strain immediately (beverage will turn bitter if fruit and spices remain after cooking is complete). Remove and discard cinnamon sticks. Serve with additional fresh orange and lemon slices, if desired.

Makes 8 servings

Minted Hot Cocoa

6 cups milk

¾ cup semisweet chocolate pieces

½ cup sugar

½ cup unsweetened cocoa powder

1 teaspoon vanilla

½ teaspoon mint extract

10 sprigs fresh mint, tied together with kitchen string, plus additional for garnish

Whipped cream (optional)

1. Combine milk, chocolate, sugar, cocoa, vanilla and mint extract in **CROCK-POT®** slow cooker; stir to blend. Add 10 mint sprigs. Cover; cook on LOW 3 to 4 hours.

2. Uncover; remove and discard mint sprigs. Whisk cocoa mixture well. Cover until ready to serve. Garnish each serving with whipped cream and additional mint sprigs.

Makes 6 to 8 servings

Mucho Mocha Cocoa

4 cups whole milk

4 cups half-and-half

1 cup chocolate syrup

⅓ cup instant coffee granules

2 tablespoons sugar

2 whole cinnamon sticks

1. Combine milk, half-and-half, chocolate syrup, coffee granules, sugar and cinnamon sticks in **CROCK-POT®** slow cooker; stir to blend. Cover; cook on LOW 3 hours.

2. Remove and discard cinnamon sticks. Serve warm in mugs.

Makes 9 servings

Tip: This is great for a party. If desired, add 1 ounce of rum or whiskey to each serving.

Triple Delicious Hot Chocolate

3 cups milk, divided

⅓ cup sugar

¼ cup unsweetened cocoa powder

¼ teaspoon salt

¾ teaspoon vanilla

1 cup whipping cream

1 square (1 ounce) bittersweet chocolate, chopped

1 square (1 ounce) white chocolate, chopped

Whipped cream (optional)

Mini semisweet chocolate chips (optional)

1. Combine ½ cup milk, sugar, cocoa and salt in **CROCK-POT®** slow cooker; stir to blend. Stir in remaining 2½ cups milk and vanilla. Cover; cook on LOW 2 hours.

2. Stir in cream. Cover; cook on LOW 10 minutes. Stir in bittersweet and white chocolate until melted.

3. Pour hot chocolate into mugs. Top each serving with whipped cream and chocolate chips, if desired.

Makes 6 servings

Ginger-Lime Martini

2 cups sugar

1 cup water

1 (5-inch) piece fresh ginger, peeled and thinly sliced

3 cups vodka, chilled

2 cups lime juice

Crushed ice

1. Combine sugar, water and ginger in **CROCK-POT®** slow cooker. Cover; cook on LOW 6 to 8 hours or on HIGH 3 to 4 hours.

2. Strain ginger syrup; cool. Refrigerate in airtight container until needed, up to 7 days.

3. For each serving, combine 2 ounces ginger syrup, 3 ounces vodka and 2 ounces lime juice in martini shaker half filled with crushed ice. Shake to combine; strain into chilled martini glass. Repeat with remaining ingredients.

Makes 8 servings

Homemade Ginger Ale: Pour ½ cup chilled ginger syrup over ice in 16-ounce glass. Top off with 1 cup soda water and stir gently to combine.

Chai Tea

2 quarts (8 cups) water

8 bags black tea

¾ cup sugar*

8 slices fresh ginger

5 whole cinnamon sticks, plus additional for garnish

16 whole cloves

16 whole cardamom seeds, pods removed (optional)

1 cup milk

*Chai tea is typically sweet. For less-sweet tea, reduce sugar to ½ cup.

1. Combine water, tea bags, sugar, ginger, 5 cinnamon sticks, cloves and cardamom, if desired, in **CROCK-POT®** slow cooker; stir to blend. Cover; cook on HIGH 2 to 2½ hours.

2. Strain mixture; discard solids. (At this point, tea may be covered and refrigerated up to 3 days.)

3. Stir in milk just before serving. Garnish with additional cinnamon sticks.

Makes 8 to 10 servings

Mulled Wine

2 bottles (750 ml *each*) dry red wine, such as Cabernet Sauvignon

1 cup water

1 cup corn syrup

1 (8-inch) square double-thickness cheesecloth

Peel of 1 large orange

1 cinnamon stick, broken in half

8 whole cloves

1 whole nutmeg

1. Combine wine, water and corn syrup in **CROCK-POT**® slow cooker.

2. Rinse cheesecloth; squeeze out water. Wrap orange peel, cinnamon stick halves, cloves and nutmeg in cheesecloth. Tie bag securely with cotton string or additional strip of cheesecloth. Add to **CROCK-POT**® slow cooker. Cover; cook on HIGH 2 to 2½ hours.

3. Remove and discard spice bag. Ladle wine into mugs. Garnish as desired.

Makes 12 servings

Tip: Mulled wine is a wonderful and warming beverage to serve at a holiday party. The spices will fill the kitchen with festive aromas, and the sweet and fruity flavors pair well with rich holiday food and desserts.

SOUPS, STEWS & CHILIES

White Chicken Chili

- 8 ounces dried navy beans, rinsed and sorted
- 1 tablespoon vegetable oil
- 2 pounds boneless, skinless chicken breasts (about 4)
- 2 onions, chopped
- 1 tablespoon minced garlic
- 2 teaspoons ground cumin
- 2 teaspoons salt
- 1 teaspoon dried oregano
- ¼ teaspoon black pepper
- ¼ teaspoon ground red pepper (optional)
- 4 cups chicken broth
- 1 can (4 ounces) fire-roasted diced mild green chiles, rinsed and drained
- ¼ cup chopped fresh cilantro

1. Place beans on bottom of **CROCK-POT**® slow cooker. Heat oil in large skillet over medium-high heat. Add chicken; cook 8 minutes or until browned on all sides. Remove to **CROCK-POT**® slow cooker.

2. Heat same skillet over medium heat. Add onions; cook 6 minutes or until softened and lightly browned. Add garlic, cumin, salt, oregano, black pepper and ground red pepper, if desired; cook and stir 1 minute. Add broth and chiles; bring to a simmer, stirring to scrape up any browned bits from bottom of skillet. Remove onion mixture to **CROCK-POT**® slow cooker.

3. Cover; cook on LOW 5 hours. Remove chicken to large cutting board; shred with two forks. Return chicken to **CROCK-POT**® slow cooker. Stir in cilantro.

Makes 6 to 8 servings

Thai-Style Chicken Pumpkin Soup

1 tablespoon extra virgin olive oil

6 boneless, skinless chicken breasts,
  cut into 1-inch pieces

1 large white onion, thinly sliced

3 cloves garlic, minced

1 tablespoon minced fresh ginger

½ to ¾ teaspoon red pepper flakes

4 cups reduced-sodium chicken broth

2 stalks celery, diced

2 carrots, diced

1 can (15 ounces) solid-pack pumpkin*

½ cup creamy peanut butter

½ cup mango nectar

½ cup fresh lime juice

3 tablespoons rice vinegar

½ cup minced fresh cilantro, divided

½ cup whipping cream

1 tablespoon cornstarch

2 to 4 cups hot cooked rice (preferably
  jasmine or basmati)

3 green onions, minced

½ cup roasted unsalted peanuts,
  coarsely chopped

  Lime wedges (optional)

*Do not use pumpkin pie filling.

1. Heat oil in large skillet over medium heat. Add chicken and cook about 3 minutes, stirring occasionally. Add onion, garlic, ginger and red pepper flakes; cook 1 to 2 minutes or until fragrant. Remove to **CROCK-POT®** slow cooker.

2. Stir in broth, celery, carrots, pumpkin, peanut butter, mango nectar and lime juice. Cover; cook on LOW 8 hours or on HIGH 4 hours.

3. Stir in rice vinegar and ¼ cup cilantro. Stir cream into cornstarch in small bowl until smooth. Stir into soup. Simmer, uncovered, on HIGH 10 minutes or until soup is thickened.

4. To serve, place rice in bowls. Ladle soup around rice. Sprinkle with remaining ¼ cup cilantro, green onions and peanuts. Squeeze fresh lime juice over soup, if desired.

Makes 4 to 6 servings

Chicken Stew with Herb Dumplings

2 cups sliced carrots

1 cup chopped onion

1 green bell pepper, sliced

½ cup sliced celery

2 cans (about **14** ounces *each*) chicken broth, divided

⅔ cup all-purpose flour

1 pound boneless, skinless chicken breasts, cut into 1-inch pieces

1 large red potato, unpeeled and cut into 1-inch pieces

6 ounces mushrooms, halved

¾ cup frozen peas

1¼ teaspoons dried basil, divided

1 teaspoon dried rosemary, divided

½ teaspoon dried tarragon, divided

¼ cup whipping cream

¾ to 1 teaspoon salt

¼ teaspoon black pepper

1 cup biscuit baking mix

⅓ cup milk

1. Combine carrots, onion, bell pepper, celery and all but 1 cup broth in **CROCK-POT**® slow cooker. Cover; cook on LOW 2 hours.

2. Stir remaining 1 cup broth into flour in small bowl until smooth. Stir into vegetable mixture. Add chicken, potato, mushrooms, peas, 1 teaspoon basil, ¾ teaspoon rosemary and ¼ teaspoon tarragon. Cover; cook on LOW 4 hours or until vegetables and chicken are tender. Stir in cream, salt and black pepper.

3. Combine baking mix, remaining ¼ teaspoon basil, ¼ teaspoon rosemary and ¼ teaspoon tarragon in small bowl. Stir in milk until soft dough forms. Add dumpling mixture to top of stew in four large spoonfuls.

4. Cook, uncovered, on LOW 30 minutes. Cover; cook on LOW 30 to 45 minutes or until dumplings are firm and toothpick inserted into center comes out clean. Serve in shallow bowls.

Makes 4 servings

Italian Hillside Garden Soup

1 tablespoon olive oil

1 cup chopped green bell pepper

1 cup chopped onion

½ cup sliced celery

1 can (about 15 ounces) navy beans, rinsed and drained

1 can (about 14 ounces) diced tomatoes with basil, garlic and oregano

2 cans (about 14 ounces *each*) chicken broth

1 medium zucchini, chopped

1 cup frozen cut green beans

¼ teaspoon garlic powder

1 package (9 ounces) refrigerated sausage- or cheese-filled tortellini pasta

3 tablespoons chopped fresh basil

Grated Asiago or Parmesan cheese (optional)

1. Heat oil in large skillet over medium-high heat. Add bell pepper, onion and celery; cook and stir 4 minutes or until onion is translucent. Remove to **CROCK-POT**® slow cooker.

2. Add navy beans, tomatoes, broth, zucchini, green beans and garlic powder; stir to blend. Cover; cook on LOW 7 hours or on HIGH 3½ hours.

3. Add tortellini. Cover; cook on HIGH 20 to 25 minutes or until pasta is tender. Stir in basil. Garnish with cheese.

Makes 6 servings

Nana's Mini Meatball Soup

1 pound ground beef

1 pound ground pork

1½ cups finely grated Pecorino Romano or Parmesan cheese

1 cup seasoned dry bread crumbs

2 eggs, lightly beaten

1 bunch fresh Italian parsley, finely chopped

Salt and black pepper

3 quarts chicken broth

1 bunch escarole, coarsely chopped*

½ (16-ounce) package ditalini pasta, cooked and drained

*You may substitute spinach.

1. Combine beef, pork, cheese, bread crumbs, eggs, parsley, salt and pepper in large bowl until well blended. Shape into ¾-inch meatballs.

2. Add meatballs and broth to **CROCK-POT**® slow cooker. Cover; cook on LOW 9 hours or on HIGH 5 hours.

3. Add escarole. Cover; cook on LOW 15 minutes or until wilted. Stir in pasta just before serving.

Makes 6 to 8 servings

Leek and Potato Soup

6 slices bacon, crisp-cooked, chopped and divided

5 cups shredded frozen hash brown potatoes

3 leeks (white and light green parts only), cut into ¾-inch pieces

1 can (about 14 ounces) vegetable broth

1 can (10¾ ounces) condensed cream of potato soup, undiluted

2 stalks celery, sliced

1 can (5 ounces) evaporated milk

½ cup sour cream

Set aside 2 tablespoons bacon. Combine remaining bacon, potatoes, leeks, broth, soup, celery and evaporated milk in **CROCK-POT**® slow cooker; stir to blend. Cover; cook on LOW 6 to 7 hours. Stir in sour cream. Sprinkle each serving with reserved bacon.

Makes 4 to 6 servings

Hearty Chicken Chili

1 medium onion, finely chopped

1 small jalapeño pepper, seeded and minced*

1 clove garlic, minced

1½ teaspoons chili powder

¾ teaspoon salt

½ teaspoon ground cumin

½ teaspoon dried oregano

½ teaspoon black pepper

2 cans (about 15 ounces *each*) hominy, rinsed and drained**

1 can (about 15 ounces) pinto beans, rinsed and drained

1½ pounds boneless, skinless chicken thighs, cut into 1-inch pieces

1 cup chicken broth

Chopped fresh Italian parsley or cilantro (optional)

*Jalapeño peppers can sting and irritate the skin, so wear rubber gloves when handling peppers and do not touch your eyes.

**Hominy is corn that has been treated to remove the germ and hull. It can be found with the canned vegetables or beans in most supermarkets.

1. Combine onion, jalapeño pepper, garlic, chili powder, salt, cumin, oregano and black pepper in **CROCK-POT®** slow cooker.

2. Stir in hominy, beans, chicken and broth. Cover; cook on LOW 7 hours. Garnish with parsley.

Makes 6 servings

Tip: For a hotter dish, add ¼ teaspoon red pepper flakes with the seasonings. For thicker chili, stir 3 tablespoons cooking liquid into 1 tablespoon flour in small bowl until smooth. Stir into cooking liquid; cook on HIGH 10 minutes or until thickened.

Three-Bean Mole Chili

1 can (about 15 ounces) chili beans in spicy sauce, undrained

1 can (about 15 ounces) pinto beans, rinsed and drained

1 can (about 15 ounces) black beans, rinsed and drained

1 can (about 14 ounces) Mexican or chili-style diced tomatoes

1 large green bell pepper, chopped

1 small onion, chopped

½ cup vegetable broth

¼ cup prepared mole paste*

2 teaspoons minced garlic

2 teaspoons ground cumin

2 teaspoons chili powder

2 teaspoons ground coriander (optional)

Optional toppings: crushed tortilla chips, sprigs fresh cilantro, shredded Cheddar cheese

*Mole paste is available in the Mexican section of large supermarkets and at specialty markets.

Combine beans, tomatoes, bell pepper, onion, broth, mole paste, garlic, cumin, chili powder and coriander, if desired, in **CROCK-POT®** slow cooker; stir to blend. Cover; cook on LOW 5 to 6 hours. Serve with desired toppings.

Makes 4 to 6 servings

Tip: Opening the lid and checking on food in the **CROCK-POT®** slow cooker can affect both cooking time and results. Due to the nature of slow cooking, there's no need to stir the food unless the recipe method says to do so.

Chicken and Sweet Potato Stew

4 boneless, skinless chicken breasts, cut into 1-inch pieces

2 medium sweet potatoes, cubed

2 medium Yukon Gold potatoes, cubed

2 medium carrots, cut into ½-inch slices

1 can (28 ounces) whole stewed tomatoes

1 cup chicken broth

1 teaspoon salt

1 teaspoon paprika

1 teaspoon celery seeds

½ teaspoon black pepper

⅛ teaspoon ground cinnamon

⅛ teaspoon ground nutmeg

¼ cup fresh basil, chopped

Combine chicken, sweet potatoes, Yukon Gold potatoes, carrots, tomatoes, broth, salt, paprika, celery seeds, pepper, cinnamon and nutmeg in **CROCK-POT**® slow cooker; stir to blend. Cover; cook on LOW 6 to 8 hours or on HIGH 3 to 4 hours. Sprinkle with basil just before serving.

Makes 6 servings

Potato Soup

8 slices smoked bacon

1 large onion, chopped

2 stalks celery, chopped

2 carrots, chopped

3 cloves garlic, minced

1 teaspoon dried thyme

5 potatoes (about 3 pounds), cut into ½-inch cubes

4 cups chicken broth

1 cup half-and-half

¾ teaspoon salt

¼ teaspoon black pepper

1. Heat large skillet over medium heat. Add bacon; cook and stir until crisp. Remove to paper towel-lined plate using slotted spoon; crumble.

2. Pour off all but 2 tablespoons bacon fat from skillet and return to medium-high heat. Add onion, celery, carrots, garlic and thyme; cook and stir 5 to 6 minutes or until slightly softened.

3. Combine onion mixture, potatoes, half of bacon and broth in **CROCK-POT**® slow cooker. Cover; cook on LOW 7 to 8 hours or on HIGH 3 to 4 hours.

4. Mash potatoes with potato masher and stir in half-and-half, salt and pepper. Cover; cook on HIGH 15 minutes. Garnish with remaining half of bacon.

Makes 8 servings

Wild Mushroom Beef Stew

1½ to 2 pounds cubed beef stew meat

2 tablespoons all-purpose flour

½ teaspoon salt

½ teaspoon black pepper

1½ cups beef broth

4 shiitake mushrooms, sliced

2 medium carrots, sliced

2 medium potatoes, diced

1 small white onion, chopped

1 stalk celery, sliced

1 teaspoon paprika

1 clove garlic, minced

1 teaspoon Worcestershire sauce

1 whole bay leaf

Place beef in **CROCK-POT®** slow cooker. Combine flour, salt and pepper in small bowl; stir to blend. Sprinkle flour mixture over meat; toss to coat. Add broth, mushrooms, carrots, potatoes, onion, celery, paprika, garlic, Worcestershire sauce and bay leaf; stir to blend. Cover; cook on LOW 10 to 12 hours or on HIGH 4 to 6 hours. Remove and discard bay leaf.

Makes 5 servings

Note: If shiitake mushrooms are unavailable in your local grocery store, you can substitute other mushrooms of your choice. For extra punch, add a few dried porcini mushrooms.

Classic Chili

1½ pounds ground beef

1½ cups chopped onion

1 cup chopped green bell pepper

2 cloves garlic, minced

3 cans (about 15 ounces *each*) dark red kidney beans, rinsed and drained

2 cans (about 15 ounces *each*) tomato sauce

1 can (about 14 ounces) diced tomatoes

2 to 3 teaspoons chili powder

1 to 2 teaspoons ground mustard

¾ teaspoon dried basil

½ teaspoon black pepper

1 to 2 dried red chiles (optional)

Shredded Cheddar cheese (optional)

Sprigs fresh cilantro (optional)

1. Brown beef, onion, bell pepper and garlic in large skillet over medium-high heat 6 to 8 minutes, stirring to break up meat. Remove to **CROCK-POT**® slow cooker using slotted spoon.

2. Add beans, tomato sauce, tomatoes, chili powder, mustard, basil, black pepper and chiles, if desired, to **CROCK-POT**® slow cooker; stir to blend. Cover; cook on LOW 8 to 10 hours or on HIGH 4 to 5 hours. If used, remove chiles before serving. Top with cheese, if desired. Garnish with cilantro.

Makes 6 servings

Corn and Two Bean Chili

1 can (about 15 ounces) pinto or kidney beans, rinsed and drained

1 can (about 15 ounces) black beans, rinsed and drained

1 can (about 14 ounces) fire-roasted diced tomatoes

1 cup salsa

1 cup frozen corn

½ cup minced onion

1 teaspoon chili powder

1 teaspoon ground cumin

½ cup sour cream (optional)

1 cup (4 ounces) shredded Cheddar cheese (optional)

1. Coat inside of **CROCK-POT**® slow cooker with nonstick cooking spray. Combine beans, tomatoes, salsa, corn, onion, chili powder and cumin in **CROCK-POT**® slow cooker; stir to blend.

2. Cover; cook on LOW 5 to 6 hours or on HIGH 2½ to 3 hours. Top each serving with sour cream and cheese, if desired.

Makes 4 servings

Three-Bean Chili with Chorizo

2 Mexican chorizo sausages (about 6 ounces *each*), casings removed

1 tablespoon vegetable oil

1 large onion, chopped

1 tablespoon salt

1 tablespoon tomato paste

1 tablespoon minced garlic

1 tablespoon chili powder

1 tablespoon ancho chili powder

2 to 3 teaspoons chipotle chili powder

2 teaspoons ground cumin

1 teaspoon ground coriander

3 cups water

2 cans (about 14 ounces *each*) crushed tomatoes

½ cup dried pinto beans, rinsed and sorted

½ cup dried kidney beans, rinsed and sorted

½ cup dried black beans, rinsed and sorted

Chopped fresh cilantro (optional)

1. Heat large nonstick skillet over medium-high heat. Add sausages; cook 3 to 4 minutes, stirring to break up meat. Remove to **CROCK-POT®** slow cooker using slotted spoon.

2. Wipe out skillet. Heat oil in same skillet over medium heat. Add onion; cook and stir 6 minutes or until softened. Add salt, tomato paste, garlic, chili powders, cumin and coriander; cook and stir 1 minute. Remove to **CROCK-POT®** slow cooker. Stir in water, tomatoes and beans.

3. Cover; cook on LOW 10 hours. Garnish each serving with cilantro.

Makes 6 to 8 servings

Braised Pork Shanks with Israeli Couscous and Root Vegetable Stew

4 pork shanks, bone in, skin removed (about 1½ pounds *total*)

Coarse salt and black pepper

1 cup olive oil

4 large carrots, sliced diagonally into 1-inch pieces and divided

4 stalks celery, sliced diagonally into 1-inch pieces and divided

1 Spanish onion, peeled and quartered

4 cloves garlic, crushed

4 to 6 cups chicken broth

2 cups dry white wine

¼ cup tomato paste

¼ cup distilled white vinegar

1 tablespoon whole black peppercorns

Israeli Couscous (recipe follows)

1. Season pork well with salt and black pepper. Heat oil in large skillet over medium heat. Add pork; cook 7 to 10 minutes or until browned on all sides. Remove to **CROCK-POT**® slow cooker.

2. Pour off all but 2 tablespoons oil in skillet. Add half of carrots, half of celery, onion and garlic to skillet; cook and stir 5 minutes or until vegetables are soft but not browned. Remove to **CROCK-POT**® slow cooker.

3. Add broth, wine, tomato paste, vinegar and peppercorns to skillet. Bring to a boil, stirring and scraping up any browned bits from bottom of skillet. Pour over pork. Cover; cook on HIGH 2 hours, turning shanks every 20 minutes.

4. Remove pork to large bowl. Strain cooking liquid; discard solids. Return cooking liquid to **CROCK-POT**® slow cooker. Add remaining carrots and celery. Return pork to **CROCK-POT**® slow cooker. Cover; cook on HIGH 1 hour.

5. Meanwhile, prepare Israeli Couscous.

6. Add Israeli Couscous to **CROCK-POT**® slow cooker. Cover; cook on HIGH 10 minutes or until heated through. Place Israeli Couscous, carrots and celery in shallow bowls. Place pork on top; spoon cooking liquid into each bowl.

Makes 4 servings

Israeli Couscous

2 cups water

Pinch salt

1⅓ cups Israeli or regular couscous

Combine water and salt in large skillet over medium-low heat; bring to a boil over high heat. Add couscous; cook and stir 6 to 8 minutes or until tender. Rinse and drain under cold water.

Makes about 2 cups

52 SOUPS, STEWS & CHILIES

Lamb and Chickpea Stew

1 pound lamb stew meat	¼ teaspoon black pepper
2 teaspoons salt, divided	2 cups chicken broth
2 tablespoons vegetable oil, divided	1 cup diced canned tomatoes, drained
1 large onion, chopped	1 cup dried chickpeas, rinsed and sorted
1 tablespoon minced garlic	½ cup chopped dried apricots
1½ teaspoons ground cumin	¼ cup chopped fresh Italian parsley
1 teaspoon ground turmeric	2 tablespoons honey
1 teaspoon ground coriander	2 tablespoons lemon juice
1 teaspoon ground cinnamon	Hot cooked couscous

1. Season lamb with 1 teaspoon salt. Heat 1 tablespoon oil in large skillet over medium-high heat. Add lamb; cook and stir 8 minutes or until browned on all sides. Remove to **CROCK-POT**® slow cooker.

2. Heat remaining 1 tablespoon oil in same skillet over medium heat. Add onion; cook and stir 6 minutes or until softened. Add garlic, remaining 1 teaspoon salt, cumin, turmeric, coriander, cinnamon and pepper; cook and stir 1 minute. Add broth and tomatoes; cook and stir 5 minutes, scraping up any browned bits from bottom of skillet. Remove to **CROCK-POT**® slow cooker. Stir in chickpeas.

3. Cover; cook on LOW 7 hours. Stir in apricots. Cover; cook on LOW 1 hour. Turn off heat. Let stand 10 minutes. Skim off and discard fat. Stir in parsley, honey and lemon juice. Serve over couscous.

Makes 6 servings

Chicken and Mushroom Stew

4 tablespoons vegetable oil, divided

2 medium leeks (white and light green parts only), halved lengthwise and thinly sliced crosswise

1 carrot, cut into 1-inch pieces

1 stalk celery, diced

6 boneless, skinless chicken thighs (about 2 pounds)

Salt and black pepper

12 ounces cremini mushrooms, quartered

1 ounce dried porcini mushrooms, rehydrated in 1 ½ cups hot water and chopped, soaking liquid strained and reserved

1 teaspoon minced garlic

1 sprig fresh thyme

1 whole bay leaf

¼ cup all-purpose flour

½ cup dry white wine

1 cup chicken broth

1. Heat 1 tablespoon oil in large skillet over medium heat. Add leeks; cook and stir 8 minutes or until softened. Remove to **CROCK-POT**® slow cooker. Add carrot and celery.

2. Heat 1 tablespoon oil in same skillet over medium-high heat. Season chicken with salt and pepper. Add chicken to skillet in batches; cook 8 minutes or until browned on all sides. Remove to **CROCK-POT**® slow cooker.

3. Heat remaining 2 tablespoons oil in same skillet. Add cremini mushrooms; cook 7 minutes or until mushrooms have released their liquid and started to brown. Add porcini mushrooms, garlic, thyme, bay leaf and flour; cook and stir 1 minute. Add wine; cook and stir until evaporated, stirring to scrape up any browned bits from bottom of skillet. Add reserved mushroom soaking liquid and broth; bring to a simmer. Pour mixture into **CROCK-POT**® slow cooker.

4. Cover; cook on HIGH 2 to 3 hours. Remove thyme sprig and bay leaf before serving.

Makes 6 servings

Curried Chicken and Coconut Soup

- 8 boneless, skinless chicken thighs
- 6 cups chicken broth
- 2 cans (about 13 ounces *each*) unsweetened coconut milk
- 2 bunches green onions, sliced
- 3 to 4 tablespoons curry powder
- 4 stalks lemongrass, minced
- 2 tablespoons peeled and minced fresh ginger
- 2 packages (6 ounces *each*) baby spinach
- 3 large limes, divided
  Salt and black pepper
- 1 bunch fresh cilantro, chopped

1. Combine chicken, broth, coconut milk, green onions, curry powder, lemongrass and ginger in **CROCK-POT**® slow cooker; stir to blend. Cover; cook on LOW 10 hours or on HIGH 6 hours.

2. Remove chicken to large cutting board. Remove bones; cut chicken into ½-inch cubes. Return chicken to soup; add spinach. Cover; cook on HIGH 10 minutes or until spinach is wilted.

3. Juice 2 limes; add juice to **CROCK-POT**® slow cooker. Season soup with salt and pepper. Cut remaining lime into 6 to 8 wedges. Sprinkle each serving with cilantro and serve with lime wedges.

Makes 6 to 8 servings

Roasted Tomato-Basil Soup

2 cans (28 ounces *each*) whole tomatoes, drained, 3 cups liquid reserved

2½ tablespoons packed dark brown sugar

1 medium onion, finely chopped

3 cups vegetable broth

3 tablespoons tomato paste

¼ teaspoon ground allspice

1 can (5 ounces) evaporated milk

¼ cup shredded fresh basil (about 10 large leaves)

Salt and black pepper

Sprigs fresh basil (optional)

1. Preheat oven to 450°F. Line baking sheet with foil; spray with nonstick cooking spray. Arrange tomatoes on foil in single layer. Sprinkle with brown sugar; top with onion. Roast 25 minutes or until tomatoes look dry and light brown. Let tomatoes cool slightly; finely chop.

2. Combine tomato mixture, 3 cups reserved liquid from tomatoes, broth, tomato paste and allspice in **CROCK-POT®** slow cooker; stir to blend. Cover; cook on LOW 8 hours or on HIGH 4 hours.

3. Add evaporated milk and shredded basil; season with salt and pepper. Cover; cook on HIGH 30 minutes or until heated through. Garnish each serving with basil.

Makes 6 servings

Double Thick Potato-Cheese Soup

2 pounds baking potatoes, cut into ½-inch cubes

2 cans (10½ ounces *each*) condensed cream of mushroom soup

1½ cups finely chopped green onions, divided

¼ teaspoon garlic powder

⅛ teaspoon ground red pepper

1½ cups (6 ounces) shredded sharp Cheddar cheese

1 cup (8 ounces) sour cream

1 cup milk

Black pepper

1. Combine potatoes, soup, 1 cup green onions, garlic powder and ground red pepper in **CROCK-POT®** slow cooker; stir to blend. Cover; cook on LOW 8 hours or on HIGH 4 hours.

2. Stir cheese, sour cream and milk into **CROCK-POT®** slow cooker until cheese is melted. Cover; cook on HIGH 10 minutes. Season with black pepper. Top with remaining ½ cup green onions.

Makes 6 servings

Cincinnati Chili

1 tablespoon vegetable oil	**2** teaspoons salt
2 onions, chopped	**1½** teaspoons ground cumin
2 pounds ground beef	**1½** teaspoons Worcestershire sauce
1 can (28 ounces) diced tomatoes	**1¼** teaspoons ground allspice
1 cup tomato sauce	**¾** teaspoon ground red pepper
½ cup water	**12** ounces cooked spaghetti
3 cloves garlic, minced	Optional toppings: chopped onions, shredded Cheddar cheese, kidney beans and/or oyster crackers
1 tablespoon unsweetened cocoa powder	
1 tablespoon chili powder	
2½ teaspoons ground cinnamon	

1. Heat oil in large skillet over medium-high heat. Add onions; cook 2 to 3 minutes or until translucent. Add beef; cook until beef is browned, stirring to break up meat. Drain fat. Remove to **CROCK-POT**® slow cooker using slotted spoon.

2. Stir tomatoes, tomato sauce, water, garlic, cocoa, chili powder, cinnamon, salt, cumin, Worcestershire sauce, allspice and ground red pepper into **CROCK-POT**® slow cooker. Cover; cook on LOW 7 to 8 hours or on HIGH 3½ to 4 hours. Spoon chili over spaghetti. Top as desired.

Makes 6 servings

Black and White Chili

1 pound boneless, skinless chicken breasts, cut into ¾-inch pieces

1 cup chopped onion

1 can (about 15 ounces) Great Northern beans, rinsed and drained

1 can (about 15 ounces) black beans, rinsed and drained

1 can (about 14 ounces) stewed tomatoes

2 tablespoons Texas-style chili seasoning mix

1. Spray large skillet with nonstick cooking spray; heat over medium heat. Add chicken and onion; cook and stir 5 minutes or until chicken is browned.

2. Combine chicken mixture, beans, tomatoes and chili seasoning mix in **CROCK-POT**® slow cooker; stir to blend. Cover; cook on LOW 4 to 4½ hours.

Makes 6 servings

Serving Suggestion: For a change of pace, this delicious chili is excellent served over cooked rice or pasta.

Hearty Chicken Noodle Soup

1¼ pounds boneless, skinless chicken breasts, cut into 1-inch pieces

1¼ pounds boneless, skinless chicken thighs

4 cans (about 14 ounces *each*) chicken broth

12 baby carrots, cut into ½-inch pieces

4 stalks celery, cut into ½-inch pieces

¾ cup finely chopped onion

4 cubes chicken bouillon

1 teaspoon dried Italian parsley flakes

½ teaspoon black pepper

¼ teaspoon ground red pepper

1 teaspoon salt

2 cups uncooked egg noodles

1. Place chicken in **CROCK-POT**® slow cooker. Add broth, carrots, celery, onion, bouillon cubes, parsley flakes, black pepper, ground red pepper and salt. Cover; cook on LOW 5 to 6 hours.

2. Stir in egg noodles. Turn **CROCK-POT**® slow cooker to HIGH. Cover; cook on HIGH 30 minutes or until noodles are tender.

Makes 8 to 10 servings

French Onion Soup

¼ cup (½ stick) butter

3 pounds yellow onions, sliced

1 tablespoon sugar

2 to 3 tablespoons dry white wine or water (optional)

8 cups beef broth

8 to 16 slices French bread

1 cup (4 ounces) shredded Gruyère or Swiss cheese

1. Melt butter in large skillet over medium-low heat. Add onions; cover and cook 10 minutes or just until onions are tender and transparent, but not browned.

2. Remove cover. Sprinkle sugar over onions; cook and stir 8 to 10 minutes or until onions are caramelized. Remove to **CROCK-POT**® slow cooker. Add wine, if desired, to skillet. Bring to a boil, scraping up any browned bits from bottom of skillet. Add to **CROCK-POT**® slow cooker. Stir in broth. Cover; cook on LOW 8 hours or on HIGH 6 hours.

3. Preheat broiler. To serve, ladle soup into individual ovenproof soup bowls. Top each serving with 1 or 2 bread slices and cheese. Place under broiler until cheese is melted and bubbly.

Makes 8 servings

Variation: Substitute 1 cup dry white wine for 1 cup of beef broth.

Pasta Fagioli Soup

2 cans (about **14** ounces *each*) beef or vegetable broth

1 can (about **15** ounces) Great Northern beans, rinsed and drained

1 can (about **14** ounces) diced tomatoes

2 zucchini, quartered lengthwise and sliced

1 tablespoon olive oil

1½ teaspoons minced garlic

½ teaspoon dried basil

½ teaspoon dried oregano

½ cup uncooked ditalini, tubetti or small shell pasta

½ cup garlic-seasoned croutons

½ cup grated Asiago or Romano cheese

3 tablespoons chopped fresh basil or Italian parsley (optional)

1. Combine broth, beans, tomatoes, zucchini, oil, garlic, dried basil and oregano in **CROCK-POT®** slow cooker; stir to blend. Cover; cook on LOW 3 to 4 hours.

2. Stir in pasta. Cover; cook on LOW 1 hour or until pasta is tender. Serve soup with croutons and cheese. Garnish with fresh basil.

Makes 5 to 6 servings

Tip: Only small pasta varieties should be used in this recipe. The low heat of a **CROCK-POT®** slow cooker will not allow larger pasta shapes to cook completely.

Hearty Meatball Stew

3 pounds ground beef or ground turkey

1 cup seasoned dry bread crumbs

4 eggs

½ cup milk

¼ cup grated Romano cheese

2 teaspoons salt

2 teaspoons garlic salt

2 teaspoons black pepper

2 tablespoons olive oil

2 cups water

2 cups beef broth

1 can (about 14 ounces) stewed tomatoes, undrained

1 can (12 ounces) tomato paste

1 cup chopped carrots

1 cup chopped onion

¼ cup chopped celery

1 tablespoon Italian seasoning

1. Combine beef, bread crumbs, eggs, milk, cheese, salt, garlic salt and pepper in large bowl. Shape into 2-inch-round meatballs. Heat oil in skillet over medium-high heat. Brown meatballs on all sides. Remove to **CROCK-POT®** slow cooker.

2. Add water, broth, tomatoes, tomato paste, carrots, onion, celery and Italian seasoning; stir to blend. Cover; cook on LOW 4 to 6 hours or on HIGH 2 to 4 hours.

Makes 6 to 8 servings

Greek-Style Chicken Stew

2 cups sliced mushrooms

2 cups cubed peeled eggplant

1¼ cups chicken broth

¾ cup coarsely chopped onion

2 cloves garlic, minced

1½ teaspoons all-purpose flour, plus additional for dusting

1 teaspoon dried oregano

½ teaspoon dried basil

½ teaspoon dried thyme

6 skinless chicken breasts (about 2 pounds)

3 tablespoons dry sherry or chicken broth

¼ teaspoon salt

¼ teaspoon black pepper

1 can (14 ounces) artichoke hearts, drained

12 ounces uncooked wide egg noodles

1. Combine mushrooms, eggplant, broth, onion, garlic, 1½ teaspoons flour, oregano, basil and thyme in **CROCK-POT**® slow cooker. Cover; cook on HIGH 1 hour.

2. Coat chicken very lightly with flour. Generously spray large skillet with nonstick cooking spray; heat over medium heat. Add chicken; cook 10 to 15 minutes or until browned on all sides.

3. Remove vegetables from **CROCK-POT**® slow cooker to medium bowl with slotted spoon. Layer chicken in **CROCK-POT**® slow cooker; return vegetables to **CROCK-POT**® slow cooker. Add sherry, salt and pepper. Turn **CROCK-POT**® slow cooker to LOW. Cover; cook on LOW 6 to 6½ hours or until chicken is no longer pink in center and vegetables are tender.

4. Stir artichokes into **CROCK-POT**® slow cooker. Cover; cook on LOW 45 minutes to 1 hour or until heated through. Cook noodles according to package directions. Serve chicken stew over noodles.

Makes 6 servings

Mushroom-Beef Stew

1 pound cubed beef stew meat

1 can (10¾ ounces) condensed cream of mushroom soup, undiluted

2 cans (4 ounces *each*) sliced mushrooms, drained

1 package (1 ounce) onion soup mix

Hot cooked noodles

Combine beef, soup, mushrooms and dry soup mix in **CROCK-POT**® slow cooker; stir to blend. Cover; cook on LOW 8 to 10 hours. Serve over noodles.

Makes 4 servings

CHICKEN & TURKEY

Greek Chicken and Orzo

2   medium green bell peppers, cut into thin strips

1   cup chopped onion

2   teaspoons extra virgin olive oil

8   chicken thighs, rinsed and patted dry

1   tablespoon dried oregano

½   teaspoon dried rosemary

½   teaspoon garlic powder

¾   teaspoon salt, divided

½   teaspoon black pepper, divided

8   ounces uncooked orzo pasta

Juice and grated peel of 1 medium lemon

½   cup water

2   ounces crumbled feta cheese (optional)

Chopped fresh parsley (optional)

1. Coat inside of **CROCK-POT**® slow cooker with nonstick cooking spray. Add bell peppers and onion.

2. Heat oil in large skillet over medium-high heat. Brown chicken on all sides. Remove to **CROCK-POT**® slow cooker, overlapping slightly if necessary. Sprinkle chicken with oregano, rosemary, garlic powder, ¼ teaspoon salt and ¼ teaspoon black pepper. Cover; cook on LOW 5 to 6 hours or on HIGH 3 to 4 hours or until chicken is tender.

3. Remove chicken to plate. Stir orzo, lemon juice, lemon peel, water, and remaining ½ teaspoon salt and ¼ teaspoon black pepper into **CROCK-POT**® slow cooker. Top with chicken. Cover; cook on HIGH 30 minutes or until pasta is tender. Garnish with cheese and parsley.

Makes 4 servings

Tip: Browning skin-on chicken not only adds flavor and color, but also prevents the skin from shrinking and curling during the long, slow cooking process.

Indian-Style Apricot Chicken

6 skinless chicken thighs (about 2 pounds)

¼ teaspoon salt, plus additional for seasoning

¼ teaspoon black pepper, plus additional for seasoning

1 tablespoon vegetable oil

1 large onion, chopped

2 cloves garlic, minced

2 tablespoons grated fresh ginger

½ teaspoon ground cinnamon

⅛ teaspoon ground allspice

1 can (about 14 ounces) diced tomatoes

1 cup chicken broth

1 package (8 ounces) dried apricots

Pinch saffron threads (optional)

Hot cooked basmati rice

2 tablespoons chopped fresh Italian parsley (optional)

1. Coat inside of **CROCK-POT**® slow cooker with nonstick cooking spray. Season chicken with ¼ teaspoon salt and ¼ teaspoon pepper. Heat oil in large skillet over medium-high heat. Add chicken; cook until browned on all sides. Remove to **CROCK-POT**® slow cooker.

2. Add onion to skillet; cook and stir 3 to 5 minutes or until translucent. Stir in garlic, ginger, cinnamon and allspice; cook and stir 15 to 30 seconds or until mixture is fragrant. Add tomatoes and broth; cook 2 to 3 minutes or until mixture is heated through. Pour into **CROCK-POT**® slow cooker.

3. Add apricots and saffron, if desired. Cover; cook on LOW 5 to 6 hours or on HIGH 3 to 4 hours. Season with additional salt and pepper, if desired. Serve with basmati rice and garnish with parsley.

Makes 4 to 6 servings

Tip: To skin chicken easily, grasp skin with paper towel and pull away. Repeat with fresh paper towel for each piece of chicken, discarding skins and towels.

Chipotle Chicken Stew

1 pound boneless, skinless chicken thighs, cubed

1 can (about 15 ounces) navy beans, rinsed and drained

1 can (about 15 ounces) black beans, rinsed and drained

1 can (about 14 ounces) crushed tomatoes, undrained

1½ cups chicken broth

½ cup orange juice

1 medium onion, diced

1 canned chipotle pepper in adobo sauce, minced

1 teaspoon salt

1 teaspoon ground cumin

1 whole bay leaf

Sprigs fresh cilantro (optional)

1. Combine chicken, beans, tomatoes, broth, orange juice, onion, chipotle pepper, salt, cumin and bay leaf in **CROCK-POT®** slow cooker.

2. Cover; cook on LOW 7 to 8 hours or on HIGH 3½ to 4 hours. Remove and discard bay leaf. Garnish with cilantro.

Makes 6 servings

Zesty Chicken and Rice Supper

2 boneless, skinless chicken breasts, cut into 1-inch pieces

1 can (about 28 ounces) diced tomatoes

2 large green bell peppers, coarsely chopped

1 small onion, chopped

1 cup uncooked converted long grain rice

1 cup water

1 package (about 1 ounce) taco seasoning

1 teaspoon salt

1 teaspoon black pepper

1 teaspoon ground red pepper

Shredded Cheddar cheese (optional)

Combine all ingredients except cheese in **CROCK-POT®** slow cooker; stir to blend. Cover; cook on LOW 6 to 8 hours or on HIGH 3 to 4 hours. Garnish with cheese.

Makes 3 to 4 servings

Turkey Ropa Vieja

12 ounces turkey tenderloin (2 large or 3 small) or boneless, skinless chicken thighs

1 can (8 ounces) tomato sauce

2 medium tomatoes, chopped

1 small yellow onion, thinly sliced

1 small green bell pepper, chopped

4 pimiento-stuffed green olives, sliced

1 clove garlic, minced

¾ teaspoon ground cumin

½ teaspoon dried oregano

⅛ teaspoon black pepper

2 teaspoons lemon juice

¼ teaspoon salt (optional)

1 cup hot cooked rice (optional)

1 cup cooked black beans (optional)

1. Place turkey in **CROCK-POT®** slow cooker. Add tomato sauce, tomatoes, onion, bell pepper, olives, garlic, cumin, oregano and black pepper. Cover; cook on LOW 6 to 7 hours.

2. Remove turkey to cutting board; shred with two forks. Return turkey to **CROCK-POT®** slow cooker. Stir in lemon juice and salt, if desired. Serve with rice and black beans, if desired.

Makes 4 servings

Creole Vegetables and Chicken

1 can (about 14 ounces) diced tomatoes

8 ounces frozen cut okra

2 cups chopped green bell pepper

1 cup chopped yellow onion

1 cup chicken broth

¾ cup sliced celery

2 teaspoons Worcestershire sauce

1 teaspoon dried thyme

1 whole bay leaf

1 pound chicken tenders, cut into bite-size pieces

1 tablespoon extra virgin olive oil

¾ teaspoon Creole seasoning

1½ teaspoons sugar

Hot pepper sauce

¼ cup chopped fresh Italian parsley

1. Coat **CROCK-POT**® slow cooker with nonstick cooking spray. Add tomatoes, okra, bell pepper, onion, broth, celery, Worcestershire sauce, thyme and bay leaf. Cover; cook on LOW 9 hours or on HIGH 4½ hours.

2. Coat medium nonstick skillet with cooking spray. Heat over medium-high heat. Add chicken; cook and stir 6 minutes or until beginning to brown. Remove chicken to **CROCK-POT**® slow cooker. Stir in oil, Creole seasoning, sugar and hot pepper sauce. Cover; cook on HIGH 15 minutes to blend flavors. Stir in parsley. Remove and discard bay leaf.

Makes 8 servings

Tip: To slightly thicken stews in the **CROCK-POT**® slow cooker, remove the solid foods and leave the cooking liquid in the stoneware. Stir ¼ cup cold water into 2 to 4 tablespoons cornstarch in a small bowl until smooth. Stir into the **CROCK-POT**® slow cooker and cook on HIGH until the mixture is smooth.

Mediterranean Chicken

- 1 tablespoon olive oil
- 2 pounds boneless, skinless chicken breasts
- 1 can (28 ounces) diced tomatoes
- 2 onions, chopped
- ½ cup dry sherry
- 6 teaspoons minced garlic

- Juice of 2 lemons
- 2 whole cinnamon sticks
- 1 whole bay leaf
- ½ teaspoon black pepper
- 1 pound cooked egg noodles
- ½ cup feta cheese

1. Heat oil in large skillet. Add chicken; cook until lightly browned on all sides.

2. Combine tomatoes, onions, sherry, garlic, lemon juice, cinnamon sticks, bay leaf and pepper in **CROCK-POT**® slow cooker; stir to blend. Add chicken. Cover; cook on LOW 8 to 10 hours or on HIGH 4 to 5 hours.

3. Remove and discard cinnamon sticks and bay leaf. Serve chicken and sauce over cooked noodles. Sprinkle with cheese just before serving.

Makes 6 servings

Chicken Soup

- 6 cups chicken broth
- 1½ pounds boneless, skinless chicken breasts, cubed
- 2 cups sliced carrots
- 1 cup sliced mushrooms
- 1 red bell pepper, chopped

- 1 onion, chopped
- 2 tablespoons grated fresh ginger
- 3 teaspoons minced garlic
- ½ teaspoon red pepper flakes
- Salt and black pepper

Combine all ingredients in **CROCK-POT**® slow cooker; stir to blend. Cover; cook on LOW 6 to 7 hours or on HIGH 3 to 3½ hours.

Makes 4 to 6 servings

Lemon and Herb Turkey Breast

1 split turkey breast (about 3 pounds)

½ cup lemon juice

½ cup dry white wine

6 cloves garlic, minced

¼ teaspoon salt

¼ teaspoon dried parsley flakes

¼ teaspoon dried tarragon

¼ teaspoon dried rosemary

¼ teaspoon dried sage

¼ teaspoon black pepper

  Sprigs fresh sage and rosemary (optional)

  Lemon slices (optional)

1. Place turkey in **CROCK-POT**® slow cooker. Combine lemon juice, wine, garlic, salt, parsley flakes, tarragon, dried rosemary, dried sage and pepper in medium bowl; stir to blend. Pour lemon juice mixture over turkey in **CROCK-POT**® slow cooker.

2. Cover; cook on LOW 8 to 10 hours or on HIGH 4 to 5 hours. Garnish with fresh sage, fresh rosemary and lemon slices.

Makes 4 servings

Old World Chicken and Vegetables

1 tablespoon dried oregano

1 teaspoon salt, divided

1 teaspoon paprika

½ teaspoon garlic powder

¼ teaspoon black pepper

2 green bell peppers, cut into thin strips

1 yellow onion, thinly sliced

1 cut-up whole chicken (about 3 pounds)

⅓ cup ketchup

  Hot cooked egg noodles

1. Combine oregano, ½ teaspoon salt, paprika, garlic powder and black pepper in small bowl.

2. Place bell peppers and onion in **CROCK-POT**® slow cooker. Add chicken thighs and legs; sprinkle with half of spice blend. Add chicken breasts; sprinkle with remaining spice blend. Cover; cook on LOW 8 hours or on HIGH 4 hours. Stir in ketchup and remaining ½ teaspoon salt.

3. Serve chicken and vegetables over noodles.

Makes 4 servings

Spanish Paella
with Chicken and Sausage

1 tablespoon olive oil

4 chicken thighs (about 2 pounds *total*)

1 medium onion, chopped

4 cups chicken broth

1 pound hot smoked sausage, sliced
    into rounds

1 can (about 14 ounces) stewed
    tomatoes, undrained

1 cup uncooked Arborio rice

1 clove garlic, minced

1 pinch saffron (optional)

½ cup frozen peas, thawed

1. Heat oil in large skillet over medium-high heat. Add chicken in batches; cook until browned well on all sides. Remove chicken to **CROCK-POT**® slow cooker as it browns.

2. Add onion to same skillet; cook and stir until translucent. Stir broth, sausage, tomatoes, rice and garlic into skillet. Stir in saffron, if desired. Pour over chicken in **CROCK-POT**® slow cooker. Cover; cook on LOW 6 to 8 hours or on HIGH 3 to 4 hours or until chicken is fully cooked and rice is tender.

3. Remove chicken pieces to serving platter; fluff rice with fork. Stir peas into rice. Spoon rice into bowls; top with chicken.

Makes 4 servings

Slow-Simmered Curried Chicken

1½ cups chopped onions

1 medium green bell pepper, chopped

1 pound boneless, skinless chicken breasts or thighs, cut into bite-size pieces

1 cup medium salsa

2 teaspoons grated fresh ginger

½ teaspoon garlic powder

½ teaspoon red pepper flakes

¼ cup chopped fresh cilantro

1 teaspoon sugar

1 teaspoon curry powder

½ teaspoon salt

Hot cooked rice

1. Place onions and bell pepper in **CROCK-POT®** slow cooker. Top with chicken.

2. Combine salsa, ginger, garlic powder and red pepper flakes in small bowl; spoon over chicken. Cover; cook on LOW 5 to 6 hours or until chicken is tender.

3. Combine cilantro, sugar, curry powder and salt in small bowl; stir into **CROCK-POT®** slow cooker. Turn **CROCK-POT®** slow cooker to HIGH. Cover; cook on HIGH 15 minutes or until heated through. Serve over rice.

Makes 4 servings

Greek-Style Chicken

6 boneless, skinless chicken thighs, trimmed

½ teaspoon salt

½ teaspoon black pepper

1 tablespoon olive oil

½ cup chicken broth

1 lemon, thinly sliced

¼ cup pitted kalamata olives

1 clove garlic, minced

½ teaspoon dried oregano

Hot cooked orzo or rice

1. Season chicken with salt and pepper. Heat oil in large skillet over medium-high heat. Add chicken; cook until browned on all sides. Remove to **CROCK-POT®** slow cooker.

2. Stir in broth, lemon, olives, garlic and oregano. Cover; cook on LOW 5 to 6 hours or until chicken is tender. Serve with orzo.

Makes 4 to 6 servings

Chicken Meatballs in Spicy Tomato Sauce

3 tablespoons olive oil, divided

1 medium onion, chopped

6 cloves garlic, minced

1½ teaspoons dried basil

¼ teaspoon red pepper flakes

2 cans (about 14 ounces *each*) diced tomatoes

3 tablespoons tomato paste

2 teaspoons salt, divided

1½ pounds ground chicken

2 egg yolks

1 teaspoon dried oregano

¼ teaspoon black pepper

1. Heat 2 tablespoons oil in large skillet over medium-high heat. Add onion, garlic, basil and red pepper flakes; cook and stir 5 minutes or until onion is softened. Remove half of mixture to **CROCK-POT®** slow cooker. Stir in diced tomatoes, tomato paste and 1 teaspoon salt.

2. Remove remaining onion mixture to large bowl. Add chicken, egg yolks, oregano, remaining 1 teaspoon salt and black pepper; mix well. Shape mixture into 24 (1-inch) balls.

3. Heat remaining 1 tablespoon oil in large skillet. Add meatballs in batches; cook 7 minutes or until browned. Remove to **CROCK-POT®** slow cooker using slotted spoon. Cover; cook on LOW 4 to 5 hours.

Makes 4 servings

Hearty Cassoulet

1 tablespoon olive oil

1 onion, finely chopped

4 boneless, skinless chicken thighs, chopped

¼ pound smoked turkey sausage, finely chopped

3 cloves garlic, minced

1 teaspoon dried thyme

½ teaspoon black pepper

¼ cup tomato paste

2 tablespoons water

3 cans (about 15 ounces *each*) Great Northern beans, rinsed and drained

½ cup plain dry bread crumbs

3 tablespoons minced fresh Italian parsley

1. Heat oil in large skillet over medium heat. Add onion; cook and stir 5 minutes or until tender. Add chicken, sausage, garlic, thyme and pepper; cook and stir 5 minutes or until chicken and sausage are browned.

2. Remove from heat; stir in tomato paste and water until blended. Remove to **CROCK-POT**® slow cooker. Stir in beans. Cover; cook on LOW 4 to 4½ hours.

3. Combine bread crumbs and parsley in small bowl. Sprinkle over top of cassoulet just before serving.

Makes 6 servings

Tip: When preparing ingredients for the **CROCK-POT**® slow cooker, cut into uniform pieces so everything will cook evenly.

Chicken Tangier

2	tablespoons dried oregano	1	cup pitted prunes
2	teaspoons seasoned salt	½	cup pitted green olives
2	teaspoons puréed garlic	¼	cup currants or raisins
¼	teaspoon black pepper	2	tablespoons capers
8	skinless chicken thighs (about 3 pounds)		Hot cooked couscous
1	lemon, thinly sliced		Chopped fresh Italian parsley or cilantro (optional)
½	cup dry white wine		
2	tablespoons olive oil		

1. Stir oregano, salt, garlic and pepper in small bowl. Rub onto chicken, coating all sides.

2. Coat inside of **CROCK-POT**® slow cooker with nonstick cooking spray. Arrange chicken in **CROCK-POT**® slow cooker, tucking lemon slices between pieces. Pour wine over chicken; drizzle with oil. Add prunes, olives, currants and capers. Cover; cook on LOW 7 to 8 hours or on HIGH 4 to 5 hours. Serve over couscous. Garnish with parsley.

Makes 8 servings

Tip: It may seem like a lot, but this recipe does call for 2 tablespoons dried oregano in order to more accurately represent the powerfully seasoned flavors of Morocco.

Chutney Curried Chicken with Yogurt Sauce

1 container (6 to 8 ounces) plain yogurt

2 teaspoons curry powder

1 teaspoon garlic salt

⅛ teaspoon ground red pepper

4 bone-in chicken breasts, skin removed (2 to 2¼ pounds)

1 small onion, sliced

⅓ cup mango chutney

1 tablespoon lime juice

2 cloves garlic, minced

2 tablespoons water

2 tablespoons cornstarch

3 cups hot cooked linguine

Optional garnishes: chopped fresh cilantro, chopped peanuts, toasted coconut

1. Place yogurt in paper towel-lined strainer over medium bowl. Drain in refrigerator until ready to serve.

2. Combine curry powder, garlic salt and ground red pepper in small bowl; sprinkle over chicken. Place onion in **CROCK-POT**® slow cooker; top with chicken. Combine chutney, lime juice and garlic in medium bowl; spoon over chicken. Cover; cook on LOW 5 to 6 hours or on HIGH 2½ to 3 hours or until chicken is tender.

3. Remove chicken to serving platter; cover with foil to keep warm. Stir water into cornstarch in small bowl until smooth; whisk into cooking liquid. Cover; cook on HIGH 15 minutes or until thickened. Spoon sauce over chicken; serve over linguine. Top with thickened yogurt. Garnish as desired.

Makes 4 servings

Chicken and Vegetable Soup

1 tablespoon olive oil

2 medium parsnips, cut into ½-inch pieces

2 medium carrots, cut into ½-inch pieces

2 medium onions, chopped

2 stalks celery, cut into ½-inch pieces

1 whole chicken (3 to 3½ pounds)

4 cups chicken broth

10 sprigs fresh Italian parsley *or* 1½ teaspoons dried parsley flakes

4 sprigs fresh thyme *or* ½ teaspoon dried thyme

1. Coat inside of **CROCK-POT**® slow cooker with nonstick cooking spray. Heat oil in large skillet over medium-high heat. Add parsnips, carrots, onions and celery; cook and stir 5 minutes or until vegetables are softened. Remove to **CROCK-POT**® slow cooker. Add chicken, broth, parsley and thyme.

2. Cover; cook on LOW 6 to 7 hours. Remove chicken to large cutting board; let stand 10 minutes. Remove and discard skin and bones from chicken. Shred chicken using two forks. Stir shredded chicken back into **CROCK-POT**® slow cooker.

Makes 10 servings

Turkey Chili

2 tablespoons olive oil, divided

1½ pounds ground turkey

2 medium onions, chopped

1 medium red bell pepper, chopped

1 medium green bell pepper, chopped

5 cloves garlic, minced

1 jalapeño pepper, finely chopped*

2 cans (about 14 ounces *each*) fire-roasted diced tomatoes

4 teaspoons chili powder

1 teaspoon ground cumin

1 teaspoon dried oregano

½ teaspoon salt

*Jalapeño peppers can sting and irritate the skin, so wear rubber gloves when handling peppers and do not touch your eyes.

1. Heat 1 tablespoon oil in large skillet over medium-high heat. Add turkey; cook 7 to 8 minutes, stirring to break up meat. Remove to **CROCK-POT**® slow cooker using slotted spoon.

2. Heat remaining 1 tablespoon oil in same skillet over medium-high heat. Add onions, bell peppers, garlic and jalapeño pepper; cook and stir 4 to 5 minutes or until softened. Stir in tomatoes, chili powder, cumin, oregano and salt; cook 1 minute. Remove to **CROCK-POT**® slow cooker. Cover; cook on LOW 6 hours.

Makes 6 servings

Country Chicken and Vegetables with Creamy Herb Sauce

1 pound new potatoes, cut into ½-inch wedges

1 medium onion, cut into 8 wedges

½ cup coarsely chopped celery

4 bone-in chicken drumsticks, skinned

4 bone-in chicken thighs, skinned

1 can (10¾ ounces) cream of chicken soup

1 packet (1 ounce) ranch-style dressing mix

½ teaspoon dried thyme

¼ teaspoon black pepper

½ cup whipping cream

Salt (optional)

¼ cup finely chopped green onions (green and white parts)

1. Coat inside of **CROCK-POT®** slow cooker with nonstick cooking spray. Arrange potatoes, onion and celery in bottom. Add chicken. Combine soup, dressing mix, thyme and pepper in small bowl. Spoon mixture evenly over chicken and vegetables. Cover; cook on HIGH 3½ hours.

2. Remove chicken to shallow serving bowl with slotted spoon. Add cream and salt, if desired, to cooking liquid; stir to blend. Pour sauce over chicken. Garnish with green onions.

Makes 4 servings

Chicken and Mushroom Fettuccine Alfredo

1½ pounds boneless, skinless chicken breasts, cut into 1-inch strips

2 packages (8 ounces *each*) cremini mushrooms, cut into thirds

½ teaspoon salt

¼ teaspoon black pepper

¼ teaspoon garlic powder

2 packages (8 ounces *each*) cream cheese, cut into cubes

1½ cups grated Parmesan cheese, plus additional for garnish

1½ cups whole milk

1 cup (2 sticks) butter, cubed

1 package (16 ounces) uncooked fettuccine

Chopped fresh basil (optional)

1. Coat inside of **CROCK-POT®** slow cooker with nonstick cooking spray. Arrange chicken in single layer in bottom of **CROCK-POT®** slow cooker. Top with mushrooms. Sprinkle salt, pepper and garlic powder over mushrooms.

2. Cook and stir cream cheese, 1½ cups Parmesan cheese, milk and butter in medium saucepan over medium heat until smooth and heated through. Pour over mushrooms, pushing down any that float to surface. Cover; cook on LOW 4 to 5 hours or on HIGH 2 to 2½ hours.

3. Cook fettuccine according to package directions; drain. Add fettuccine to Alfredo sauce; toss gently to combine. Garnish with additional Parmesan cheese and basil.

Makes 6 to 8 servings

Simple Coq au Vin

4 chicken legs
Salt and black pepper
2 tablespoons olive oil
8 ounces mushrooms, sliced
1 onion, sliced into rings
½ cup dry red wine
½ teaspoon dried basil
½ teaspoon dried thyme
½ teaspoon dried oregano
Hot cooked rice

1. Season chicken with salt and pepper. Heat oil in large skillet over medium-high heat. Add chicken; cook until browned on all sides. Remove to **CROCK-POT**® slow cooker.

2. Add mushrooms and onion slices to skillet; cook and stir until tender. Add wine, stirring to scrape up any browned bits from bottom of skillet. Add to **CROCK-POT**® slow cooker. Sprinkle with basil, thyme and oregano. Cover; cook on LOW 8 to 10 hours or on HIGH 3 to 4 hours.

3. Serve chicken and sauce over rice.

Makes 4 servings

Tandoori Chicken

8 boneless, skinless chicken breasts
    (2 pounds *total*), cut into 1-inch pieces
1 cup chicken broth
1 can (6 ounces) tomato paste
½ cup chopped onion
½ cup chopped green bell pepper
½ cup (1 stick) butter
2 tablespoons fresh chopped cilantro

1 tablespoon chopped garlic
1 teaspoon ground cumin
1 teaspoon tandoori powder
1 teaspoon chili powder
1 teaspoon paprika
Salt and black pepper
Hot cooked rice

Combine chicken, broth, tomato paste, onion, bell pepper, butter, cilantro, garlic, cumin, tandoori powder, chili powder, paprika, salt and black pepper in **CROCK-POT**® slow cooker; stir to blend. Cover; cook on LOW 6 hours or on HIGH 4 hours. Serve over rice.

Makes 4 to 5 servings

Curry Chicken with Mango and Red Pepper

6 boneless, skinless chicken thighs or breasts (1½ pounds *total*)

Salt and black pepper

2 tablespoons olive oil

1 bag (8 ounces) frozen mango chunks, thawed and drained

2 red bell peppers, diced

⅓ cup raisins

1 shallot, thinly sliced

¾ cup chicken broth

1 tablespoon cider vinegar

2 cloves garlic, crushed

4 thin slices fresh ginger

1 teaspoon ground cumin

½ teaspoon curry powder

½ teaspoon whole cloves

¼ teaspoon ground red pepper (optional)

Fresh cilantro (optional)

1. Season chicken with salt and black pepper. Heat oil in large skillet over medium heat. Add chicken; cook 5 to 7 minutes or until lightly browned. Remove to **CROCK-POT**® slow cooker.

2. Add mango, bell peppers, raisins and shallot to **CROCK-POT**® slow cooker. Combine broth, vinegar, garlic, ginger, cumin, curry powder, cloves and ground red pepper, if desired, in large bowl; pour over chicken. Cover; cook on LOW 6 to 8 hours or on HIGH 3 to 4 hours. To serve, spoon mango, bell peppers, raisins, shallot and cooking liquid over chicken. Garnish with cilantro.

Makes 6 servings

Turkey Stroganoff

- **4** cups sliced mushrooms
- **2** stalks celery, thinly sliced
- **2** medium shallots *or* ½ small onion, minced
- **1** cup reduced-sodium chicken broth
- **½** teaspoon dried thyme
- **¼** teaspoon black pepper
- **2** turkey tenderloins, turkey breasts *or* boneless, skinless chicken thighs (about 10 ounces *each*), cut into 1-inch pieces
- **½** cup sour cream
- **1** tablespoon plus 1 teaspoon all-purpose flour
- **¼** teaspoon salt
- **1⅓** cups hot cooked wide whole wheat egg noodles

1. Spray large skillet with nonstick cooking spray; heat over medium heat. Add mushrooms, celery and shallots; cook and stir 5 minutes or until mushrooms and shallots are tender. Remove to **CROCK-POT**® slow cooker. Stir broth, thyme and pepper into **CROCK-POT**® slow cooker. Stir in turkey. Cover; cook on LOW 5 to 6 hours.

2. Stir sour cream into flour in small bowl until smooth. Spoon 2 tablespoons liquid from **CROCK-POT**® slow cooker into sour cream mixture; stir until blended. Stir sour cream mixture into **CROCK-POT**® slow cooker. Cover; cook on LOW 10 minutes.

3. Season with salt. Spoon noodles onto each plate. Top with turkey mixture.

Makes 4 servings

Provençal Lemon and Olive Chicken

2 cups chopped onions

8 chicken thighs (about 2½ pounds)

1 lemon, thinly sliced

1 cup pitted green olives

1 tablespoon olive brine from jar or white vinegar

2 teaspoons herbes de Provence

1 whole bay leaf

½ teaspoon salt

⅛ teaspoon black pepper

1 cup chicken broth

½ cup minced fresh Italian parsley

1. Place onions in **CROCK-POT®** slow cooker. Arrange chicken over onions. Place lemon slice on each thigh. Add olives, brine, herbes de Provence, bay leaf, salt and pepper; slowly pour in broth.

2. Cover; cook on LOW 5 to 6 hours or on HIGH 3 to 3½ hours or until chicken is tender. Remove and discard bay leaf. Stir in parsley before serving.

Makes 8 servings

Coconut-Curry Chicken Thighs

8 chicken thighs (about 2 to 2½ pounds)

½ teaspoon salt

¼ teaspoon black pepper

1 tablespoon olive oil

1 medium onion, chopped

1 medium red bell pepper, chopped

3 cloves garlic, minced

1 tablespoon grated fresh ginger

1 can (about 13 ounces) unsweetened coconut milk

3 tablespoons honey

1 tablespoon Thai red curry paste

2 teaspoons Thai roasted red chili paste

2 tablespoons chopped fresh cilantro (optional)

½ cup chopped cashew nuts (optional)

1. Coat inside of **CROCK-POT**® slow cooker with nonstick cooking spray. Season chicken with salt and black pepper. Heat oil in large skillet over medium-high heat. Add chicken; cook 6 to 8 minutes or until browned on all sides. Remove to **CROCK-POT**® slow cooker.

2. Pour off all but 1 tablespoon fat from skillet. Heat skillet over medium-high heat. Add onion, bell pepper, garlic and ginger; cook and stir 1 to 2 minutes or until vegetables begin to soften. Remove skillet from heat. Stir in coconut milk, honey, curry paste and chili paste until smooth. Pour over chicken in **CROCK-POT**® slow cooker.

3. Cover; cook on LOW 4 hours. Serve chicken with sauce. Garnish with cilantro and cashews.

Makes 4 servings

Boneless Chicken Cacciatore

1 tablespoon olive oil

6 boneless, skinless chicken breasts, sliced in half horizontally

4 cups tomato-basil or marinara pasta sauce

1 cup coarsely chopped yellow onion

1 cup coarsely chopped green bell pepper

1 can (6 ounces) sliced mushrooms

¼ cup dry red wine (optional)

2 teaspoons minced garlic

2 teaspoons dried oregano

2 teaspoons dried thyme

1 teaspoon salt

2 teaspoons black pepper

Hot cooked pasta (optional)

1. Heat oil in large skillet over medium heat. Add chicken; cook until browned on all sides. Remove to **CROCK-POT**® slow cooker.

2. Add pasta sauce, onion, bell pepper, mushrooms, wine, if desired, garlic, oregano, thyme, salt and black pepper to **CROCK-POT**® slow cooker; stir to blend. Cover; cook on LOW 5 to 7 hours or on HIGH 2 to 3 hours. Serve over pasta, if desired.

Makes 6 servings

Forty-Clove Chicken

1 cut-up whole chicken (about 3 pounds)

Salt and black pepper

1 to 2 tablespoons olive oil

¼ cup dry white wine

2 tablespoons chopped fresh Italian parsley *or* 2 teaspoons dried parsley flakes

2 tablespoons dry vermouth

2 teaspoons dried basil

1 teaspoon dried oregano

Pinch red pepper flakes

40 cloves garlic (about 2 heads)

4 stalks celery, sliced

Juice and peel of 1 lemon

1. Season chicken with salt and black pepper. Heat oil in large skillet over medium heat. Add chicken in batches; cook until browned on all sides. Remove to plate.

2. Combine wine, parsley, vermouth, basil, oregano and red pepper flakes in large bowl. Add garlic and celery; stir to coat. Remove garlic and celery to **CROCK-POT**® slow cooker with slotted spoon. Add chicken to remaining herb mixture; stir to coat. Arrange chicken on top of garlic mixture in **CROCK-POT**® slow cooker. Sprinkle lemon juice and peel over chicken in **CROCK-POT**® slow cooker. Cover; cook on LOW 6 hours.

Makes 4 to 6 servings

Herbed Turkey Breast with Orange Sauce

1 large onion, chopped

3 cloves garlic, minced

1 teaspoon dried rosemary

½ teaspoon black pepper

1 boneless, skinless turkey breast (3 pounds)*

1½ cups orange juice

*Unless you have a 5-, 6- or 7-quart **CROCK-POT**® slow cooker, cut any piece of meat larger than 2½ pounds in half so it cooks completely.

1. Place onion in **CROCK-POT**® slow cooker. Combine garlic, rosemary and pepper in small bowl.

2. Cut slices about three fourths of the way through turkey at 2-inch intervals. Rub garlic mixture between slices. Place turkey, cut side up, in **CROCK-POT**® slow cooker. Pour orange juice over turkey. Cover; cook on LOW 7 to 8 hours.

3. Slice turkey. Serve with orange sauce.

Makes 4 to 6 servings

Tip: Don't peek! The **CROCK-POT**® slow cooker can take as long as 30 minutes to regain heat lost when the cover is removed. Only remove the cover when instructed to do so by the recipe.

Basque Chicken with Peppers

1 cut-up whole chicken (4 pounds)

2 teaspoons salt, divided

1 teaspoon black pepper, divided

1½ tablespoons olive oil

1 onion, chopped

1 medium green bell pepper, cut into strips

1 medium yellow bell pepper, cut into strips

1 medium red bell pepper, cut into strips

8 ounces small brown mushrooms, halved

1 can (about 14 ounces) stewed tomatoes, undrained

½ cup chicken broth

½ cup Rioja wine

3 ounces tomato paste

2 cloves garlic, minced

1 sprig fresh marjoram

1 teaspoon smoked paprika

4 ounces chopped prosciutto

1. Season chicken with 1 teaspoon salt and ½ teaspoon black pepper. Heat oil in large skillet over medium-high heat. Add chicken in batches; cook 6 to 8 minutes or until browned on all sides. Remove to **CROCK-POT**® slow cooker.

2. Heat same skillet over medium-low heat. Add onion; cook and stir 3 minutes or until softened. Add bell peppers and mushrooms; cook 3 minutes. Add tomatoes, broth, wine, tomato paste, garlic, marjoram, remaining 1 teaspoon salt, paprika and remaining ½ teaspoon black pepper to skillet; bring to a simmer. Cook 3 to 4 minutes; pour over chicken in **CROCK-POT**® slow cooker. Cover; cook on LOW 5 to 6 hours or on HIGH 4 hours.

3. Ladle vegetables and sauce over chicken. Sprinkle with prosciutto.

Makes 4 to 6 servings

Chinese Chicken Stew

1 pound boneless, skinless chicken thighs, cut into 1-inch pieces

1 teaspoon Chinese five-spice powder*

½ to ¾ teaspoon red pepper flakes

1 tablespoon peanut or vegetable oil

1 large onion, coarsely chopped

1 package (8 ounces) mushrooms, sliced

2 cloves garlic, minced

1 can (about 14 ounces) chicken broth, divided

1 tablespoon cornstarch

1 large red bell pepper, cut into ¾-inch pieces

2 tablespoons soy sauce

2 large green onions, cut into ½-inch pieces

1 tablespoon sesame oil

3 cups hot cooked rice (optional)

¼ cup coarsely chopped fresh cilantro (optional)

*Chinese five-spice powder is a blend of cinnamon, cloves, fennel seed, anise and Szechuan peppercorns. It is available in most supermarkets and Asian grocery stores.

1. Toss chicken with five-spice powder and red pepper flakes in large bowl. Heat peanut oil in large skillet. Add chicken and onion; cook and stir about 5 minutes or until chicken is browned. Add mushrooms and garlic; cook and stir until chicken is no longer pink.

2. Stir ¼ cup broth into cornstarch in small bowl until smooth; set aside. Combine chicken mixture, remaining broth, bell pepper and soy sauce in **CROCK-POT**® slow cooker. Cover; cook on LOW 3½ hours or until peppers are tender.

3. Whisk cornstarch mixture, green onions and sesame oil into **CROCK-POT**® slow cooker. Cover; cook on LOW 30 to 45 minutes or until thickened. Ladle into soup bowls. Scoop ½ cup rice into each bowl. Sprinkle with cilantro.

Makes 6 servings

Three Onion Chicken

3 tablespoons butter

3 onions, chopped

3 leeks (white and light green parts only), sliced

2 cloves garlic, chopped

½ cup dry white wine

2 tablespoons lemon juice

½ cup reduced-sodium chicken broth

6 boneless, skinless chicken breasts (6 ounces *each*)

1 teaspoon salt

¼ teaspoon black pepper

½ teaspoon dried thyme

2 green onions, sliced

1. Melt butter in large skillet over medium-high heat. Add onions; cook and stir 3 to 5 minutes or until translucent. Add leeks; cook and stir 5 minutes or until onions are golden brown and leeks are tender. Add garlic; cook and stir 30 seconds. Add wine and lemon juice; cook and stir until most liquid is evaporated. Remove to **CROCK-POT**® slow cooker. Pour in broth.

2. Sprinkle chicken with salt and pepper. Add to **CROCK-POT**® slow cooker. Sprinkle with thyme. Cover; cook on HIGH 1½ hours or until chicken is cooked through. Sprinkle with green onions before serving.

Makes 6 servings

Chicken Mozambique

2½ pounds boneless, skinless chicken breasts

1 cup dry white wine

½ cup (1 stick) butter, cut into small pieces

1 small onion, chopped

2 tablespoons minced garlic

2 tablespoons lemon juice

2 tablespoons hot pepper sauce

1 teaspoon salt

Hot cooked rice

Zucchini slices (optional)

Paprika (optional)

Combine chicken, wine, butter, onion, garlic, lemon juice, hot pepper sauce and salt in **CROCK-POT**® slow cooker; stir to blend. Cover; cook on LOW 8 hours or on HIGH 6 hours. Serve chicken and sauce with rice and zucchini, if desired. Sprinkle with paprika, if desired.

Makes 10 servings

Spanish Chicken with Rice

2 tablespoons olive oil

11 ounces cooked linguiça or kielbasa sausage, sliced into ½-inch rounds

6 boneless, skinless chicken thighs (about 1 pound)

1 onion, chopped

5 cloves garlic, minced

2 cups uncooked converted long grain rice

½ cup diced carrots

1 red bell pepper, chopped

½ teaspoon salt

¼ teaspoon black pepper

¼ teaspoon saffron threads (optional)

3½ cups hot chicken broth

½ cup peas

1. Heat oil in medium skillet over medium heat. Add sausage; cook and stir until browned. Remove to **CROCK-POT**® slow cooker using slotted spoon.

2. Add chicken to skillet; cook until browned on all sides. Remove to **CROCK-POT**® slow cooker. Add onion to skillet; cook and stir 5 minutes or until softened. Stir in garlic; cook 30 seconds. Remove to **CROCK-POT**® slow cooker.

3. Stir rice, carrots, bell pepper, salt, black pepper and saffron, if desired, into **CROCK-POT**® slow cooker. Pour broth over mixture. Cover; cook on HIGH 3½ to 4 hours.

4. Stir in peas. Cover; cook on HIGH 15 minutes or until heated through.

Makes 6 servings

HEARTY BEEF

Asian Beef with Mandarin Oranges

- **2** tablespoons vegetable oil
- **2** pounds boneless beef chuck roast, cut into ½-inch strips
- **1** onion, thinly sliced
- **1** head bok choy, chopped
- **1** green bell pepper, sliced
- **1** can (5 ounces) sliced water chestnuts, drained
- **1** package (about 3 ounces) shiitake mushrooms, sliced
- **⅓** cup soy sauce
- **2** teaspoons minced fresh ginger
- **¼** teaspoon salt
- **1** can (11 ounces) mandarin oranges, drained and syrup reserved
- **2** tablespoons cornstarch
- **2** cups beef broth
- **6** cups steamed rice

1. Heat oil in large skillet over medium-high heat. Add beef in batches; cook until browned on all sides. Remove to **CROCK-POT**® slow cooker.

2. Add onion to skillet; cook and stir over medium heat until softened. Add bok choy, bell pepper, water chestnuts, mushrooms, soy sauce, ginger and salt; cook and stir 5 minutes or until bok choy is wilted. Remove to **CROCK-POT**® slow cooker.

3. Stir reserved mandarin orange syrup into cornstarch in medium bowl until smooth. Whisk into broth in large bowl; pour into **CROCK-POT**® slow cooker. Cover; cook on LOW 10 hours or on HIGH 5 to 6 hours or until beef is tender.

4. Stir in mandarin oranges. Spoon over rice in shallow serving bowls.

Makes 6 servings

Classic Beef Stew

2½ pounds cubed beef stew meat

¼ cup all-purpose flour

2 tablespoons olive oil, divided

3 cups beef broth

16 baby carrots

8 fingerling potatoes, halved crosswise

1 medium onion, chopped

1 ounce dried oyster mushrooms, chopped

2 teaspoons garlic powder

1 teaspoon dried basil

1 teaspoon dried oregano

½ teaspoon dried rosemary

½ teaspoon dried marjoram

½ teaspoon dried sage

½ teaspoon dried thyme

Salt and black pepper (optional)

Chopped fresh Italian parsley (optional)

1. Combine beef and flour in large bowl; toss to coat. Heat 1 tablespoon oil in large skillet over medium-high heat. Add half of beef; cook and stir 4 minutes or until browned. Remove to **CROCK-POT®** slow cooker. Repeat with remaining oil and beef.

2. Add broth, carrots, potatoes, onion, mushrooms, garlic powder, basil, oregano, rosemary, marjoram, sage and thyme to **CROCK-POT®** slow cooker; stir to blend. Cover; cook on LOW 10 to 12 hours or on HIGH 5 to 6 hours. Season with salt and pepper, if desired. Garnish with parsley.

Makes 8 servings

Easy Beef Burgundy

1½ pounds boneless beef round steak, cut into 1-inch pieces

1 can (10¾ ounces) condensed cream of mushroom soup, undiluted

1 cup dry red wine

1 onion, chopped

1 can (4 ounces) sliced mushrooms, drained

1 package (about 1 ounce) onion soup mix

1 tablespoon minced garlic

Hot cooked egg noodles (optional)

Combine beef, mushroom soup, wine, onion, mushrooms, dry soup mix and garlic in **CROCK-POT®** slow cooker; stir to blend. Cover; cook on LOW 6 to 8 hours or until beef is tender. Serve over noodles, if desired.

Makes 4 to 6 servings

Cajun Pot Roast

1 boneless beef chuck roast (3 pounds)*

1 to 2 tablespoons Cajun seasoning

1 tablespoon vegetable oil

1 can (about 14 ounces) diced tomatoes

1 can (about 14 ounces) diced tomatoes with mild green chiles

1 medium onion, chopped

1 cup chopped rutabaga

1 cup chopped mushrooms

1 cup chopped turnip

1 cup chopped parsnip

1 cup chopped green bell pepper

1 cup green beans

1 cup sliced carrots

1 cup corn

2 tablespoons hot pepper sauce

1 teaspoon sugar

½ teaspoon black pepper

¾ cup water

*Unless you have a 5-, 6- or 7-quart **CROCK-POT**® slow cooker, cut any roast larger than 2½ pounds in half so it cooks completely.

1. Coat inside of **CROCK-POT**® slow cooker with nonstick cooking spray. Season beef with Cajun seasoning. Heat oil in large skillet over medium-high heat. Add beef; cook 5 minutes on each side or until browned.

2. Combine beef, tomatoes, onion, rutabaga, mushrooms, turnip, parsnip, bell pepper, green beans, carrots, corn, hot pepper sauce, sugar and black pepper in **CROCK-POT**® slow cooker. Pour in water. Cover; cook on LOW 6 hours.

Makes 6 servings

Beef and Black Bean Chili

1 tablespoon vegetable oil

1 pound boneless beef round steak, cut into 1-inch cubes

1 package (14 ounces) frozen green and red bell pepper strips with onions

1 can (about 15 ounces) black beans, rinsed and drained

1 can (about 14 ounces) fire-roasted diced tomatoes

2 tablespoons chili powder

1 tablespoon minced garlic

2 teaspoons ground cumin

½ ounce semisweet chocolate, chopped

Hot cooked rice

Shredded Cheddar cheese (optional)

1. Heat oil in large skillet over medium-high heat. Add beef; cook until browned on all sides. Remove to **CROCK-POT**® slow cooker using slotted spoon.

2. Stir pepper strips with onions, beans, tomatoes, chili powder, garlic and cumin into **CROCK-POT**® slow cooker. Cover; cook on LOW 8 to 9 hours. Turn off heat; stir in chocolate until melted. Serve over rice; garnish with cheese.

Makes 4 servings

Best Ever Chili

1½ pounds ground beef

1 cup chopped onion

2 cans (about 15 ounces *each*) kidney beans, drained and liquid reserved

1½ pounds plum tomatoes, diced

1 can (15 ounces) tomato paste

3 to 6 tablespoons chili powder

Sour cream and chopped green onion (optional)

1. Brown beef and onion 6 to 8 minutes in large skillet over medium-high heat, stirring to break up meat. Drain fat. Remove to **CROCK-POT**® slow cooker using slotted spoon.

2. Add beans, tomatoes, tomato paste, 1 cup reserved bean liquid and chili powder to **CROCK-POT**® slow cooker; mix well. Cover; cook on LOW 10 to 12 hours. Top with sour cream and green onion, if desired.

Makes 8 servings

Beef and Veal Meat Loaf

1 tablespoon olive oil

1 small onion, chopped

½ red bell pepper, chopped

3 cloves garlic, minced

1 teaspoon dried oregano

1 pound ground beef

1 pound ground veal

1 egg

3 tablespoons tomato paste

1 teaspoon salt

½ teaspoon black pepper

1. Coat inside of **CROCK-POT®** slow cooker with nonstick cooking spray. Heat oil in large skillet over medium-high heat. Add onion, bell pepper, garlic and oregano; cook and stir 5 minutes or until vegetables are softened. Remove to large bowl; cool 6 minutes.

2. Add beef, veal, egg, tomato paste, salt and black pepper; mix well. Shape into 9×5-inch loaf; place in **CROCK-POT®** slow cooker. Cover; cook on LOW 5 to 6 hours. Remove meat loaf to large cutting board; let stand 10 minutes before slicing.

Makes 6 servings

Beef and Beet Borscht

6 slices bacon

1 boneless beef chuck roast (1½ pounds), trimmed and cut into ½-inch pieces

1 medium onion, chopped

4 cloves garlic, minced

4 medium beets, peeled and cut into ½-inch pieces

3 cups beef broth

2 large carrots, sliced

6 sprigs fresh dill

3 tablespoons honey

3 tablespoons red wine vinegar

2 whole bay leaves

3 cups shredded green cabbage

1. Heat large skillet over medium heat. Add bacon; cook and stir until crisp. Remove to paper towel-lined plate using slotted spoon; crumble.

2. Return skillet to medium-high heat. Add beef; cook 5 minutes or until browned. Remove to **CROCK-POT**® slow cooker.

3. Pour off all but 1 tablespoon fat from skillet. Add onion and garlic; cook and stir 4 minutes or until onion is softened. Remove to **CROCK-POT**® slow cooker. Stir in bacon, beets, broth, carrots, dill, honey, vinegar and bay leaves.

4. Cover; cook on LOW 5 to 6 hours. Stir in cabbage. Cover; cook on LOW 30 minutes. Remove and discard bay leaves before serving.

Makes 6 to 8 servings

Hearty Chili Mac

1 pound ground beef

1 can (about 14 ounces) diced tomatoes, drained

1 cup chopped onion

1 tablespoon chili powder

1 clove garlic, minced

½ teaspoon salt

½ teaspoon ground cumin

½ teaspoon dried oregano

¼ teaspoon red pepper flakes

¼ teaspoon black pepper

2 cups hot cooked elbow macaroni

1. Brown beef 6 to 8 minutes in large skillet over medium-high heat, stirring to break up meat. Drain fat. Remove to **CROCK-POT**® slow cooker.

2. Add tomatoes, onion, chili powder, garlic, salt, cumin, oregano, red pepper flakes and black pepper to **CROCK-POT**® slow cooker; mix well. Cover; cook on LOW 4 hours.

3. Stir in macaroni. Cover; cook on LOW 1 hour.

Makes 4 servings

Beef Fajita Soup

1 pound cubed beef stew meat

1 can (about 15 ounces) pinto beans, rinsed and drained

1 can (about 15 ounces) black beans, rinsed and drained

1 can (about 14 ounces) diced tomatoes with roasted garlic

1 can (about 14 ounces) beef broth

1½ cups water

1 green bell pepper, thinly sliced

1 red bell pepper, thinly sliced

1 onion, thinly sliced

2 teaspoons ground cumin

1 teaspoon seasoned salt

1 teaspoon black pepper

Optional toppings: sour cream, shredded cheese and/or chopped olives

Combine beef, beans, tomatoes, broth, water, bell peppers, onion, cumin, salt and black pepper in **CROCK-POT**® slow cooker; stir to blend. Cover; cook on LOW 8 hours. Top as desired.

Makes 8 servings

Meatballs and Spaghetti Sauce

2 pounds ground beef

1 cup plain dry bread crumbs

1 onion, chopped

2 eggs, beaten

¼ cup minced fresh Italian parsley

4 teaspoons minced garlic, divided

½ teaspoon ground mustard

½ teaspoon black pepper

4 tablespoons olive oil, divided

1 can (28 ounces) whole tomatoes

½ cup chopped fresh basil

1 teaspoon sugar

Salt and black pepper

Hot cooked spaghetti

1. Combine beef, bread crumbs, onion, eggs, parsley, 2 teaspoons garlic, ground mustard and ½ teaspoon pepper in large bowl. Shape into walnut-sized balls. Heat 2 tablespoons oil in large skillet over medium heat. Add meatballs; cook until browned on all sides. Remove to **CROCK·POT**® slow cooker.

2. Combine tomatoes, basil, remaining 2 tablespoons oil, 2 teaspoons garlic, sugar, salt and black pepper in medium bowl; stir to blend. Pour over meatballs, turn to coat. Cover; cook on LOW 3 to 5 hours or on HIGH 2 to 4 hours. Serve over spaghetti.

Makes 6 to 8 servings

Beefy Tortellini

½ pound ground beef or turkey

1 jar (24 to 26 ounces) roasted tomato and garlic pasta sauce

1 package (12 ounces) uncooked three-cheese tortellini

8 ounces sliced button or exotic mushrooms, such as oyster, shiitake and cremini

½ cup water

½ teaspoon red pepper flakes (optional)

¾ cup grated Asiago or Romano cheese
Chopped fresh Italian parsley (optional)

1. Coat inside of **CROCK-POT**® slow cooker with nonstick cooking spray. Brown beef in large skillet over medium-high heat 6 to 8 minutes, stirring to break up meat. Remove to **CROCK-POT**® slow cooker using slotted spoon.

2. Stir pasta sauce, tortellini, mushrooms, water and red pepper flakes, if desired, into **CROCK-POT**® slow cooker. Cover; cook on LOW 2 hours or on HIGH 1 hour. Stir.

3. Cover; cook on LOW 2 to 2½ hours or on HIGH ½ to 1 hour. Serve in bowls topped with cheese and parsley, if desired.

Makes 6 servings

Corned Beef and Cabbage

12 new red potatoes, quartered

4 carrots, sliced

1 corned beef brisket (about 4 pounds)*

2 onions, sliced

3 whole bay leaves

8 whole black peppercorns

1 head cabbage, cut into wedges

*Unless you have a 5-, 6- or 7-quart **CROCK-POT®** slow cooker, cut any roast larger than 2½ pounds in half so it cooks completely.

1. Place potatoes and carrots in bottom of **CROCK-POT®** slow cooker. Add brisket, onions, bay leaves, peppercorns and enough water to cover brisket. Cover; cook on LOW 4 to 5 hours or on HIGH 2 to 2½ hours.

2. Add cabbage. Cover; cook on LOW 4 to 5 hours or on HIGH 2 to 2½ hours. Remove and discard bay leaves. Remove brisket to large cutting board; slice against the grain. Serve with vegetables.

Makes 6 to 8 servings

Shepherd's Pie

1 pound ground beef

1 pound ground lamb

1 package (12 ounces) frozen chopped onions

2 teaspoons minced garlic

1 package (16 ounces) frozen peas and carrots

1 can (about 14 ounces) diced tomatoes, drained

3 tablespoons quick-cooking tapioca

2 teaspoons dried oregano

1 teaspoon salt

½ teaspoon black pepper

2 packages (24 ounces *each*) prepared mashed potatoes

1. Brown beef and lamb in large nonstick skillet over medium-high heat 6 to 8 minutes, stirring to break up meat. Drain fat. Remove to **CROCK-POT**® slow cooker using slotted spoon. Return skillet to heat. Add onions and garlic; cook and stir until onions are tender. Remove to **CROCK-POT**® slow cooker.

2. Stir peas and carrots, tomatoes, tapioca, oregano, salt and pepper into **CROCK-POT**® slow cooker. Cover; cook on LOW 7 to 8 hours.

3. Top with prepared mashed potatoes. Cover; cook on LOW 30 minutes or until potatoes are heated through.

Makes 6 servings

Asian Ginger Beef over Bok Choy

2 tablespoons peanut oil

1½ pounds boneless beef chuck roast, cut into 1-inch pieces

3 green onions, cut into ½-inch slices

6 cloves garlic

1 cup chicken broth

½ cup water

¼ cup soy sauce

2 teaspoons ground ginger

1 teaspoon Asian chili paste

9 ounces fresh udon noodles or vermicelli, cooked and drained

3 cups bok choy, trimmed, washed and cut into 1-inch pieces

½ cup minced fresh cilantro

1. Heat oil in large skillet over medium-high heat. Add beef in batches; cook until browned on all sides. Brown last batch of beef with green onions and garlic.

2. Remove to **CROCK-POT**® slow cooker. Add broth, water, soy sauce, ginger and chili paste; stir to blend. Cover; cook on LOW 7 to 8 hours or on HIGH 3 to 4 hours or until beef is very tender.

3. Just before serving, add noodles to **CROCK-POT**® slow cooker; stir to blend. Add bok choy and stir again. Cover; cook on HIGH 15 minutes or until bok choy is tender-crisp. Garnish with cilantro.

Makes 6 to 8 servings

Thai Steak Salad

STEAK

¼ cup soy sauce

3 cloves garlic, minced

3 tablespoons honey

1 pound boneless beef chuck steak, about ¾ inch thick

DRESSING

¼ cup hoisin sauce

2 tablespoons creamy peanut butter

½ cup water

1 tablespoon minced fresh ginger

1 tablespoon ketchup or tomato paste

2 teaspoons lime juice

2 cloves garlic, minced

1 teaspoon sugar

¼ teaspoon hot chili sauce or sriracha*

SALAD

½ head savoy cabbage, shredded

1 bag (10 ounces) romaine lettuce with carrots and red cabbage

1 cup fresh cilantro leaves

¾ cup chopped mango

½ cup chopped peanuts

Fresh lime wedges

*Sriracha is a Thai hot sauce, sometimes called "rooster sauce" because of the label on the bottle, and is available in Asian specialty markets.

1. Prepare steak: Coat inside of **CROCK-POT®** slow cooker with nonstick cooking spray. Combine soy sauce, garlic and honey in small bowl. Pour into **CROCK-POT®** slow cooker. Add steak, turning to coat. Cover; cook on HIGH 3 hours or until steak is tender.

2. Transfer steak to cutting board and let stand 10 minutes. Slice against the grain into ¼-inch strips. Cover with plastic wrap and refrigerate until needed.

3. Prepare dressing: Blend hoisin sauce and peanut butter until smooth. Add remaining dressing ingredients; stir until well blended.

4. Assemble salad: Toss cabbage and romaine salad mixture with dressing in large bowl. Top with reserved steak. Sprinkle with cilantro, mango and peanuts. Serve with lime wedges.

Makes 4 to 6 servings

Tip: Because the **CROCK-POT®** slow cooker cooks at a low heat for a long time, it's perfect for dishes calling for less-tender cuts of meat.

Beef Roast with Dark Rum Sauce

1 teaspoon ground allspice

½ teaspoon salt

½ teaspoon black pepper

¼ teaspoon ground cloves

1 beef rump roast (about 3 pounds)*

2 tablespoons extra virgin olive oil

1 cup dark rum, divided

½ cup beef broth

2 cloves garlic, minced

2 whole bay leaves, broken in half

½ cup packed dark brown sugar

¼ cup lime juice

*Unless you have a 5-, 6- or 7-quart **CROCK-POT**®
slow cooker, cut any roast larger than 2½ pounds
in half so it cooks completely.

1. Combine allspice, salt, pepper and cloves in small bowl. Rub spices onto all sides of roast.

2. Heat oil in large skillet over medium heat. Add beef; cook until browned on all sides. Remove to **CROCK-POT**® slow cooker. Add ½ cup rum, broth, garlic and bay leaves. Cover; cook on LOW 1 hour.

3. Combine remaining ½ cup rum, brown sugar and lime juice in small bowl; stir to blend. Pour over beef. Cover; cook on LOW 4 to 6 hours.

4. Remove beef to large cutting board. Cover loosely with foil; let stand 10 to 15 minutes before slicing. Remove and discard bay leaves. Serve with sauce.

Makes 6 servings

Braised Short Ribs with Aromatic Spices

1 tablespoon olive oil

3 pounds bone-in beef short ribs, trimmed

1 teaspoon ground cumin, divided

1 teaspoon salt

½ teaspoon black pepper

2 medium onions, halved and thinly sliced

10 cloves garlic, thinly sliced

2 tablespoons balsamic vinegar

2 tablespoons honey

1 whole cinnamon stick

2 whole star anise pods

2 large sweet potatoes, peeled and cut into ¾-inch cubes

1 cup beef broth

1. Heat oil in large skillet over medium-high heat. Season ribs with ½ teaspoon cumin, salt and pepper. Add to skillet; cook 8 minutes or until browned, turning occasionally. Remove ribs to large plate.

2. Heat same skillet over medium heat. Add onions and garlic; cook 12 to 14 minutes or until onions are lightly browned. Stir in vinegar; cook 1 minute. Add remaining ½ teaspoon cumin, honey, cinnamon stick and star anise; cook and stir 30 seconds. Remove mixture to **CROCK-POT**® slow cooker. Stir in potatoes; top with ribs. Pour in broth.

3. Cover; cook on LOW 8 to 9 hours or until meat is falling off the bones. Remove and discard bones from ribs. Remove and discard cinnamon stick and star anise. Turn off heat. Let mixture stand 5 to 10 minutes. Skim off and discard fat. Serve beef with sauce and vegetables.

Makes 4 servings

Delicious Pepper Steak

- 2 tablespoons toasted sesame oil
- 2 pounds beef round steak, cut into strips
- ½ medium red bell pepper, sliced
- ½ medium green bell pepper, sliced
- ½ medium yellow bell pepper, sliced
- 1 medium onion, sliced
- 14 grape tomatoes
- ⅓ cup hoisin sauce
- ¼ cup water
- 3 tablespoons all-purpose flour
- 3 tablespoons reduced-sodium soy sauce
- 2 teaspoons garlic powder
- 1 teaspoon ground cumin
- 1 teaspoon dried oregano
- 1 teaspoon paprika
- ⅛ teaspoon ground red pepper
- Hot cooked rice (optional)

1. Heat oil in large skillet over medium-high heat. Add beef in batches; cook 4 to 5 minutes or until browned. Remove to large paper towel-lined plate.

2. Add bell peppers, onion and tomatoes to **CROCK-POT**® slow cooker. Combine hoisin sauce, water, flour, soy sauce, garlic powder, cumin, oregano, paprika and ground red pepper in medium bowl; stir to blend. Add to **CROCK-POT**® slow cooker. Add beef. Cover; cook on LOW 8 to 9 hours or on HIGH 4 to 4½ hours. Serve with rice, if desired.

Makes 8 servings

Sauvignon Blanc Beef with Beets and Thyme

1 pound red or yellow beets, scrubbed and quartered

2 tablespoons extra virgin olive oil

1 boneless beef chuck roast (about 3 pounds)*

1 medium yellow onion, peeled and quartered

2 cloves garlic, minced

5 sprigs fresh thyme

1 whole bay leaf

2 whole cloves

1 cup chicken broth

1 cup Sauvignon Blanc or dry white wine

2 tablespoons tomato paste

Salt and black pepper

*Unless you have a 5-, 6- or 7-quart **CROCK-POT**® slow cooker, cut any roast larger than 2½ pounds in half so it cooks completely.

1. Layer beets evenly in **CROCK-POT**® slow cooker.

2. Heat oil in large skillet over medium heat. Add beef; cook 4 to 5 minutes on each side or until browned. Add onion and garlic during last few minutes of browning. Remove to **CROCK-POT**® slow cooker.

3. Add thyme, bay leaf and cloves to **CROCK-POT**® slow cooker. Combine broth, wine and tomato paste in medium bowl. Season broth mixture with salt and pepper; stir to blend. Pour over beef and beets in **CROCK-POT**® slow cooker. Cover; cook on LOW 8 to 10 hours or until beef is fork-tender and beets are tender. Remove and discard bay leaf.

Makes 6 servings

Brisket with Sweet Onions

2 large sweet onions, cut into 10 (½-inch) slices*

1 flat-cut boneless beef brisket (about 3½ pounds)**

Salt and black pepper

2 cans (about 14 ounces *each*) beef broth

1 teaspoon cracked black peppercorns

¾ cup crumbled blue cheese (optional)

*Preferably Maui, Vidalia or Walla Walla onions.

Unless you have a 5-, 6- or 7-quart **CROCK·POT® slow cooker, cut any roast larger than 2½ pounds in half so it cooks completely.

1. Coat inside of **CROCK·POT**® slow cooker with nonstick cooking spray. Line bottom with onion slices.

2. Season brisket with salt and black pepper. Heat large skillet over medium-high heat. Add brisket; cook 10 to 12 minutes or until browned on all sides. Remove to **CROCK·POT**® slow cooker.

3. Pour broth into **CROCK·POT**® slow cooker. Sprinkle brisket with peppercorns. Cover; cook on HIGH 5 to 7 hours.

4. Remove brisket to large cutting board. Cover loosely with foil; let stand 10 to 15 minutes. Slice evenly against the grain. To serve, arrange onions on serving platter and spread slices of brisket on top. Sprinkle with blue cheese, if desired. Serve with cooking liquid.

Makes 10 servings

Simple Beef Chili

3 pounds ground beef

2 cans (about **14** ounces *each*) diced tomatoes

2 cans (about **15** ounces *each*) kidney beans, rinsed and drained

2 cups chopped onions

1 package (**10** ounces) frozen corn

1 cup chopped green bell pepper

1 can (8 ounces) tomato sauce

3 tablespoons chili powder

1 teaspoon garlic powder

½ teaspoon ground cumin

½ teaspoon dried oregano

Prepared corn bread (optional)

1. Brown beef 6 to 8 minutes in large skillet over medium-high heat, stirring to break up meat. Remove to **CROCK-POT**® slow cooker using slotted spoon.

2. Add tomatoes, beans, onions, corn, bell pepper, tomato sauce, chili powder, garlic powder, cumin and oregano to **CROCK-POT**® slow cooker; stir to blend. Cover; cook on LOW 4 hours. Serve with corn bread, if desired.

Makes 8 servings

Tip: The flavor and aroma of crushed or ground herbs and spices may lessen during a longer cooking time. So, when slow cooking in your **CROCK-POT**® slow cooker, be sure to taste and adjust seasonings, if necessary, before serving.

PLEASING PORK

Jerk Pork and Sweet Potato Stew

1¼ pounds boneless pork shoulder, cut into bite-size pieces

2 tablespoons all-purpose flour

¼ teaspoon salt

¼ teaspoon black pepper

2 tablespoons vegetable oil

1 large sweet potato, diced

1 cup frozen or canned corn

¼ cup minced green onions (green parts only), divided

1 clove garlic, minced

½ medium Scotch bonnet pepper or jalapeño pepper, seeded and minced (about 1 teaspoon)*

⅛ teaspoon ground allspice

1 cup chicken broth

1 tablespoon lime juice

2 cups cooked rice (optional)

*Scotch bonnet and jalapeño peppers can sting and irritate the skin, so wear rubber gloves when handling peppers and do not touch your eyes.

1. Combine pork, flour, salt and black pepper in large resealable food storage bag; seal bag. Shake to coat pork. Heat oil in large skillet over medium heat. Add pork in batches; cook 5 minutes or until browned. Remove to **CROCK-POT**® slow cooker.

2. Stir in sweet potato, corn, 2 tablespoons green onions, garlic, Scotch bonnet pepper and allspice. Stir in broth. Cover; cook on LOW 5 to 6 hours.

3. Stir in lime juice and remaining 2 tablespoons green onions. Top stew with rice, if desired.

Makes 4 servings

Tip: To reduce the amount of fat in **CROCK-POT**® slow cooker meals, trim excess fat from meats and degrease canned broth before using.

Pork Soup with Soba Noodles and Bok Choy

2 tablespoons olive oil

1 boneless pork loin roast (about 2½ pounds), cut into matchstick pieces

2 tablespoons hoisin sauce

1 tablespoon sugar

1 to 2 teaspoons Chinese five-spice powder

6 cups chicken broth

1½ tablespoons fresh ginger, peeled and cut into thin slices

3 cloves garlic, thinly sliced

2 tablespoons soy sauce

1 head bok choy, sliced

1 pound soba noodles, cooked

1. Heat oil in large skillet. Add pork, hoisin sauce, sugar and five-spice powder; cook and stir 5 to 7 minutes or until pork is browned. Remove to **CROCK-POT**® slow cooker.

2. Add broth, ginger, garlic, soy sauce and bok choy to **CROCK-POT**® slow cooker. Cover; cook on LOW 6 to 7 hours or on HIGH 3 to 4 hours.

3. Stir in soba noodles. Cover; cook on HIGH 10 minutes or until just heated through.

Makes 6 to 8 servings

Pork Loin Stuffed with Stone Fruits

1 boneless pork loin roast
   (about 4 pounds)*

   Salt and black pepper

2 tablespoons vegetable oil

2 tablespoons butter

1 onion, chopped

½ cup Madeira or sherry wine

1½ cups dried stone fruits (½ cup *each*
   plums, peaches and apricots)

2 cloves garlic, minced

¾ teaspoon salt

½ teaspoon black pepper

¼ teaspoon dried thyme

   Kitchen string, cut into 15-inch
   lengths

1 tablespoon olive oil

*Unless you have a 5-, 6- or 7-quart **CROCK-POT®**
slow cooker, cut any roast larger than 2½ pounds
in half so it cooks completely.

1. Coat **CROCK-POT®** slow cooker with nonstick cooking spray. Season pork with salt and pepper. Heat vegetable oil in large skillet over medium-high heat. Add pork; cook until browned on all sides. Remove to cutting board. Cover loosely with foil; let stand 10 to 15 minutes.

2. Melt butter in same skillet over medium heat. Add onion; cook and stir until translucent. Add Madeira; cook 2 to 3 minutes until mixture reduces slightly. Stir in dried fruit, garlic, ¾ teaspoon salt, ½ teaspoon black pepper and thyme; cook 1 minute. Remove from heat.

3. Cut strings from pork, if any. Butterfly pork lengthwise (use sharp knife to cut meat; cut to within 1½ inches of edge). Spread pork flat on cutting board, browned side down. Spoon fruit mixture onto pork. Bring sides together to close roast. Slide kitchen string under pork and tie roast shut, allowing 2 inches between ties. If any fruit escapes, push back gently. Place pork in **CROCK-POT®** slow cooker. Pour olive oil over pork. Cover; cook on LOW 5 to 6 hours or on HIGH 2 to 3 hours or until pork is tender.

4. Remove pork to cutting board. Cover loosely with foil; let stand 10 to 15 minutes. Pour cooking liquid into small saucepan (strain through fine-mesh sieve first, if desired). Cook over high heat about 3 minutes to reduce sauce. Add salt and black pepper to sauce, if desired. Slice pork and serve with sauce.

Makes 8 to 10 servings

Mediterranean Meatball Ratatouille

1 pound bulk mild Italian sausage

1 package (8 ounces) sliced mushrooms

1 small eggplant, diced

1 zucchini, diced

½ cup chopped yellow onion

1 clove garlic, minced

1 teaspoon dried oregano

1 teaspoon salt

½ teaspoon black pepper

2 tomatoes, diced

1 tablespoon tomato paste

2 tablespoons chopped fresh basil

1 teaspoon fresh lemon juice

1. Shape sausage into 1-inch meatballs. Brown meatballs in large skillet over medium heat. Place half of meatballs in **CROCK-POT®** slow cooker. Add half each of mushrooms, eggplant and zucchini. Top with onion, garlic, ½ teaspoon oregano, ½ teaspoon salt and ¼ teaspoon pepper.

2. Add remaining meatballs, mushrooms, eggplant, zucchini, ½ teaspoon oregano, ½ teaspoon salt and ¼ teaspoon pepper. Cover; cook on LOW 6 to 7 hours.

3. Stir diced tomatoes and tomato paste into **CROCK-POT®** slow cooker. Cover; cook on LOW 15 minutes. Stir in basil and lemon juice just before serving.

Makes 6 servings

Stew Provençal

2 cans (about 14 ounces *each*) beef broth, divided

⅓ cup all-purpose flour

1 to 2 pork tenderloins (about 2 pounds *total*), trimmed and diced

4 red potatoes, unpeeled and cut into cubes

2 cups frozen cut green beans, thawed

1 onion, chopped

2 cloves garlic, minced

1 teaspoon salt

1 teaspoon dried thyme

½ teaspoon black pepper

Sprigs fresh thyme (optional)

1. Combine ¾ cup beef broth and flour in small bowl; cover and refrigerate. Add remaining broth, pork, potatoes, beans, onion, garlic, salt, dried thyme and pepper to **CROCK-POT**® slow cooker; stir to blend. Cover; cook on LOW 8 to 10 hours or on HIGH 4 to 5 hours.

2. Whisk flour mixture into **CROCK-POT**® slow cooker. Cook, uncovered, on HIGH 30 minutes or until thickened. Garnish with thyme sprigs.

Makes 8 servings

Pork in Chile Sauce

2 cups tomato purée

2 large tomatoes, chopped

2 small poblano peppers, seeded and chopped

2 large shallots *or* 1 small onion, chopped

2 cloves garlic, minced

½ teaspoon dried oregano

¼ teaspoon chipotle chili powder or regular chili powder*

¼ teaspoon black pepper

2 boneless pork chops (6 ounces *each*), cut into 1-inch pieces

½ teaspoon salt

4 whole wheat or corn tortillas, warmed (optional)

*Chipotle chili powder is available in the spice section of most supermarkets.

Combine tomato purée, tomatoes, poblano peppers, shallots, garlic, oregano, chili powder and black pepper in **CROCK-POT**® slow cooker; stir to blend. Add pork. Cover; cook on LOW 5 to 6 hours. Stir in salt. Serve with tortillas, if desired.

Makes 4 servings

Boneless Pork Roast with Garlic

1 boneless pork rib roast
    (2 to 2½ pounds)
    Salt and black pepper
3 tablespoons olive oil, divided
4 cloves garlic, minced
¼ cup chopped fresh rosemary
½ lemon, cut into ⅛- to ¼-inch slices
½ cup chicken broth
¼ cup dry white wine

1. Season pork with salt and pepper. Combine 2 tablespoons oil, garlic and rosemary in small bowl. Rub over pork. Roll and tie pork with kitchen string. Tuck lemon slices under string and into ends of roast.

2. Heat remaining 1 tablespoon oil in skillet over medium heat. Add pork; cook 6 to 8 minutes or until browned on all sides. Remove to **CROCK-POT**® slow cooker.

3. Return skillet to heat. Add broth and wine, scraping up any browned bits from bottom of skillet. Pour over pork in **CROCK-POT**® slow cooker. Cover; cook on LOW 8 to 9 hours or on HIGH 3½ to 4 hours.

4. Remove roast to large cutting board. Cover loosely with foil; let stand 10 to 15 minutes before removing kitchen string and slicing. Pour pan juices over sliced pork.

Makes 4 to 6 servings

Knockwurst and Cabbage

2 tablespoons olive oil
8 to 10 knockwurst sausage links
1 head red cabbage, cut into ¼-inch slices
½ cup thinly sliced white onion

2 teaspoons caraway seeds
1 teaspoon salt
4 cups chicken broth
    Chopped fresh Italian parsley (optional)

1. Heat oil in large skillet over medium heat. Cook sausages 5 to 7 minutes or until browned on all sides. Remove to **CROCK-POT**® slow cooker.

2. Add cabbage and onion to **CROCK-POT**® slow cooker. Sprinkle with caraway seeds and salt. Add broth. Cover; cook on LOW 4 hours or on HIGH 2 hours. Garnish with parsley.

Makes 8 servings

Spiced Pork and Apple Stew

1 teaspoon canola oil

1¼ pounds cubed pork stew meat

1 medium sweet onion, cut into
½-inch-thick slices

2 cloves garlic, minced

1 can (28 ounces) crushed tomatoes

2 large or 3 small red or white potatoes,
cut into 1-inch pieces

1½ cups baby carrots, cut into ½-inch pieces

2 small apples, cored and cubed

1 cup reduced-sodium chicken broth

2 tablespoons spicy brown mustard

1 tablespoon packed brown sugar

2 teaspoons ground cinnamon

1 teaspoon ground cumin

¼ teaspoon salt

2 tablespoons chopped fresh Italian
parsley (optional)

1. Heat oil in large skillet over medium-high heat. Add pork; cook until browned on all sides. Add onion and garlic; cook and stir 5 minutes. Remove to **CROCK-POT**® slow cooker.

2. Add tomatoes, potatoes, carrots, apples, broth, mustard, brown sugar, cinnamon, cumin and salt to **CROCK-POT**® slow cooker. Cover; cook on LOW 6 to 8 hours or until pork and potatoes are tender. Garnish with parsley.

Makes 8 servings

Asian Pork Tenderloin

½ cup bottled garlic ginger sauce

¼ cup sliced green onions

1 pork tenderloin (about 1 pound)

1 large red onion, cut into slices

1 medium red bell pepper, cut into 1-inch
pieces

1 medium zucchini, cut into ¼-inch slices

1 tablespoon olive oil

1. Combine sauce and green onions in large resealable food storage bag. Add pork. Seal bag; turn to coat. Place bag on large baking sheet; refrigerate 30 minutes or overnight.

2. Combine red onion, bell pepper, zucchini and oil in large bowl; toss to coat. Place vegetables in **CROCK-POT**® slow cooker. Remove pork from bag; place on top of vegetables. Discard marinade. Cover; cook on LOW 6 to 7 hours or on HIGH 4 to 5 hours.

3. Remove pork to large cutting board. Cover loosely with foil; let stand 10 to 15 minutes before slicing. Serve pork with vegetables.

Makes 4 servings

Pulled Pork with Honey-Chipotle Barbecue Sauce

1 tablespoon chili powder, divided

1 teaspoon chipotle chili powder, divided

1 teaspoon ground cumin, divided

1 teaspoon garlic powder, divided

1 teaspoon salt

1 bone-in pork shoulder (3½ pounds), trimmed*

1 can (15 ounces) tomato sauce

5 tablespoons honey, divided

*Unless you have a 5-, 6- or 7-quart **CROCK-POT**® slow cooker, cut any roast larger than 2½ pounds in half so it cooks completely.

1. Coat inside of **CROCK-POT**® slow cooker with nonstick cooking spray. Combine 1 teaspoon chili powder, ½ teaspoon chipotle chili powder, ½ teaspoon cumin, ½ teaspoon garlic powder and salt in small bowl. Rub pork with chili powder mixture. Place in **CROCK-POT**® slow cooker.

2. Combine tomato sauce, 4 tablespoons honey, remaining 2 teaspoons chili powder, ½ teaspoon chipotle chili powder, ½ teaspoon cumin and ½ teaspoon garlic powder in large bowl; stir to blend. Pour over pork in **CROCK-POT**® slow cooker. Cover; cook on LOW 8 hours.

3. Remove pork to large bowl; cover loosely with foil. Turn **CROCK-POT**® slow cooker to HIGH. Cover; cook on HIGH 30 minutes or until sauce is thickened. Stir in remaining 1 tablespoon honey. Turn off heat.

4. Remove bone from pork and discard. Shred pork using two forks. Stir shredded pork back into **CROCK-POT**® slow cooker to coat well with sauce.

Makes 8 servings

Maple-Dry Rubbed Ribs

2 teaspoons chili powder, divided

1 teaspoon ground coriander

1 teaspoon garlic powder, divided

½ teaspoon salt

¼ teaspoon black pepper

3 to 3½ pounds pork baby back ribs, trimmed and cut in half

3 tablespoons maple syrup, divided

1 can (about 8 ounces) tomato sauce

¼ teaspoon ground cinnamon

¼ teaspoon ground ginger

1. Coat inside of **CROCK-POT**® slow cooker with nonstick cooking spray. Combine 1 teaspoon chili powder, coriander, ½ teaspoon garlic powder, salt and pepper in small bowl. Brush ribs with 1 tablespoon syrup; rub with spice mixture. Remove to **CROCK-POT**® slow cooker.

2. Combine tomato sauce, remaining 1 teaspoon chili powder, ½ teaspoon garlic powder, 2 tablespoons syrup, cinnamon and ginger in medium bowl; stir to blend. Pour over ribs in **CROCK-POT**® slow cooker. Cover; cook on LOW 8 to 9 hours.

3. Remove ribs to large serving platter; cover with foil to keep warm. Turn **CROCK-POT**® slow cooker to HIGH. Cover; cook on HIGH 10 to 15 minutes or until sauce is thickened. Brush ribs with sauce and serve any remaining sauce on the side.

Makes 4 servings

Pozole Rojo

4 dried ancho chiles, stemmed and seeded

3 dried guajillo chiles, stemmed and seeded*

2 cups boiling water

2½ pounds boneless pork shoulder, trimmed and cut in half

3 teaspoons salt, divided

1 tablespoon vegetable oil

2 medium onions, chopped

1½ tablespoons minced garlic

2 teaspoons ground cumin

2 teaspoons Mexican oregano**

4 cups chicken broth

2 cans (30 ounces *each*) white hominy, rinsed and drained

Optional toppings: sliced radishes, lime wedges, sliced romaine lettuce, chopped onion, tortilla chips and/or diced avocado

*Guajillo chiles can be found in the ethnic section of large supermarkets.

**Mexican oregano has a stronger flavor than regular oregano. It can be found in the spices and seasonings section of most large supermarkets.

1. Place ancho and guajillo chiles in medium bowl; pour boiling water over top. Weigh down chiles with small plate or bowl; soak 30 minutes.

2. Meanwhile, season pork with 1 teaspoon salt. Heat oil in large skillet over medium-high heat. Add pork; cook 8 to 10 minutes or until browned on all sides. Remove to **CROCK-POT**® slow cooker.

3. Heat same skillet over medium heat. Add onions; cook 6 minutes or until softened. Add garlic, cumin, oregano and remaining 2 teaspoons salt; cook and stir 1 minute. Stir in broth; bring to a simmer, scraping up any browned bits from bottom of skillet. Pour over pork in **CROCK-POT**® slow cooker.

4. Place softened chiles and soaking liquid in food processor or blender; blend until smooth. Pour through fine-mesh sieve into medium bowl, pressing with spoon to extract liquid. Discard solids. Stir mixture into **CROCK-POT**® slow cooker.

5. Cover; cook on LOW 5 hours. Stir in hominy. Cover; cook on LOW 1 hour. Turn off heat. Let stand 10 to 15 minutes. Skim off fat and discard. Remove pork to large cutting board; shred with two forks. Ladle hominy mixture into bowls; top each serving with pork and desired toppings.

Makes 8 servings

Cajun Pork Sausage and Shrimp Stew

1 can (28 ounces) diced tomatoes

1 package (16 ounces) frozen mixed vegetables (potatoes, carrots, celery and onions)

1 package (14 to 16 ounces) kielbasa or smoked sausage, cut diagonally into ¾-inch slices

2 teaspoons Cajun seasoning

¾ pound large raw shrimp, peeled and deveined (with tails on)

2 cups (8 ounces) frozen sliced okra, thawed

Hot cooked rice or grits

1. Coat inside of **CROCK-POT®** slow cooker with nonstick cooking spray. Combine tomatoes, vegetables, sausage and Cajun seasoning in **CROCK-POT®** slow cooker; stir to blend. Cover; cook on LOW 5 to 6 hours or on HIGH 2 to 2½ hours.

2. Stir shrimp and okra into **CROCK-POT®** slow cooker. Cover; cook on HIGH 30 to 35 minutes or until shrimp are pink and opaque. Serve over rice.

Makes 6 servings

Pork Tenderloin Chili

1½ to 2 pounds pork tenderloin, cooked and cut into 2-inch pieces

2 cans (about 15 ounces *each*) pinto beans, rinsed and drained

2 cans (about 15 ounces *each*) black beans, rinsed and drained

2 cans (about 14 ounces *each*) whole tomatoes

2 cans (4 ounces *each*) diced mild green chiles

1 package (1¼ ounces) taco seasoning mix

Diced avocado (optional)

Combine pork, beans, tomatoes, chiles and taco seasoning mix in **CROCK-POT®** slow cooker; stir to blend. Cover; cook on LOW 4 hours. Top with avocado, if desired.

Makes 8 servings

Spicy Citrus Pork with Pineapple Salsa

1 tablespoon ground cumin

½ teaspoon salt

1 teaspoon black pepper

3 pounds center-cut pork loin, rinsed and patted dry*

2 tablespoons vegetable oil

4 cans (8 ounces *each*) pineapple tidbits in own juice, drained, ½ cup juice reserved**

3 tablespoons lemon juice, divided

2 teaspoons grated lemon peel

1 cup finely chopped orange or red bell pepper

4 tablespoons finely chopped red onion

2 tablespoons chopped fresh cilantro or mint

1 teaspoon grated fresh ginger (optional)

¼ teaspoon red pepper flakes (optional)

*Unless you have a 5-, 6- or 7-quart **CROCK-POT**® slow cooker, cut any roast larger than 2½ pounds in half so it cooks completely.

**If tidbits are unavailable, purchase pineapple chunks and coarsely chop.

1. Coat inside of **CROCK-POT**® slow cooker with nonstick cooking spray. Combine cumin, salt and black pepper in small bowl. Rub pork with spice mixture. Heat oil in medium skillet over medium-high heat. Add pork; cook 1 to 2 minutes on each side or until browned. Remove to **CROCK-POT**® slow cooker.

2. Spoon 4 tablespoons reserved pineapple juice and 2 tablespoons lemon juice over pork. Cover; cook on LOW 2 to 2¼ hours or on HIGH 1 hour and 10 minutes or until meat is tender.

3. Meanwhile, combine pineapple, remaining 4 tablespoons pineapple juice, 1 tablespoon lemon juice, lemon peel, bell pepper, onion, cilantro, ginger, if desired, and red pepper flakes, if desired, in medium bowl. Toss gently to blend.

4. Remove pork to cutting board. Cover loosely with foil; let stand 10 to 15 minutes before slicing. Arrange pork slices on serving platter. Pour sauce evenly over slices. Serve with salsa.

Makes 12 servings

Asian Noodles with Pork and Vegetables

¾ cup soy sauce

¾ cup honey

4 cloves garlic, chopped

1 tablespoon ground ginger

1 boneless pork shoulder roast (2½ pounds), trimmed

¾ cup Asian sweet chili sauce

¼ cup water

3 tablespoons cornstarch

2 packages (16 ounces *each*) frozen mixed Asian vegetables

1 tablespoon toasted sesame oil

Hot cooked soba noodles, rice or spaghetti

1. Combine soy sauce, honey, garlic and ginger in **CROCK-POT**® slow cooker. Add pork. Cover; cook on LOW 8 to 10 hours or on HIGH 5 to 6 hours or until pork is fork-tender. Remove pork to cutting board.

2. Stir chili sauce into **CROCK-POT**® slow cooker; bring to a boil. Stir water into cornstarch in small bowl until smooth. Whisk cornstarch mixture into **CROCK-POT**® slow cooker until thickened. Meanwhile, shred pork.

3. Add vegetables and shredded pork to **CROCK-POT**® slow cooker. Cover; cook on HIGH 10 to 20 minutes. Stir in oil. Serve over soba noodles.

Makes 6 servings

Sweet and Spicy Pork Picadillo

1 tablespoon olive oil

1 yellow onion, cut into ¼-inch pieces

2 cloves garlic, minced

1 pound boneless pork country-style ribs, trimmed and cut into 1-inch cubes

1 can (about 14 ounces) diced tomatoes

3 tablespoons cider vinegar

2 canned chipotle peppers in adobo sauce, chopped*

½ cup raisins

½ teaspoon ground cumin

½ teaspoon ground cinnamon

Hot cooked rice (optional)

Black beans (optional)

*You may substitute dried chipotle peppers, soaked in warm water about 20 minutes to soften before chopping.

1. Heat oil in large skillet over medium-low heat. Add onion and garlic; cook and stir 4 minutes. Add pork; cook and stir 5 to 7 minutes or until browned. Remove to **CROCK-POT**® slow cooker.

2. Combine tomatoes, vinegar, chipotle peppers, raisins, cumin and cinnamon in medium bowl; stir to blend. Pour over pork in **CROCK-POT**® slow cooker. Cover; cook on LOW 5 hours or on HIGH 3 hours. Remove pork to large cutting board; shred with two forks. Serve with rice and beans, if desired.

Makes 4 servings

Harvest Ham Supper

6 carrots, cut into 2-inch pieces

3 medium sweet potatoes, quartered

1 to 1½ pounds boneless ham

1 cup maple syrup

Chopped fresh Italian parsley (optional)

1. Arrange carrots and potatoes in bottom of **CROCK-POT**® slow cooker.

2. Place ham on top of vegetables. Pour syrup over ham and vegetables. Cover; cook on LOW 6 to 8 hours. Garnish with parsley.

Makes 6 servings

Fall-Apart Pork Roast with Mole

⅔ cup whole almonds

⅔ cup raisins

3 tablespoons vegetable oil, divided

½ cup chopped onion

4 cloves garlic, chopped

1 boneless pork shoulder roast (2¾ pounds), well trimmed*

1 can (about 14 ounces) diced fire-roasted tomatoes or diced tomatoes

1 cup cubed bread, any variety

½ cup chicken broth

2 ounces Mexican chocolate, chopped

2 tablespoons canned chipotle peppers in adobo sauce, chopped

1 teaspoon salt

Chopped fresh cilantro (optional)

*Unless you have a 5-, 6- or 7-quart **CROCK-POT**® slow cooker, cut any roast larger than 2½ pounds in half so it cooks completely.

1. Heat large skillet over medium-high heat. Add almonds; cook and stir 3 to 4 minutes until fragrant. Add raisins; cook and stir 1 to 2 minutes or until raisins begin to plump. Place half of almond mixture in large bowl. Reserve remaining half for garnish.

2. Heat 1 tablespoon oil in same skillet. Add onion and garlic; cook and stir 2 minutes or until softened. Add to almond mixture; set aside.

3. Heat remaining 2 tablespoons oil in same skillet. Add pork; cook 5 to 7 minutes or until browned on all sides. Remove to **CROCK-POT**® slow cooker.

4. Add tomatoes, bread, broth, chocolate, chipotle peppers and salt to almond mixture. Add tomato mixture in batches to food processor or blender; process until smooth. Pour purée mixture over pork in **CROCK-POT**® slow cooker. Cover; cook on LOW 7 to 8 hours or on HIGH 3 to 4 hours.

5. Remove pork to large serving platter. Whisk sauce until smooth before spooning over pork. Garnish with reserved almond mixture and chopped cilantro.

Makes 6 servings

Apple-Cherry Glazed Pork Chops

½ to 1 teaspoon dried thyme

¼ teaspoon salt

¼ teaspoon black pepper

4 boneless pork loin chops (3 ounces *each*), trimmed

1⅓ cups unsweetened apple juice

1 small apple, unpeeled and sliced

¼ cup sliced green onions

¼ cup dried tart cherries

2 tablespoons water

2 teaspoons cornstarch

1. Combine thyme, salt and pepper in small bowl. Rub both sides of pork chops with spice mixture. Spray large skillet with nonstick cooking spray; heat over medium-high heat. Add pork to skillet in batches; cook until browned on both sides. Remove to **CROCK-POT**® slow cooker.

2. Add apple juice, apple slices, green onions and cherries to same skillet. Cook, uncovered, 2 to 3 minutes or until apple and onions are tender. Stir water into cornstarch in small bowl until smooth; whisk into skillet. Bring to a boil; cook and stir until thickened. Spoon over pork chops.

3. Cover; cook on LOW 3½ to 4 hours or until pork chops are tender. Spoon fruit and cooking liquid over pork chops.

Makes 4 servings

Pork Roast with Currant Cherry Salsa

1½ teaspoons chili powder

¾ teaspoon salt

½ teaspoon garlic powder

½ teaspoon paprika

¼ teaspoon ground allspice

1 boneless pork loin roast (2 pounds)

½ cup water

1 package (1 pound) frozen pitted dark cherries, thawed, drained and halved

¼ cup currants or dark raisins

1 teaspoon grated orange peel

1 teaspoon balsamic vinegar

⅛ to ¼ teaspoon red pepper flakes

1. Combine chili powder, salt, garlic powder, paprika and allspice in small bowl. Rub pork with spice mixture, pressing spices into pork.

2. Spray large skillet with nonstick cooking spray; heat over medium-high heat. Add pork; cook 6 to 8 minutes or until browned on all sides. Remove to **CROCK-POT**® slow cooker.

3. Pour water into skillet, stirring to scrape up any browned bits from bottom of skillet. Pour into **CROCK-POT**® slow cooker around pork. Cover; cook on LOW 6 to 8 hours.

4. Remove pork to large cutting board. Cover loosely with foil; let stand 10 to 15 minutes. Strain juices from **CROCK-POT**® slow cooker; discard solids. Keep warm.

5. Turn **CROCK-POT**® slow cooker to HIGH. Add cherries, currants, orange peel, vinegar and red pepper flakes to **CROCK-POT**® slow cooker. Cover; cook on HIGH 30 minutes. Slice pork; spoon warm juices over meat. Serve with salsa.

Makes 8 servings

Sauerkraut Pork Ribs

1 tablespoon vegetable oil

3 to 4 pounds pork country-style ribs

1 large onion, thinly sliced

1 teaspoon caraway seeds

½ teaspoon garlic powder

¼ to ½ teaspoon black pepper

¾ cup water

2 jars (about 28 ounces *each*) sauerkraut

12 medium red potatoes, quartered

1. Heat oil in large skillet over medium-low heat. Add ribs; cook until browned on all sides. Remove to **CROCK-POT**® slow cooker. Drain fat.

2. Add onion to skillet; cook until tender. Add caraway seeds, garlic powder and pepper; cook 15 minutes. Remove to **CROCK-POT**® slow cooker.

3. Add water to skillet, stirring to scrape up any browned bits. Pour into **CROCK-POT**® slow cooker. Partially drain sauerkraut, leaving some liquid; pour over pork. Top with potatoes. Cover; cook on LOW 6 to 8 hours or until potatoes are tender, stirring once during cooking.

Makes 12 servings

Savory Slow Cooker Pork Roast

1 boneless pork blade or sirloin roast (3 to 4 pounds)

Salt and black pepper

2 tablespoons vegetable oil

1 medium onion, cut into ¼-inch-thick rings

2 to 3 cloves garlic, chopped

1 can (15 ounces) chicken broth

Sprigs fresh oregano (optional)

1. Season pork with salt and pepper. Heat oil in large skillet over medium heat. Add pork; cook until browned on all sides.

2. Place onion slices on bottom of **CROCK-POT**® slow cooker; sprinkle with garlic. Place pork on onions; pour broth over pork.

3. Cover; cook on LOW 10 hours or on HIGH 6 to 7 hours. Garnish with oregano.

Makes 8 servings

Country Sausage and Bean Soup

2 cans (about 14 ounces *each*) chicken broth

1½ cups hot water

1 cup dried black beans, rinsed and sorted

1 cup chopped onion

2 whole bay leaves

1 teaspoon sugar

⅛ teaspoon ground red pepper

6 ounces country pork sausage

1 cup chopped tomato

1 tablespoon chili powder

1 tablespoon Worcestershire sauce

2 teaspoons extra virgin olive oil

1½ teaspoons ground cumin

½ teaspoon salt

¼ cup chopped fresh cilantro

1. Combine broth, water, beans, onion, bay leaves, sugar and ground red pepper in **CROCK-POT®** slow cooker; stir to blend. Cover; cook on LOW 8 hours or on HIGH 4 hours.

2. Spray large skillet with nonstick cooking spray; heat over medium-high heat. Add sausage; cook until beginning to brown, stirring to break up meat.

3. Add sausage, tomato, chili powder, Worcestershire sauce, oil, cumin and salt to **CROCK-POT®** slow cooker. Cover; cook on HIGH 15 minutes to blend flavors. Sprinkle with cilantro.

Makes 9 servings

Pork Roast with Fruit Medley

1 boneless pork loin roast
  (about 4 pounds)*

1 tablespoon black pepper

2 teaspoons salt

2 cups green grapes

1 cup dried apricots

1 cup dried prunes

1 cup dry red wine

  Juice of ½ lemon

2 whole bay leaves

2 cloves garlic, minced

1 teaspoon dried thyme

*Unless you have a 5-, 6- or 7-quart **CROCK-POT**®
slow cooker, cut any roast larger than 2½ pounds
in half so it cooks completely.

1. Season pork with pepper and salt. Spray large skillet with nonstick cooking spray; heat over medium-high heat. Add pork; cook 5 to 7 minutes or until browned on all sides.

2. Combine grapes, apricots, prunes, wine, lemon juice, bay leaves, garlic and thyme in **CROCK-POT**® slow cooker; stir to blend. Add pork to **CROCK-POT**® slow cooker; turn to coat. Cover; cook on LOW 7 to 9 hours or on HIGH 3 to 5 hours. Remove and discard bay leaves. Remove pork to large cutting board. Cover loosely with foil; let stand 10 to 15 minutes before slicing.

Makes 8 servings

Golden Harvest Pork Stew

- 1 pound boneless pork cutlets, cut into 1-inch pieces
- 2 tablespoons all-purpose flour, divided
- 1 tablespoon vegetable oil
- 2 medium Yukon Gold potatoes, unpeeled and cut into 1-inch cubes
- 1 large sweet potato, cut into 1-inch cubes
- 1 cup chopped carrots
- 1 ear corn, broken into 4 pieces *or* ½ cup corn
- ½ cup chicken broth
- 1 jalapeño pepper, seeded and finely chopped*
- 1 clove garlic, minced
- 1 teaspoon salt
- ¼ teaspoon black pepper
- ¼ teaspoon dried thyme
- Chopped fresh Italian parsley

*Jalapeño peppers can sting and irritate the skin, so wear rubber gloves when handling peppers and do not touch your eyes.

1. Toss pork pieces with 1 tablespoon flour in medium bowl. Heat oil in large skillet over medium-high heat. Add pork; cook until browned on all sides. Remove to **CROCK-POT®** slow cooker.

2. Add remaining ingredients except parsley and 1 tablespoon flour. Cover; cook on LOW 5 to 6 hours.

3. Stir ¼ cup cooking liquid into remaining 1 tablespoon flour in small bowl. Whisk flour mixture into stew. Turn **CROCK-POT®** slow cooker to HIGH. Cook on HIGH 10 minutes or until thickened. Adjust seasonings, if desired. Sprinkle with parsley.

Makes 4 servings

Saucy Pork Loin and Potatoes

1 tablespoon olive oil

1 pork tenderloin (2 pounds)

½ cup chicken broth

3 tablespoons cornstarch

½ cup packed brown sugar

⅓ cup soy sauce

¼ cup lemon juice

¼ cup dry white wine

2 cloves garlic, minced

1 tablespoon mustard

1 tablespoon Worcestershire sauce

3 cups potatoes, cut into wedges

Chopped fresh Italian parsley (optional)

1. Heat oil in large skillet over medium-high heat. Add pork; cook 4 to 6 minutes on each side or until browned. Stir broth into cornstarch in small bowl until smooth. Combine pork, broth mixture, brown sugar, soy sauce, lemon juice, wine, garlic, mustard and Worcestershire sauce in **CROCK-POT**® slow cooker. Cover; cook on LOW 4 hours.

2. Stir potatoes into **CROCK-POT**® slow cooker; turn pork. Cover; cook on LOW 2 hours. Garnish with parsley.

Makes 6 servings

Mango Ginger Pork Roast

1 boneless pork shoulder roast (about 4 pounds)*

½ to 1 teaspoon ground ginger

Salt and black pepper

2 cups mango salsa

2 tablespoons honey

¼ cup apricot preserves

Hot cooked rice

*Unless you have a 5-, 6- or 7-quart **CROCK-POT**® slow cooker, cut any roast larger than 2½ pounds in half so it cooks completely.

1. Season pork with ginger, salt and pepper. Add to **CROCK-POT**® slow cooker.

2. Combine salsa, honey and preserves in medium bowl; stir to blend. Pour over pork. Cover; cook on LOW 6 to 8 hours.

3. Turn **CROCK-POT**® slow cooker to HIGH. Cover; cook on HIGH 3 to 4 hours or until pork is tender. Serve with rice.

Makes 4 to 6 servings

Pork Chops with Dried Fruit and Onions

6 bone-in end-cut pork chops
(about 2½ pounds)

Salt and black pepper

3 tablespoons vegetable oil

2 onions, diced

2 cloves garlic, minced

¼ teaspoon dried sage

¾ cup quartered pitted dried plums

¾ cup chopped mixed dried fruit

3 cups unsweetened unfiltered apple juice

1 whole bay leaf

1. Season pork chops with salt and pepper. Heat oil in large skillet over medium-high heat. Add pork in batches; cook 6 to 8 minutes or until browned on all sides. Remove to **CROCK-POT**® slow cooker.

2. Add onions to skillet. Reduce heat to medium; cook and stir until softened. Add garlic; cook 30 seconds. Sprinkle sage over mixture. Add dried plums, mixed fruit and juice. Bring mixture to a boil. Reduce heat to low and cook, uncovered, 3 minutes, stirring to scrape up any browned bits from bottom of skillet. Spoon mixture over pork.

3. Add bay leaf. Cover; cook on LOW 3½ to 4 hours. Remove and discard bay leaf. Season with salt and pepper, if desired. Spoon fruit and cooking liquid over pork.

Makes 6 servings

Pork Roast with Dijon Tarragon Glaze

1½ to 2 pounds boneless pork loin, trimmed

1 teaspoon ground paprika

½ teaspoon black pepper

⅓ cup reduced-sodium chicken or
vegetable broth

2 tablespoons Dijon mustard

2 tablespoons lemon juice

1 teaspoon minced fresh tarragon

1. Sprinkle pork with paprika and pepper. Place pork in **CROCK-POT**® slow cooker. Combine broth, mustard, lemon juice and tarragon in small bowl; spoon over pork.

2. Cover; cook on LOW 6 to 8 hours or on HIGH 3 to 4 hours. Remove pork to large cutting board. Cover loosely with foil; let stand 10 to 15 minutes before slicing. Serve with cooking liquid.

Makes 4 to 6 servings

SATISFYING SEAFOOD

Cape Cod Stew

2 pounds medium raw shrimp, peeled and deveined

2 pounds fresh cod or other white fish

3 lobsters (1½ to 2½ pounds *each*), uncooked

1 pound mussels or clams, scrubbed

2 cans (about 14 ounces *each*) chopped tomatoes

4 cups beef broth

½ cup chopped onions

½ cup chopped carrots

½ cup chopped fresh cilantro

2 tablespoons sea salt

2 teaspoons crushed or minced garlic

2 teaspoons lemon juice

4 whole bay leaves

1 teaspoon dried thyme

½ teaspoon saffron threads

1. Cut shrimp and fish into bite-size pieces and place in large bowl; refrigerate. Remove lobster tails and claws. Chop tail into 2-inch pieces and separate claws at joints. Place lobster and mussels in large bowl; refrigerate.

2. Combine remaining ingredients in **CROCK-POT®** slow cooker. Cover; cook on LOW 7 hours.

3. Add seafood. Turn **CROCK-POT®** slow cooker to HIGH. Cover; cook on HIGH 45 minutes to 1 hour or until seafood is just cooked through. Remove and discard bay leaves. Discard any mussels that do not open.

Makes 8 servings

Scallops in Fresh Tomato and Herb Sauce

2 tablespoons vegetable oil

1 medium red onion, peeled and diced

1 clove garlic, minced

3½ cups fresh tomatoes, peeled*

1 can (12 ounces) tomato pureé

1 can (6 ounces) tomato paste

¼ cup dry red wine

2 tablespoons chopped fresh Italian parsley

1 tablespoon chopped fresh oregano

¼ teaspoon black pepper

1½ pounds fresh scallops, cleaned and drained

Hot cooked pasta or rice

*To peel tomatoes, place one at a time in simmering water about 10 seconds. (Add 30 seconds if tomatoes are not fully ripened.) Immediately plunge into a bowl of cold water for another 10 seconds. Peel skin with a knife.

1. Heat oil in medium skillet over medium heat. Add onion and garlic; cook and stir 7 to 8 minutes or until onion is soft and translucent. Remove to **CROCK-POT®** slow cooker.

2. Add tomatoes, tomato purée, tomato paste, wine, parsley, oregano and pepper. Cover; cook on LOW 6 to 8 hours.

3. Turn **CROCK-POT®** slow cooker to HIGH. Add scallops. Cook on HIGH 15 minutes or until scallops are cooked through. Serve over pasta.

Makes 4 servings

Seafood and Tomato Herb Ragoût

1 can (28 ounces) crushed tomatoes

1 can (8 ounces) tomato sauce

1 cup water

1 cup dry white wine

1 leek, chopped

1 green bell pepper, chopped

½ cup chopped celery

⅓ cup chopped fresh Italian parsley, plus additional for garnish

¼ cup extra virgin olive oil

3 cloves garlic, minced

2 tablespoons chopped fresh basil

1 tablespoon chopped fresh thyme

1 tablespoon chopped fresh oregano

1 teaspoon salt

½ teaspoon paprika

¼ teaspoon ground red pepper

1 pound orange roughy fillets or other white fish, such as cod or haddock, cubed

12 prawns, peeled and deveined

12 scallops, cleaned

1. Stir all ingredients except fish, prawns and scallops into **CROCK-POT**® slow cooker until well combined. Cover; cook on LOW 6 to 8 hours or on HIGH 3 to 4 hours.

2. Add fish, prawns and scallops to **CROCK-POT**® slow cooker. Cover; cook on HIGH 15 to 30 minutes or just until seafood is cooked through. Garnish with additional parsley.

Makes 6 to 8 servings

Braised Sea Bass
with Aromatic Vegetables

2 tablespoons butter or olive oil

2 fennel bulbs, thinly sliced

3 large carrots, julienned

3 large leeks, cleaned and thinly sliced

Salt and black pepper

6 sea bass fillets or other firm-fleshed white fish (2 to 3 pounds *total*)

1. Melt butter in large skillet over medium-high heat. Add fennel, carrots and leeks; cook and stir 6 to 8 minutes or until beginning to soften and lightly brown. Season with salt and pepper. Arrange half of vegetables in bottom of **CROCK-POT®** slow cooker.

2. Season bass with salt and pepper; place on top of vegetables in **CROCK-POT®** slow cooker. Top with remaining vegetables. Cover; cook on LOW 2 to 3 hours or on HIGH 1 to 1½ hours.

Makes 6 servings

Lemon and Garlic Shrimp

1 pound large raw shrimp, peeled and deveined (with tails on)

½ cup (1 stick) butter, cubed

3 cloves garlic, crushed

2 tablespoons lemon juice

½ teaspoon paprika

Salt and black pepper

2 tablespoons finely chopped fresh Italian parsley

Crusty bread, sliced (optional)

1. Coat inside of **CROCK-POT®** slow cooker with nonstick cooking spray. Add shrimp, butter and garlic; mix well. Cover; cook on HIGH 1¼ hours.

2. Turn off heat. Stir in lemon juice, paprika, salt and pepper. Spoon shrimp and liquid into large serving bowl. Sprinkle with parsley. Serve with crusty bread for dipping, if desired.

Makes 6 to 8 servings

Italian Fish Soup

1 can (about 14 ounces) Italian-seasoned diced tomatoes

1 can (about 14 ounces) reduced-sodium chicken broth

1 small fennel bulb, chopped (about 1 cup), fronds reserved for garnish

3 cloves garlic, minced

1 tablespoon olive oil

½ teaspoon dried basil

½ teaspoon crushed saffron threads (optional)

¼ teaspoon red pepper flakes

½ pound (8 ounces) skinless halibut or cod fillets, cut into 1-inch pieces

½ pound (8 ounces) raw medium shrimp, peeled and deveined (with tails on)

1. Combine tomatoes, broth, fennel bulb, garlic, oil, basil, saffron, if desired, and red pepper flakes in **CROCK-POT**® slow cooker; stir to blend. Cover; cook on LOW 4 to 5 hours or on HIGH 2½ to 3 hours or until fennel is tender.

2. Stir in halibut and shrimp. Cover; cook on HIGH 15 to 30 minutes or until shrimp are pink and opaque and fish begins to flake when tested with fork. Ladle soup evenly into shallow bowls. Garnish with chopped fennel fronds.

Makes 4 servings

Thai Shrimp Soup Infused with Lemongrass, Ginger and Chiles

¾ pound large shrimp, peeled and deveined, shells reserved

8 cups fish or chicken broth

1 cup diced carrots

3 stalks lemongrass, thinly sliced

2 to 3 tablespoons fresh ginger, peeled and grated

2 tablespoons minced garlic

1½ tablespoons finely chopped fresh Thai basil or basil

1½ tablespoons finely chopped fresh mint

1½ tablespoons finely chopped fresh cilantro

1 serrano pepper, stemmed and thinly sliced*

1 to 2 limes, juiced

1 can (about 13 ounces) unsweetened coconut milk

¼ to ½ teaspoon sambal oelek chile paste**

6 thin lime slices

*Serrano peppers can sting and irritate the skin, so wear rubber gloves when handling peppers and do not touch your eyes.

**Chile pepper pastes, such as sambal oelek, are commonly used condiments in Southeast Asia. You can find them in the ethnic section of many grocery stores, in Asian markets or online.

1. Halve shrimp lengthwise. Place in refrigerator.

2. Place shrimp shells, broth, carrots, lemongrass, ginger and garlic in **CROCK-POT**® slow cooker. Cover; cook on LOW 3½ to 4½ hours or on HIGH 2 to 3 hours.

3. Strain broth and return to **CROCK-POT**® slow cooker; discard solids. Add shrimp, Thai basil, mint, cilantro, serrano pepper, lime juice, coconut milk and chile paste. Cover; cook on HIGH 15 minutes or until shrimp are cooked through. Garnish with lime slices.

Makes 6 servings

Zuppa de Clams

1 package (8 ounces) shiitake mushrooms

1 red onion, diced

½ pound cooked chorizo sausage, thinly sliced

1½ cups tomato sauce

1 cup dry white wine

½ cup sweet red vermouth

24 littleneck clams, scrubbed and rinsed

Hot cooked pasta (optional)

Crusty Italian bread (optional)

1. Heat large skillet over medium heat. Add mushrooms, onion and sausage; cook 8 minutes or until onion is softened, stirring frequently. Remove to **CROCK-POT**® slow cooker.

2. Add tomato sauce, wine and vermouth to **CROCK-POT**® slow cooker. Cover; cook on LOW 6 to 7 hours or on HIGH 3½ hours. Add clams; cover and cook on HIGH 10 to 15 minutes or until clams open. Discard any clams that do not open. Serve over pasta and with bread, if desired.

Makes 3 to 4 servings

Slow Cooker Salmon with Beer

4 salmon fillets (6 ounces *each*)

Salt and black pepper

1 cup Italian dressing

3 tablespoons olive oil

1 yellow bell pepper, sliced

1 red bell pepper, sliced

1 orange bell pepper, sliced

1 large onion, sliced

2 cloves garlic, minced

1 teaspoon lemon peel

½ teaspoon dried basil

2 cups spinach, stems removed

¾ cup amber ale

½ lemon, cut into quarters

1. Season both sides of salmon with salt and black pepper. Place in baking dish; pour Italian dressing over salmon. Cover and refrigerate 30 minutes or up to 2 hours. Discard marinade.

2. Pour oil into **CROCK-POT**® slow cooker; lay salmon on top of oil, stacking as necessary. Top with bell peppers, onion, garlic, lemon peel and basil. Cover with spinach. Pour ale into **CROCK-POT**® slow cooker. Cover; cook on HIGH 1½ hours.

3. Remove salmon to large serving platter; top with vegetables. Squeeze lemon over salmon.

Makes 4 servings

Cod Tapenade

4 cod fillets or other firm white fish (2 to 3 pounds *total*)

Salt and black pepper

2 lemons, thinly sliced

Tapenade (recipe follows)

1. Season cod with salt and pepper. Arrange half of lemon slices in bottom of **CROCK-POT®** slow cooker. Top with cod; cover with remaining lemon slices. Cover; cook on HIGH 1 hour or until fish is just cooked through. Prepare Tapenade.

2. Remove fish to serving plates; discard lemon. Top with Tapenade.

Makes 4 servings

Tapenade

½ pound pitted kalamata olives

2 tablespoons chopped fresh thyme or Italian parsley

2 tablespoons capers, drained

2 tablespoons anchovy paste

1 clove garlic

¼ teaspoon grated orange peel

⅛ teaspoon ground red pepper

½ cup olive oil

Combine olives, thyme, capers, anchovy paste, garlic, orange peel and ground red pepper in food processor or blender; pulse to roughly chop. Add oil; pulse briefly to form a chunky paste.

Makes about 1 cup

Tip: In a hurry? Substitute store-brought tapenade for homemade!

Mediterranean Shrimp Soup

2 cans (about **14 ounces** *each*) reduced-sodium chicken broth

1 can (about **14 ounces**) diced tomatoes

1 can (8 ounces) tomato sauce

1 medium onion, chopped

½ medium green bell pepper, chopped

½ cup orange juice

½ cup dry white wine (optional)

1 jar (2½ ounces) sliced mushrooms

¼ cup sliced pitted black olives

2 cloves garlic, minced

1 teaspoon dried basil

2 whole bay leaves

¼ teaspoon whole fennel seeds, crushed

⅛ teaspoon black pepper

1 pound medium raw shrimp, peeled and deveined (with tails on)

1. Combine broth, tomatoes, tomato sauce, onion, bell pepper, orange juice, wine, if desired, mushrooms, olives, garlic, basil, bay leaves, fennel seeds and black pepper in **CROCK-POT**® slow cooker; stir to blend. Cover; cook on LOW 4 to 4½ hours or until vegetables are crisp-tender.

2. Stir shrimp into **CROCK-POT**® slow cooker. Cover; cook on LOW 15 to 30 minutes or until shrimp are pink and opaque. Remove and discard bay leaves.

Makes 6 servings

Note: For a heartier soup, add 1 pound firm white fish (such as cod or haddock), cut into 1-inch pieces, 45 minutes before end of cooking time.

Cod Fish Stew

- ½ pound bacon, coarsely chopped
- 1 large carrot, diced
- 1 large onion, diced
- 2 stalks celery, diced
- 2 cloves garlic, minced
  Salt and black pepper
- 3 cups water
- 2 cups clam juice or fish broth
- 1 can (28 ounces) plum tomatoes, drained
- 2 potatoes, diced
- ½ cup dry white wine
- 3 tablespoons chopped fresh Italian parsley
- 3 tablespoons tomato paste
- 3 saffron threads
- 2½ pounds fresh cod, skinned and cut into bite-size pieces

1. Heat medium skillet over medium heat. Add bacon; cook and stir until crisp. Add carrot, onion, celery and garlic to skillet; season with salt and pepper. Cook until vegetables soften, stirring frequently.

2. Remove bacon and vegetables to **CROCK-POT**® slow cooker. Stir in water, clam juice, tomatoes, potatoes, wine, parsley, tomato paste and saffron. Cover; cook on LOW 6 to 7 hours or on HIGH 3 to 4 hours.

3. Add cod. Cover; cook on HIGH 10 to 20 minutes or until cod is just cooked through.

Makes 6 to 8 servings

Note: Cod is a great fish to use for a soup or stew. The thick creamy white fish becomes a hearty meal when paired with bacon and tomato.

Seafood Cioppino

1 tablespoon olive oil

1 medium fennel bulb, thinly sliced

1 medium onion, chopped

4 cloves garlic, minced

1 teaspoon dried basil

¼ teaspoon saffron threads, crushed (optional)

1 can (about 14 ounces) diced tomatoes

1 bottle (8 ounces) clam juice

16 little neck clams, scrubbed

24 mussels, scrubbed

1 pound cod fillet, cut into 8 pieces

8 ounces large raw shrimp, peeled and deveined (with tails on)

½ teaspoon salt

⅛ teaspoon black pepper

1. Coat inside of **CROCK-POT**® slow cooker with nonstick cooking spray. Heat oil in large skillet over medium-high heat. Add fennel, onion, garlic, basil and saffron, if desired; cook and stir 4 to 5 minutes or until vegetables are softened. Remove to **CROCK-POT**® slow cooker. Stir in tomatoes and clam juice.

2. Cover; cook on HIGH 2 to 3 hours. Add clams. Cover; cook on HIGH 30 minutes. Add mussels. Cover; cook on HIGH 15 minutes.

3. Season cod and shrimp with salt and pepper. Place on top of shellfish. Cover; cook on HIGH 25 to 30 minutes until clams and mussels have opened and fish is cooked through. Discard any unopened clams or mussels.

Makes 4 servings

Shrimp and Okra Gumbo

1 tablespoon olive oil

8 ounces kielbasa, halved lengthwise and cut into ¼-inch-thick half slices

1 green bell pepper, chopped

1 medium onion, chopped

3 stalks celery, cut into ¼-inch slices

6 green onions, chopped

4 cloves garlic, minced

1 cup chicken broth

1 can (about 14 ounces) diced tomatoes

1 teaspoon Cajun seasoning

½ teaspoon dried thyme

1 pound large raw shrimp, peeled and deveined (with tails on)

2 cups frozen cut okra, thawed

1. Coat inside of **CROCK-POT**® slow cooker with nonstick cooking spray. Heat oil in large skillet over medium-high heat. Add kielbasa; cook and stir 4 minutes or until browned. Remove to **CROCK-POT**® slow cooker using slotted spoon.

2. Return skillet to medium-high heat. Add bell pepper, chopped onion, celery, green onions and garlic; cook and stir 5 to 6 minutes or until vegetables are crisp-tender. Remove to **CROCK-POT**® slow cooker. Stir in broth, tomatoes, Cajun seasoning and thyme.

3. Cover; cook on LOW 4 hours. Stir in shrimp and okra. Cover; cook on LOW 30 to 35 minutes.

Makes 6 servings

Bacon-Wrapped Scallops

24 sea scallops, side muscle removed

½ cup Belgian white ale

3 tablespoons chopped fresh cilantro

2 tablespoons honey

¼ teaspoon chipotle chili powder

12 slices bacon, halved

1. Pour ½ inch of water in bottom of **CROCK-POT**® slow cooker. Combine scallops, ale, cilantro, honey and chipotle chili powder in medium bowl; stir to coat. Refrigerate 30 minutes.

2. Place 1 scallop on end of 1 bacon half. Roll up jelly-roll style and secure with toothpick. Remove to large baking sheet. Repeat with remaining bacon and scallops. Brush tops of scallops with ale mixture.

3. Heat large skillet over medium heat. Add wrapped scallops; cook 5 to 7 minutes or until bacon is just beginning to brown. Remove to **CROCK-POT**® slow cooker. Cover; cook on LOW 1 hour.

Makes 12 servings

VEGETARIAN DELIGHTS

Open-Face Provençal Vegetable Sandwich

2 cups sliced shiitake mushroom caps

1 large zucchini, halved lengthwise and sliced ¼ inch thick

1 large red bell pepper, quartered lengthwise and thinly sliced

1 small onion, sliced lengthwise ¼ inch thick

1 small jalapeño pepper, seeded and minced*

¼ cup vegetable broth

¼ cup pitted kalamata olives

2 tablespoons capers

1 clove garlic, minced

1½ tablespoons olive oil, divided

½ teaspoon dried oregano

Salt and black pepper

4 teaspoons white wine vinegar

Crusty bread, cut into thick slices

½ cup (3 ounces) shredded mozzarella cheese (optional)

*Jalapeño peppers can sting and irritate the skin, so wear rubber gloves when handling peppers and do not touch your eyes.

1. Combine mushrooms, zucchini, bell pepper, onion, jalapeño pepper, broth, olives, capers, garlic, 1 tablespoon oil, oregano, salt and black pepper in **CROCK-POT**® slow cooker; stir to blend. Cover; cook on LOW 5 to 6 hours.

2. Turn off heat. Stir in vinegar and remaining ½ tablespoon oil. Let stand, uncovered, 15 to 30 minutes or until vegetables absorb some of liquid. (Vegetable mixture should be lukewarm.) Season with additional salt and black pepper, if desired.

3. Spoon vegetables onto bread. Sprinkle each serving with 2 tablespoons cheese and broil 30 seconds or until cheese melts and browns, if desired.

Makes 6 servings

Vegetarian Paella

2 teaspoons canola oil

1 cup chopped onion

2 cloves garlic, minced

1 cup uncooked brown rice

2¼ cups vegetable broth

1 can (about 14 ounces) stewed tomatoes, undrained

1 small zucchini, halved lengthwise and sliced to ½-inch thickness (about 1¼ cups)

1 cup coarsely chopped carrots

1 cup chopped red bell pepper

1 teaspoon Italian seasoning

½ teaspoon ground turmeric

⅛ teaspoon ground red pepper

1 can (about 14 ounces) quartered artichoke hearts, drained

½ cup frozen baby peas

1. Heat oil in large skillet over medium-high heat. Add onion; cook and stir 6 to 7 minutes or until tender. Stir in garlic.

2. Combine onion mixture and rice in **CROCK-POT®** slow cooker. Add broth, tomatoes, zucchini, carrots, bell pepper, Italian seasoning, turmeric and ground red pepper; stir to blend. Cover; cook on LOW 4 hours or on HIGH 2 hours or until liquid is absorbed.

3. Stir in artichokes and peas. Cover; cook on LOW 5 to 10 minutes or until vegetables are tender.

Makes 6 servings

Black Bean and Mushroom Chilaquiles

2 tablespoons olive oil

1 medium onion, chopped

1 medium green bell pepper, chopped

1 jalapeño or serrano pepper, seeded and minced*

2 cans (about 15 ounces *each*) black beans, rinsed and drained

1 can (about 14 ounces) diced tomatoes

10 ounces white mushrooms, cut into quarters

1½ teaspoons ground cumin

1½ teaspoons dried oregano

1 cup (4 ounces) shredded sharp white Cheddar cheese, plus additional for garnish

6 cups baked tortilla chips

*Jalapeño and serrano peppers can sting and irritate the skin, so wear rubber gloves when handling peppers and do not touch your eyes.

1. Heat oil in medium skillet over medium heat. Add onion, bell pepper and jalapeño pepper; cook and stir 5 minutes or until onion is softened. Remove to **CROCK-POT®** slow cooker. Add beans, tomatoes, mushrooms, cumin and oregano. Cover; cook on LOW 6 hours or on HIGH 3 hours.

2. Sprinkle 1 cup cheese over beans and mushrooms. Cover; cook on HIGH 15 minutes or until cheese is melted. Stir to combine.

3. For each serving, coarsely crush 1 cup tortilla chips into individual serving bowls. Top with black bean mixture. Garnish with additional cheese.

Makes 6 servings

Mediterranean Stew

1 medium butternut squash, cut into 1-inch cubes

2 cups unpeeled eggplant, cut into 1-inch cubes

2 cups sliced zucchini

1 can (about 15 ounces) chickpeas, rinsed and drained

1 package (10 ounces) frozen cut okra

1 cup chopped onion

1 can (8 ounces) tomato sauce

1 medium fresh tomato, chopped

1 medium carrot, sliced

½ cup vegetable broth

⅓ cup raisins

1 clove garlic, minced

½ teaspoon ground cumin

½ teaspoon ground turmeric

¼ teaspoon ground red pepper

¼ teaspoon paprika

¼ teaspoon ground cinnamon

6 to 8 cups hot cooked couscous

Chopped fresh Italian parsley (optional)

1. Combine squash, eggplant, zucchini, chickpeas, okra, onion, tomato sauce, fresh tomato, carrot, broth, raisins, garlic, cumin, turmeric, ground red pepper, paprika and cinnamon in **CROCK-POT®** slow cooker; stir to blend.

2. Cover; cook on LOW 8 to 10 hours. Serve over couscous. Garnish with parsley.

Makes 6 servings

Curried Cauliflower and Potatoes

3 tablespoons vegetable oil

1 medium onion, chopped

1 tablespoon minced garlic

1 tablespoon curry powder

1½ teaspoons salt

1½ teaspoons grated fresh ginger

1 teaspoon ground turmeric

1 teaspoon yellow or brown mustard seeds

¼ teaspoon red pepper flakes

1 medium head cauliflower, cut into 1-inch pieces

2 pounds fingerling potatoes, cut into halves

½ cup water

1. Heat oil in medium skillet over medium heat. Add onion; cook and stir 8 minutes or until softened. Add garlic, curry powder, salt, ginger, turmeric, mustard seeds and red pepper flakes; cook and stir 1 minute. Remove to **CROCK-POT**® slow cooker.

2. Stir in cauliflower, potatoes and water. Cover; cook on HIGH 4 hours.

Makes 6 servings

Risi Bisi

1½ cups uncooked converted long grain rice

¾ cup chopped onion

2 cloves garlic, minced

2 cans (about 14 ounces *each*) vegetable broth

⅓ cup water

¾ teaspoon Italian seasoning

½ teaspoon dried basil

½ cup frozen peas, thawed

¼ cup grated Parmesan cheese

¼ cup toasted pine nuts (optional)

1. Combine rice, onion and garlic in **CROCK-POT**® slow cooker.

2. Bring broth and water to a boil in small saucepan. Stir broth mixture, Italian seasoning and basil into rice mixture in **CROCK-POT**® slow cooker. Cover; cook on LOW 2 to 3 hours or until liquid is absorbed.

3. Add peas to **CROCK-POT**® slow cooker. Cover; cook on LOW 1 hour. Stir in cheese. Garnish with pine nuts.

Makes 6 servings

Bean and Vegetable Burritos

2 tablespoons chili powder

2 teaspoons dried oregano

1½ teaspoons ground cumin

1 sweet potato, diced

1 can (about 15 ounces) black beans, rinsed and drained

4 cloves garlic, minced

1 onion, halved and thinly sliced

1 jalapeño pepper, seeded and minced*

1 green bell pepper, chopped

1 cup frozen corn, thawed and drained

3 tablespoons lime juice

1 tablespoon chopped fresh cilantro

½ cup (3 ounces) shredded Monterey Jack cheese

4 (10-inch) flour tortillas

*Jalapeño peppers can sting and irritate the skin, so wear rubber gloves when handling peppers and do not touch your eyes.

1. Combine chili powder, oregano and cumin in small bowl.

2. Layer potato, beans, half of chili powder mixture, garlic, onion, jalapeño pepper, bell pepper, remaining half of chili powder mixture and corn in **CROCK-POT®** slow cooker. Cover; cook on LOW 5 hours or until potato is tender. Stir in lime juice and cilantro.

3. Preheat oven to 350°F. Spoon 2 tablespoons cheese down center of each tortilla. Top with 1 cup filling. Fold up bottom edges of tortillas over filling; fold in sides and roll to enclose filling. Place burritos, seam side down, on baking sheet. Cover with foil; bake 20 minutes or until heated through.

Makes 4 servings

Channa Chat (Indian-Spiced Snack Mix)

2 teaspoons canola oil

1 medium onion, finely chopped and divided

2 cloves garlic, minced

2 cans (about 15 ounces *each*) chickpeas, rinsed and drained

¼ cup vegetable broth or water

2 teaspoons tomato paste

¼ teaspoon ground cinnamon

¼ teaspoon ground cumin

¼ teaspoon black pepper

1 whole bay leaf

½ cup balsamic vinegar

1 tablespoon packed brown sugar

1 plum tomato, chopped

½ jalapeño pepper, seeded and minced *or* ¼ teaspoon ground red pepper (optional)*

½ cup crisp rice cereal

3 tablespoons chopped fresh cilantro (optional)

*Jalapeño peppers can sting and irritate the skin, so wear rubber gloves when handling peppers and do not touch your eyes.

1. Heat oil in small skillet over medium-high heat. Add half of onion and garlic. Reduce heat to medium; cook and stir 2 minutes or until softened. Remove to **CROCK-POT**® slow cooker. Stir in chickpeas, broth, tomato paste, cinnamon, cumin, black pepper and bay leaf. Cover; cook on LOW 6 hours or on HIGH 3 hours. Remove and discard bay leaf.

2. Remove chickpeas to large bowl using slotted spoon. Cool 15 minutes. Meanwhile, combine vinegar and brown sugar in small saucepan; cook over medium-low heat until vinegar is reduced by half and mixture becomes syrupy, stirring frequently.

3. Add tomato, remaining onion and jalapeño pepper, if desired, to chickpeas; toss to coat. Gently fold in cereal. Drizzle with balsamic syrup and garnish with cilantro.

Makes 6 to 8 servings

Southwestern Stuffed Peppers

4 green bell peppers

1 can (about 15 ounces) black beans, rinsed and drained

1 cup (4 ounces) shredded pepper jack cheese

¾ cup salsa

½ cup frozen corn, thawed

½ cup chopped green onions

⅓ cup uncooked long grain rice

1 teaspoon chili powder

½ teaspoon ground cumin

Sour cream (optional)

1. Cut thin slice off top of each bell pepper. Carefully remove seeds and membranes, leaving peppers whole.

2. Combine beans, cheese, salsa, corn, green onions, rice, chili powder and cumin in medium bowl. Spoon bean mixture evenly into each pepper. Place peppers in **CROCK-POT**® slow cooker.

3. Cover; cook on LOW 4 to 6 hours. Serve with sour cream, if desired.

Makes 4 servings

Caribbean Sweet Potato and Bean Stew

2 sweet potatoes (about 1 pound), cut into 1-inch cubes

2 cups frozen cut green beans

1 can (about 15 ounces) black beans, rinsed and drained

1 can (about 14 ounces) vegetable broth

1 onion, sliced

2 teaspoons Caribbean jerk seasoning

½ teaspoon dried thyme

¼ teaspoon salt

¼ teaspoon ground cinnamon

⅓ cup slivered almonds, toasted*

*To toast almonds, spread in single layer in heavy skillet. Cook over medium heat 1 to 2 minutes or until nuts are lightly browned, stirring frequently.

Combine potatoes, beans, broth, onion, jerk seasoning, thyme, salt and cinnamon in **CROCK-POT**® slow cooker. Cover; cook on LOW 5 to 6 hours or until vegetables are tender. Sprinkle with almonds.

Makes 4 servings

Minestrone alla Milanese

2 cans (about **14** ounces *each*) reduced-sodium beef broth

1 can (about **14** ounces) diced tomatoes

1 cup diced red potatoes

1 cup coarsely chopped carrots

1 cup coarsely chopped green cabbage

1 cup sliced zucchini

½ cup chopped onion

½ cup sliced fresh green beans

½ cup coarsely chopped celery

½ cup water

2 tablespoons olive oil

1 clove garlic, minced

½ teaspoon dried basil

¼ teaspoon dried rosemary

1 whole bay leaf

1 can (about **15** ounces) cannellini beans, rinsed and drained

Grated Parmesan cheese (optional)

1. Combine broth, tomatoes, potatoes, carrots, cabbage, zucchini, onion, green beans, celery, water, oil, garlic, basil, rosemary and bay leaf in **CROCK-POT**® slow cooker; stir to blend. Cover; cook on LOW 5 to 6 hours.

2. Add cannellini beans. Cover; cook on LOW 1 hour or until vegetables are tender.

3. Remove and discard bay leaf. Top with cheese, if desired.

Makes 8 servings

Saag Paneer

2 onions, finely chopped

8 cloves garlic, minced

1 teaspoon ground coriander

1 teaspoon ground cumin

½ teaspoon pumpkin pie spice

½ teaspoon ground cardamom

½ teaspoon salt

2 packages (10 ounces *each*) frozen chopped spinach, thawed and squeezed dry

2 packages (9 ounces *each*) frozen chopped creamed spinach, thawed

2 tablespoons butter

8 ounces paneer, cut into ½-inch cubes*

*Paneer is a firm, fresh cheese used in South Asian cuisines. Substitute any firm white cheese or extra firm tofu.

1. Combine onions, garlic, coriander, cumin, pumpkin pie spice, cardamom and salt in **CROCK-POT®** slow cooker. Stir in spinach, creamed spinach and butter. Cover; cook on LOW 4½ to 5 hours or until onions are soft.

2. Add paneer; cover and cook on LOW 30 minutes or until paneer is heated through.

Makes 10 servings

Ratatouille with Parmesan Cheese

1 cup diced eggplant

2 medium tomatoes, chopped

1 small zucchini, diced

1 cup sliced mushrooms

½ cup tomato purée

1 large shallot *or* ½ small onion, chopped

1 clove garlic, minced

¾ teaspoon dried oregano

⅛ teaspoon dried rosemary

⅛ teaspoon black pepper

2 tablespoons shredded fresh basil

2 teaspoons lemon juice

¼ teaspoon salt

Grated Parmesan cheese

1. Spray large skillet with nonstick cooking spray; heat over medium-high heat. Add eggplant; cook and stir 5 minutes or until lightly browned. Remove to **CROCK-POT®** slow cooker.

2. Add tomatoes, zucchini, mushrooms, tomato purée, shallot, garlic, oregano, rosemary and pepper; stir to blend. Cover; cook on LOW 6 hours or on HIGH 3 hours.

3. Stir in basil, lemon juice and salt. Turn off heat; let stand 5 minutes. Top with cheese.

Makes 4 servings

Mushroom and Vegetable Ragoût over Polenta

RAGOÛT

- 3 tablespoons extra virgin olive oil
- 8 ounces sliced mushrooms
- 8 ounces shiitake mushrooms, stemmed and thinly sliced
- ½ cup Madeira wine
- 1 can (28 ounces) crushed tomatoes
- 1 can (about 15 ounces) chickpeas, rinsed and drained
- 1 medium onion, chopped
- 1 can (about 6 ounces) tomato paste
- 4 cloves garlic, minced
- 1 sprig fresh rosemary

POLENTA

- 2 cups water
- 2 cups whole milk
- ¼ teaspoon salt
- 2 cups instant polenta
- ½ cup grated Parmesan cheese

1. For ragoût, heat oil in large skillet over medium-high heat. Add mushrooms; cook and stir 8 to 10 minutes or until mushrooms are brown. Add Madeira; cook 1 minute or until liquid is reduced by half. Remove to **CROCK-POT**® slow cooker.

2. Stir crushed tomatoes, chickpeas, onion, tomato paste, garlic and rosemary into **CROCK-POT**® slow cooker. Cover; cook on LOW 6 hours or until vegetables are tender. Remove and discard rosemary.

3. For polenta, combine water, milk and salt in large saucepan over medium-high heat. Bring to a boil; slowly whisk in polenta in slow, steady stream. Cook 4 to 5 minutes, whisking until thick and creamy.

4. Remove polenta from heat; stir in cheese. Top polenta with ragoût.

Makes 6 servings

Meatless Sloppy Joes

2 cups thinly sliced onions

2 cups chopped green bell peppers

1 can (about 15 ounces) kidney beans, drained and mashed

1 can (8 ounces) tomato sauce

2 tablespoons ketchup

1 tablespoon yellow mustard

2 cloves garlic, minced

1 teaspoon chili powder

1 tablespoon cider vinegar (optional)

4 sandwich rolls

1. Combine onions, bell peppers, beans, tomato sauce, ketchup, mustard, garlic and chili powder in **CROCK-POT**® slow cooker; stir to blend. Cover; cook on LOW 5 to 5½ hours or until vegetables are tender.

2. Season with vinegar, if desired. Serve on rolls.

Makes 4 servings

Jamaican Quinoa and Sweet Potato Stew

3 cups vegetable broth

1 large *or* 2 small sweet potatoes (12 ounces), cut into ¾-inch pieces

1 cup uncooked quinoa, rinsed and drained

1 large red bell pepper, cut into ¾-inch pieces

1 tablespoon Caribbean jerk seasoning

¼ cup chopped fresh cilantro

¼ cup sliced almonds, toasted*

Hot pepper sauce or Pickapeppa sauce (optional)

*To toast almonds, spread in single layer in heavy skillet. Cook and stir over medium heat 1 to 2 minutes or until nuts are lightly browned.

1. Coat inside of **CROCK-POT**® slow cooker with nonstick cooking spray. Combine broth, potatoes, quinoa, bell pepper and jerk seasoning in **CROCK-POT**® slow cooker; stir to blend.

2. Cover; cook on LOW 5 to 6 hours or on HIGH 2 to 2½ hours. Top with cilantro and almonds. Serve with hot pepper sauce, if desired.

Makes 4 servings

Vegetable Jollof Rice

1 eggplant (about 1¼ pounds), cut into 1-inch cubes

1¾ teaspoons salt, divided

3 tablespoons vegetable oil, plus additional as needed

1 medium onion, chopped

1 medium green bell pepper, chopped

3 medium carrots, cut into ½-inch-thick rounds

2 cloves garlic, minced

1½ cups uncooked converted rice

1 tablespoon plus ½ teaspoon chili powder

1 can (28 ounces) diced tomatoes

1 can (about 14 ounces) vegetable broth

1. Place eggplant cubes in colander. Toss with 1 teaspoon salt. Let stand in sink for 1 hour to drain. Rinse under cold water; drain and pat dry with paper towels.

2. Heat 1 tablespoon oil in large skillet over medium-high heat. Working in batches, cook eggplant until browned on all sides. Remove eggplant to plate as it is browned. Add additional oil, 1 tablespoon at a time, to skillet as needed to prepare all remaining batches of eggplant.

3. Wipe out skillet with paper towels. Add another 1 tablespoon oil to skillet; return to heat. Add onion, bell pepper, carrots and garlic; cook and stir until onion is softened but not brown. Remove to **CROCK-POT®** slow cooker. Stir in rice, chili powder and remaining ¾ teaspoon salt.

4. Drain tomatoes over 1-quart measuring cup, reserving tomato juice. Add broth to tomato juice; add water as needed to measure 4 cups total. Pour into **CROCK-POT®** slow cooker. Add drained tomatoes; stir to level rice. Top with eggplant. Cover; cook on LOW 3½ to 4 hours or until rice is tender and liquid is absorbed. Stir well. Serve warm.

Makes 6 servings

Tip: Jollof Rice (also spelled "jolof" or sometimes "djolof") is an important dish in many West African cultures.

Curried Potatoes, Cauliflower and Peas

1 tablespoon vegetable oil

1 onion, chopped

2 tablespoons minced fresh ginger

2 cloves garlic, chopped

2 pounds red potatoes, cut into ½-inch-thick rounds

1 teaspoon garam masala*

1 teaspoon salt

1 small head cauliflower (about 1¼ pounds), trimmed and broken into florets

1 cup vegetable broth

2 ripe plum tomatoes, seeded and chopped

1 cup thawed frozen peas

Hot cooked basmati or long grain rice

*Garam masala is a blend of Asian spices available in the spice aisle of many supermarkets. If garam masala is unavailable substitute ½ teaspoon ground cumin and ½ teaspoon ground coriander seeds.

1. Heat oil in large skillet over medium heat. Add onion, ginger and garlic; cook and stir 5 to 7 minutes or until onion is softened. Remove from heat.

2. Place potatoes in **CROCK-POT**® slow cooker. Blend garam masala and salt in small bowl. Sprinkle half of spice mixture over potatoes. Top with onion mixture, then cauliflower. Sprinkle remaining spice mixture over cauliflower. Pour in broth. Cover; cook on HIGH 3½ hours.

3. Remove cover and gently stir in tomatoes and peas. Cover; cook on HIGH 30 minutes or until potatoes are tender. Stir gently. Spoon over rice in bowls.

Makes 6 servings

Asian Sweet Potato and Corn Stew

1 tablespoon vegetable oil

1 large onion, chopped

2 tablespoons peeled minced fresh ginger

½ jalapeño or serrano pepper, seeded and minced*

2 cloves garlic, minced

1 cup frozen corn, thawed

2 teaspoons curry powder

1 can (13½ ounces) unsweetened coconut milk

1 teaspoon cornstarch

4 sweet potatoes, cut into ¾-inch cubes

1 can (about 14 ounces) vegetable broth

1 tablespoon soy sauce

Hot cooked jasmine or long grain rice

Chopped fresh cilantro, peanuts and green onions (optional)

*Jalapeño and serrano peppers can sting and irritate the skin, so wear rubber gloves when handling peppers and do not touch your eyes.

1. Heat oil in large skillet over medium heat. Add onion, ginger, jalapeño pepper and garlic; cook and stir 5 minutes. Remove from heat. Stir in corn and curry powder.

2. Stir coconut milk into cornstarch in **CROCK-POT®** slow cooker. Stir in potatoes, broth and soy sauce; top with curried corn. Cover; cook on LOW 5 to 6 hours. Stir gently to smooth cooking liquid. Spoon over rice in bowls. Garnish with cilantro, peanuts and green onions.

Makes 6 servings

Serving Suggestion: Garnish with coarsely chopped dry-roasted peanuts for extra flavor and crunch.

Mexican Rice, Bean and Cheese Burritos

1 can (about 15 ounces) black beans, rinsed and drained

1 can (about 14 ounces) fire-roasted diced tomatoes

1 cup uncooked converted rice

1 medium onion, chopped

1 cup ricotta cheese

½ cup water

3 cloves garlic, minced

1 jalapeño pepper, chopped*

2 teaspoons chili powder

2 cups (8 ounces) shredded Monterey Jack cheese

3 tablespoons chopped fresh cilantro

6 (10-inch) flour tortillas

¾ cup prepared black bean and corn salsa

*Jalapeño peppers can sting and irritate the skin, so wear rubber gloves when handling peppers and do not touch your eyes.

1. Coat inside of **CROCK-POT**® slow cooker with nonstick cooking spray. Add beans, tomatoes, rice, onion, ricotta cheese, water, garlic, jalapeño pepper and chili powder to **CROCK-POT**® slow cooker; stir to blend. Cover; cook on LOW 4 hours or until rice is tender.

2. Stir in Monterey Jack cheese and cilantro.

3. Warm tortillas according to package directions. Place 1 cup rice mixture on each tortilla and roll up. Serve with salsa.

Makes 6 servings

Cuban Black Beans and Rice

3¾ cups vegetable broth

1½ cups uncooked brown rice

1 onion, chopped

1 jalapeño pepper, seeded and chopped*

3 cloves garlic, minced

2 teaspoons ground cumin

1 teaspoon salt

2 cans (about 15 ounces *each*) black beans, rinsed and drained

1 tablespoon lime juice

Sour cream (optional)

Sliced green onions (optional)

*Jalapeño peppers can sting and irritate the skin, so wear rubber gloves when handling peppers and do not touch your eyes.

1. Combine broth, rice, onion, jalapeño pepper, garlic, cumin and salt in **CROCK-POT**® slow cooker; stir to blend. Cover; cook on LOW 7½ hours or until rice is tender.

2. Stir beans and lime juice into **CROCK-POT**® slow cooker. Cover; cook on LOW 15 to 20 minutes or until heated through. Top with sour cream and green onions, if desired.

Makes 4 to 6 servings

Eggplant Parmesan

¼ cup all-purpose flour

1 teaspoon dried oregano

1 teaspoon dried basil

½ teaspoon salt

1 egg

2 teaspoons cold water

2 tablespoons extra virgin olive oil, divided

1 large eggplant (about 1 pound), ends trimmed, peeled and cut crosswise into 8 slices

2¼ cups spicy marinara pasta sauce

½ cup panko bread crumbs

1½ cups (6 ounces) shredded Italian cheese blend or mozzarella cheese

Chopped fresh basil (optional)

1. Combine flour, oregano, dried basil and salt in shallow dish or pie plate. Beat egg with water in another shallow dish or pie plate.

2. Heat 1 tablespoon oil in large nonstick skillet over medium heat. Dip each slice of eggplant in egg mixture, letting excess drip back into dish. Dredge in flour mixture, coating both sides lightly. Cook 4 slices 3 to 4 minutes per side or until lightly browned. Repeat with remaining oil and 4 slices eggplant.

3. Coat inside of **CROCK-POT®** slow cooker with nonstick cooking spray. Layer ¾ cup pasta sauce in bottom of **CROCK-POT®** slow cooker. Arrange 4 slices of browned eggplant over sauce, overlapping if necessary. Top with ¼ cup panko and ½ cup cheese. Repeat layering with ¾ cup pasta sauce, 4 slices eggplant, ¼ cup panko and ½ cup cheese. Spoon remaining pasta sauce over cheese. Cover; cook on LOW 4 to 5 hours or on HIGH 2 to 2½ hours.

4. Sprinkle remaining ½ cup cheese on top. Turn off heat. Let stand, covered, 5 minutes or until cheese melts. Garnish with fresh basil.

Makes 4 servings

Curried Vegetable and Cashew Stew

- **1** medium potato, cut into ½-inch cubes
- **1** can (about 15 ounces) chickpeas, rinsed and drained
- **1** can (about 14 ounces) diced tomatoes
- **1** medium eggplant (about ½ pound), cut into ½-inch cubes
- **1** medium onion, chopped
- **1** cup reduced-sodium vegetable broth
- **2** tablespoons quick-cooking tapioca
- **2** teaspoons grated fresh ginger
- **2** teaspoons curry powder
- **½** teaspoon salt
- **¼** teaspoon black pepper
- **1** medium zucchini (about 8 ounces), cut into ½-inch cubes
- **2** tablespoons golden raisins
- **½** cup frozen peas
- **½** cup lightly salted cashew nuts

1. Combine potato, chickpeas, tomatoes, eggplant, onion, broth, tapioca, ginger, curry powder, salt and pepper in **CROCK-POT**® slow cooker; stir to blend. Cover; cook on LOW 8 to 9 hours.

2. Stir zucchini, raisins, peas and cashews into **CROCK-POT**® slow cooker. Turn **CROCK-POT**® slow cooker to HIGH. Cover; cook on HIGH 1 hour or until zucchini is tender.

Makes 8 servings

Black Bean, Zucchini and Corn Enchiladas

1 tablespoon vegetable oil

1 medium onion, chopped

2 medium zucchini

2 cups corn

1 large red bell pepper, chopped

1 teaspoon minced garlic

½ teaspoon salt

½ teaspoon ground cumin

¼ teaspoon ground coriander

1 can (about 15 ounces) black beans, rinsed and drained

2 jars (16 ounces *each*) salsa verde

12 (6-inch) corn tortillas

2½ cups (10 ounces) shredded Monterey Jack cheese

2 tablespoons chopped fresh cilantro

1. Heat oil in large skillet over medium heat. Add onion; cook 6 minutes or until softened. Add zucchini, corn and bell pepper; cook 2 minutes. Add garlic, salt, cumin and coriander; cook and stir 1 minute. Stir in beans. Remove from heat.

2. Pour 1 cup salsa in bottom of **CROCK-POT**® slow cooker. Arrange 3 tortillas in single layer, cutting the tortillas in half as needed to make them fit. Place 2 cups vegetable mixture over tortillas; sprinkle with ½ cup cheese. Repeat layering two more times. Layer with remaining 3 tortillas; top with 2 cups salsa. Sprinkle with remaining 1 cup cheese. Reserve remaining filling for another use.

3. Cover; cook on HIGH 2 hours or until cheese is bubbly and edges are lightly browned. Sprinkle with cilantro. Turn off heat. Let stand, uncovered, 10 minutes before serving.

Makes 6 servings

Greek Lemon and Rice Soup

3 cans (about 14 ounces *each*)
    vegetable broth

½ cup uncooked long grain rice
    (not converted or instant rice)

3 egg yolks

¼ cup fresh lemon juice

¼ teaspoon salt

⅛ teaspoon white pepper*

4 thin slices lemon (optional)

4 teaspoons finely chopped fresh Italian
    parsley (optional)

*Substitute black pepper, if desired.

1. Stir broth and rice in **CROCK-POT®** slow cooker. Cover; cook on HIGH 2 to 3 hours or until rice is cooked.

2. Stir egg yolks and lemon juice in medium bowl. Stir large spoonful of hot rice mixture into egg yolk mixture. Whisk back into **CROCK-POT®** slow cooker.

3. Turn **CROCK-POT®** slow cooker to LOW. Cover; cook on LOW 10 minutes. Season with salt and pepper. Ladle soup into serving bowls; garnish with lemon slices and chopped parsley.

Makes 4 servings

Arroz con Queso

1 can (about 14 ounces) crushed tomatoes

1 can (about 15 ounces) black beans,
    rinsed and drained

2 cups (8 ounces) shredded Monterey Jack
    cheese, divided

1½ cups uncooked converted long grain rice

1 onion, chopped

1 cup cottage cheese

1 can (4 ounces) chopped mild green chiles

2 tablespoons vegetable oil

3 teaspoons minced garlic

Combine tomatoes, beans, 1 cup Monterey Jack cheese, rice, onion, cottage cheese, chiles, oil and garlic in **CROCK-POT®** slow cooker; stir to blend. Cover; cook on LOW 6 to 9 hours or until liquid is absorbed. Sprinkle with remaining 1 cup Monterey Jack cheese before serving.

Makes 8 to 10 servings

Italian Escarole and White Bean Stew

1 tablespoon olive oil

1 medium onion, chopped

3 medium carrots, cut into ½-inch-thick rounds

2 cloves garlic, minced

1 can (about 14 ounces) vegetable broth

1 head (about 12 ounces) escarole, base trimmed

¼ teaspoon red pepper flakes

2 cans (about 15 ounces *each*) Great Northern beans, rinsed and drained

Grated Parmesan cheese (optional)

1. Heat oil in medium skillet over medium-high heat. Add onion and carrots; cook and stir 3 to 5 minutes or until onion softens. Add garlic; cook and stir 1 minute or until fragrant. Remove to **CROCK-POT**® slow cooker. Top with broth.

2. Roughly cut escarole crosswise into 1-inch-wide strips. Wash well in large bowl of cold water. Shake to remove excess water, leaving dirt in bottom of bowl. Add to vegetable mixture in **CROCK-POT**® slow cooker. Sprinkle with red pepper flakes. Top with beans.

3. Cover; cook on LOW 7 to 8 hours or on HIGH 3½ to 4 hours. Garnish with cheese.

Makes 4 servings

Tip: Escarole is very leafy and easily fills a 4½-quart **CROCK-POT**® slow cooker when raw, but it shrinks dramatically as it cooks down. This recipe makes four portions, but can easily be doubled. Simply double the quantities of all the ingredients listed and be sure to use a 6-quart (or larger) **CROCK-POT**® slow cooker.

Asiago and Asparagus Risotto-Style Rice

2 cups chopped onion

1 can (about 14 ounces) vegetable broth

1 cup uncooked converted rice

2 cloves garlic, minced

½ pound asparagus spears, trimmed and broken into 1-inch pieces

1 cup half-and-half, divided

½ cup (about 4 ounces) grated Asiago cheese, plus additional for garnish

¼ cup (½ stick) butter, cubed

½ cup (2 ounces) pine nuts or slivered almonds, toasted*

1 teaspoon salt

*To toast nuts, spread in single layer in heavy skillet. Cook over medium heat 1 to 2 minutes or until nuts are lightly browned, stirring frequently.

1. Combine onion, broth, rice and garlic in **CROCK-POT®** slow cooker; stir to blend. Cover; cook on HIGH 2 hours or until rice is tender.

2. Stir in asparagus and ½ cup half-and-half. Cover; cook on HIGH 20 minutes or until asparagus is crisp-tender.

3. Stir in remaining ½ cup half-and-half, ½ cup cheese, butter, pine nuts and salt. Turn off heat. Cover; let stand 5 minutes or until cheese is slightly melted. Fluff with fork. Garnish with additional cheese.

Makes 4 servings

Tip: Risotto is a classic creamy rice dish of northern Italy and can be made with a wide variety of ingredients. Fresh vegetables and cheeses such as Asiago work especially well in risotto. Parmesan cheese, shellfish, white wine and herbs are also popular additions.

COMFORTING CASSEROLES

Cerveza Chicken Enchilada Casserole

2 cups water

1 stalk celery, chopped

1 small carrot, chopped

1 can (12 ounces) Mexican beer, divided

Juice of 1 lime

1 teaspoon salt

1½ pounds boneless, skinless chicken breasts

1 can (19 ounces) enchilada sauce

7 ounces white corn tortilla chips

½ medium onion, chopped

3 cups (12 ounces) shredded Cheddar cheese

Optional toppings: sour cream, sliced black olives and chopped fresh cilantro

1. Bring water, celery, carrot, 1 cup beer, lime juice and salt to a boil in large saucepan over high heat. Add chicken breasts; reduce heat to simmer. Cook 12 to 14 minutes or until chicken is cooked through. Remove chicken to large cutting board; shred into 1-inch pieces.

2. Spread ½ cup enchilada sauce in bottom of **CROCK-POT**® slow cooker. Arrange one third of tortilla chips over sauce. Layer with one third of shredded chicken and one third of chopped onion. Sprinkle with 1 cup cheese. Repeat layers two times.

3. Pour remaining beer over casserole. Cover; cook on LOW 3½ to 4 hours. Top as desired.

Makes 4 to 6 servings

Corn Bread and Bean Casserole

1 medium onion, chopped

1 medium green bell pepper, diced

2 cloves garlic, minced

1 can (about 15 ounces) red kidney beans, rinsed and drained

1 can (about 15 ounces) pinto beans, rinsed and drained

1 can (about 15 ounces) diced tomatoes with mild green chiles

1 can (8 ounces) tomato sauce

1 teaspoon chili powder

½ teaspoon ground cumin

½ teaspoon black pepper

¼ teaspoon hot pepper sauce

1 cup yellow cornmeal

1 cup all-purpose flour

2½ teaspoons baking powder

1 tablespoon sugar

½ teaspoon salt

1¼ cups milk

2 eggs

3 tablespoons vegetable oil

1 can (8½ ounces) cream-style corn

1. Coat inside of **CROCK-POT**® slow cooker with nonstick cooking spray. Heat large skillet over medium heat. Add onion, bell pepper and garlic; cook and stir 5 minutes or until tender. Remove to **CROCK-POT**® slow cooker.

2. Stir beans, diced tomatoes, tomato sauce, chili powder, cumin, black pepper and hot pepper sauce into **CROCK-POT**® slow cooker. Cover; cook on HIGH 1 hour.

3. Combine cornmeal, flour, baking powder, sugar and salt in large bowl; stir to blend. Stir in milk, eggs and oil; mix well. Stir in corn. Spoon evenly over bean mixture in **CROCK-POT**® slow cooker. Cover; cook on HIGH 1½ to 2 hours or until corn bread topping is golden brown.

Makes 8 servings

Tip: Spoon any remaining corn bread topping into greased muffin cups. Bake 30 minutes at 375°F or until golden brown.

Cheesy Broccoli Casserole

2 packages (10 ounces *each*) frozen chopped broccoli, thawed

1 can (10½ ounces) condensed cream of celery soup, undiluted

1¼ cups (5 ounces) shredded sharp Cheddar cheese, divided

¼ cup minced onion

1 teaspoon paprika

1 teaspoon hot pepper sauce

½ teaspoon celery seed

1 cup crushed potato chips or saltine crackers

1. Coat inside of **CROCK-POT®** slow cooker with nonstick cooking spray. Combine broccoli, soup, 1 cup cheese, onion, paprika, hot pepper sauce and celery seed in **CROCK-POT®** slow cooker; stir to blend. Cover; cook on LOW 5 to 6 hours or on HIGH 2½ to 3 hours.

2. Uncover; sprinkle top with potato chips and remaining ¼ cup cheese. Cook, uncovered, on HIGH 10 to 15 minutes or until cheese is melted.

Makes 4 to 6 servings

Tuna Casserole

2 cans (10¾ ounces *each*) cream of celery soup

2 cans (5 ounces *each*) tuna in water, drained and flaked

1 cup water

2 carrots, chopped

1 small red onion, chopped

¼ teaspoon black pepper

1 raw egg, uncracked

8 ounces hot cooked egg noodles

Plain dry bread crumbs

2 tablespoons chopped fresh Italian parsley

1. Stir soup, tuna, water, carrots, onion and pepper into **CROCK-POT®** slow cooker. Place whole unpeeled egg on top. Cover; cook on LOW 4 to 5 hours or on HIGH 1½ to 3 hours.

2. Remove egg; stir in pasta. Cover; cook on HIGH 30 to 60 minutes or until onion is tender. Meanwhile, peel egg and mash in small bowl; stir in bread crumbs and parsley. Top casserole with bread crumb mixture.

Makes 6 servings

Chicken and Wild Rice Casserole

3 tablespoons olive oil

2 slices bacon, chopped

1½ pounds chicken thighs, trimmed

½ cup diced onion

½ cup diced celery

2 tablespoons Worcestershire sauce

½ teaspoon salt

¼ teaspoon black pepper

½ teaspoon dried sage

1 cup uncooked converted long grain white rice

1 package (4 ounces) wild rice

6 ounces brown mushrooms, wiped clean and quartered*

3 cups hot chicken broth**

2 tablespoons chopped fresh Italian parsley (optional)

*Use "baby bellas" or cremini mushrooms. Or you may substitute white button mushrooms.

**Use enough broth to cover chicken.

1. Spread oil in bottom of **CROCK-POT®** slow cooker. Microwave bacon on HIGH 1 minute. Remove to **CROCK-POT®** slow cooker. Place chicken in **CROCK-POT®** slow cooker, skin side down. Add onion, celery, Worcestershire sauce, salt, pepper, sage, white rice, wild rice, mushrooms and broth. Cover; cook on LOW 3 to 4 hours or until rice is tender.

2. Turn off heat. Uncover; let stand 15 minutes before serving. Remove chicken skin, if desired. Garnish with parsley.

Makes 4 to 6 servings

Slow Cooker Pizza Casserole

1½ pounds ground beef

1 pound bulk pork sausage

4 jars (14 ounces *each*) pizza sauce

2 cups (8 ounces) shredded mozzarella cheese

2 cups grated Parmesan cheese

2 cans (4 ounces *each*) mushroom stems and pieces, drained

2 packages (3 ounces *each*) sliced pepperoni

½ cup finely chopped onion

½ cup finely chopped green bell pepper

1 clove garlic, minced

1 pound corkscrew pasta, cooked and drained

1. Brown beef and sausage 6 to 8 minutes in large nonstick skillet over medium-high heat, stirring to break up meat. Remove to **CROCK-POT**® slow cooker using slotted spoon.

2. Add pizza sauce, cheeses, mushrooms, pepperoni, onion, bell pepper and garlic; stir to blend. Cover; cook on LOW 3½ hours or on HIGH 2 hours.

3. Stir in pasta. Cover; cook on HIGH 15 to 20 minutes or until pasta is heated through.

Makes 6 servings

Hot Three-Bean Casserole

2 tablespoons olive oil

1 cup coarsely chopped onion

1 cup chopped celery

2 cloves garlic, minced

1 can (about 15 ounces) chickpeas, rinsed and drained

1 can (about 15 ounces) kidney beans, rinsed and drained

1 package (10 ounces) frozen cut green beans

1 cup water

1 cup coarsely chopped tomato

1 can (8 ounces) tomato sauce

1 to 2 jalapeño peppers, seeded and minced*

1 tablespoon chili powder

2 teaspoons sugar

1½ teaspoons ground cumin

1 teaspoon salt

1 teaspoon dried oregano

¼ teaspoon black pepper

Sprigs fresh oregano (optional)

*Jalapeño peppers can sting and irritate the skin, so wear rubber gloves when handling peppers and do not touch your eyes.

1. Heat oil in large skillet over medium heat. Add onion, celery and garlic; cook and stir 5 minutes or until tender. Remove to **CROCK-POT®** slow cooker.

2. Add chickpeas, beans, water, tomato, tomato sauce, jalapeño pepper, chili powder, sugar, cumin, salt, dried oregano and black pepper to **CROCK-POT®** slow cooker; stir to blend. Cover; cook on LOW 6 to 8 hours. Garnish with fresh oregano.

Makes 12 servings

Down-Home Squash Casserole

4 cups corn bread stuffing mix
    (half of 16-ounce package)

½ cup (1 stick) butter, melted

1 can (10¾ ounces) condensed cream
    of chicken soup, undiluted

¾ cup mayonnaise

¼ cup milk

¼ teaspoon poultry seasoning
    or rubbed sage

3 medium yellow squash, cut into ½-inch
    slices (about 1 pound *total*)

1½ cups frozen seasoning blend vegetables,
    thawed*

*Seasoning blend is a mixture of chopped bell peppers, onions and celery. If seasoning blend is unavailable, use ½ cup *each* of fresh vegetables.

1. Coat inside of **CROCK-POT**® slow cooker with nonstick cooking spray. Combine stuffing and butter in large bowl; toss gently to coat. Place two thirds of stuffing in **CROCK-POT**® slow cooker. Place remaining stuffing on plate.

2. Combine soup, mayonnaise, milk and poultry seasoning in same large bowl. Add squash and vegetables; stir until well coated. Pour mixture over stuffing mix in **CROCK-POT**® slow cooker. Top evenly with remaining stuffing. Cover; cook on LOW 4 hours or until squash is tender.

3. Turn off heat. Uncover; let stand 15 minutes before serving.

Makes 8 to 10 servings

Sweet Potato and Pecan Casserole

1 can (40 ounces) sweet potatoes, drained and mashed

½ cup apple juice

⅓ cup plus 2 tablespoons butter, melted and divided

½ teaspoon salt

½ teaspoon ground cinnamon

¼ teaspoon black pepper

2 eggs, beaten

⅓ cup chopped pecans

⅓ cup packed brown sugar

2 tablespoons all-purpose flour

1. Combine potatoes, apple juice, ⅓ cup butter, salt, cinnamon and pepper in large bowl; beat in eggs. Pour mixture into **CROCK-POT®** slow cooker.

2. Combine pecans, brown sugar, flour and remaining 2 tablespoons butter in small bowl; stir to blend. Spread over sweet potatoes. Cover; cook on HIGH 3 to 4 hours.

Makes 6 to 8 servings

Chipotle Chicken Casserole

1 pound boneless, skinless chicken thighs, cubed

1 can (about 15 ounces) navy beans, rinsed and drained

1 can (about 15 ounces) black beans, rinsed and drained

1 can (about 14 ounces) crushed tomatoes

1½ cups chicken broth

½ cup orange juice

1 medium onion, diced

1 canned chipotle pepper in adobo sauce, minced

1 teaspoon salt

1 teaspoon ground cumin

1 whole bay leaf

Combine chicken, beans, tomatoes, broth, orange juice, onion, chipotle pepper, salt, cumin and bay leaf in **CROCK-POT®** slow cooker; stir to blend. Cover; cook on LOW 7 to 8 hours or on HIGH 3½ to 4 hours. Remove and discard bay leaf before serving.

Makes 6 servings

Wild Rice and Mushroom Casserole

2 tablespoons olive oil

1 large green bell pepper, finely diced

8 ounces button mushrooms, thinly sliced

½ medium red onion, finely diced

1 can (about 14 ounces) diced tomatoes, drained

2 cloves garlic, minced

1 teaspoon dried oregano

1 teaspoon paprika

2 tablespoons butter

2 tablespoons all-purpose flour

1½ cups milk

2 cups (8 ounces) shredded pepper jack, Cheddar or Swiss cheese

1 teaspoon salt

½ teaspoon black pepper

2 cups wild rice, cooked according to package directions

Sprigs fresh oregano (optional)

1. Coat inside of **CROCK-POT**® slow cooker with nonstick cooking spray. Heat oil in large skillet over medium heat. Add bell pepper, mushrooms and onion; cook 5 to 6 minutes or until vegetables soften, stirring occasionally. Add tomatoes, garlic, dried oregano and paprika; cook 3 to 5 minutes or until heated through. Remove to large bowl to cool.

2. Melt butter in same skillet over medium heat; whisk in flour. Cook and stir 4 to 5 minutes or until smooth and golden. Whisk in milk; bring to a boil. Whisk in cheese. Season with salt and black pepper.

3. Combine wild rice with vegetables in large bowl. Fold in cheese sauce; mix gently. Pour wild rice mixture into **CROCK-POT**® slow cooker. Cover; cook on LOW 4 to 6 hours or on HIGH 2 to 3 hours. Garnish with fresh oregano.

Makes 4 to 6 servings

Ravioli Casserole

8 ounces pork or turkey Italian sausage, casings removed

½ cup minced onion

1½ cups marinara sauce

1 can (about 14 ounces) Italian-style diced tomatoes

2 packages (9 ounces *each*) refrigerated meatless ravioli, such as wild mushroom or three cheese, divided

1½ cups (6 ounces) shredded mozzarella cheese, divided

Chopped fresh Italian parsley (optional)

1. Heat large skillet over medium-high heat. Brown sausage and onion 6 to 8 minutes, stirring to break up meat. Drain fat. Stir in marinara sauce and tomatoes; mix well. Remove from heat.

2. Coat inside of **CROCK-POT**® slow cooker with nonstick cooking spray. Spoon 1 cup sauce into **CROCK-POT**® slow cooker. Layer half of 1 package of ravioli over sauce; top with additional ½ cup sauce and ¼ cup cheese. Repeat layers once. Repeat layers with remaining package ravioli and all remaining sauce. Cover; cook on LOW 2½ to 3 hours or on HIGH 1½ to 2 hours or until sauce is heated through and ravioli is tender.

3. Sprinkle remaining ½ cup cheese over top of casserole. Cover; cook on HIGH 15 minutes or until cheese is melted. Garnish with parsley.

Makes 4 to 6 servings

Five-Bean Casserole

2 medium onions, chopped

8 ounces bacon, diced

2 cloves garlic, minced

½ cup packed brown sugar

½ cup cider vinegar

1 teaspoon salt

1 teaspoon dry mustard

¼ teaspoon black pepper

2 cans (about 15 ounces *each*) kidney beans, rinsed and drained

1 can (about 15 ounces) chickpeas, rinsed and drained

1 can (about 15 ounces) butter beans, rinsed and drained

1 can (about 15 ounces) Great Northern or cannellini beans, rinsed and drained

1 can (about 15 ounces) baked beans

Chopped green onions (optional)

1. Heat large nonstick skillet over medium heat. Add onions, bacon and garlic; cook and stir 5 to 7 minutes or until onions are softened. Drain fat. Stir in brown sugar, vinegar, salt, dry mustard and pepper; cook over low heat 15 minutes.

2. Combine all beans in **CROCK-POT**® slow cooker. Spoon onion mixture evenly over top of beans. Cover; cook on LOW 6 to 8 hours or on HIGH 3 to 4 hours. Serve warm. Garnish with green onions.

Makes 16 servings

Layered Mexican-Style Casserole

2 cans (about 15 ounces *each*) hominy, drained

1 can (about 15 ounces) black beans, rinsed and drained

1 can (about 14 ounces) diced tomatoes with garlic, basil and oregano

1 cup thick and chunky salsa

1 can (6 ounces) tomato paste

½ teaspoon ground cumin

3 (9-inch) flour tortillas

2 cups (8 ounces) shredded Monterey Jack cheese

¼ cup sliced black olives

1. Prepare foil handles by tearing off three 18 × 2-inch strips of heavy-duty foil or use regular foil folded to double thickness. Crisscross foil strips in spoke design and place in **CROCK-POT**® slow cooker.

2. Coat inside of **CROCK-POT**® slow cooker with nonstick cooking spray. Combine hominy, beans, tomatoes, salsa, tomato paste and cumin in large bowl; stir to blend.

3. Press 1 tortilla into bottom of **CROCK-POT**® slow cooker. Top with one third of hominy mixture and one third of cheese. Repeat layers. Press remaining tortilla on top. Top with remaining hominy mixture. Set aside remaining one third of cheese.

4. Cover; cook on LOW 6 to 8 hours or on HIGH 2 to 3 hours. Turn off heat. Sprinkle with remaining cheese and olives. Cover; let stand 5 minutes. Pull out tortilla stack with foil handles. Cut into six wedges.

Makes 6 servings

Polenta-Style Corn Casserole

1 can (about 14 ounces) vegetable broth
½ cup cornmeal
1 can (7 ounces) corn, drained
1 can (4 ounces) diced mild green chiles, drained
¼ cup diced red bell pepper
½ teaspoon salt
¼ teaspoon black pepper
1 cup (4 ounces) shredded Cheddar cheese

1. Pour broth into **CROCK-POT®** slow cooker. Whisk in cornmeal. Add corn, chiles, bell pepper, salt and black pepper. Cover; cook on LOW 4 to 5 hours or on HIGH 2 to 3 hours.

2. Stir in cheese. Cook, uncovered, on LOW 15 to 30 minutes or until cheese is melted.

Makes 6 servings

Mom's Tuna Casserole

2 cans (12 ounces *each*) solid albacore tuna, drained and flaked
3 cups diced celery
3 cups crushed potato chips, divided
6 hard-cooked eggs, chopped
1 can (10½ ounces) condensed cream of mushroom soup, undiluted

1 can (10½ ounces) condensed cream of celery soup, undiluted
1 cup mayonnaise
1 teaspoon dried tarragon
1 teaspoon black pepper

1. Combine tuna, celery, 2½ cups potato chips, eggs, soups, mayonnaise, tarragon and pepper in **CROCK-POT®** slow cooker; stir to blend. Cover; cook on LOW 5 to 7 hours.

2. Sprinkle with remaining ½ cup potato chips before serving.

Makes 8 servings

6 INGREDIENTS OR LESS

Chicken Scaloppine in Alfredo Sauce

2 tablespoons all-purpose flour

¼ teaspoon salt

¼ teaspoon black pepper

6 boneless, skinless chicken tenderloins (about 1 pound), cut lengthwise in half

1 tablespoon butter

1 tablespoon olive oil

1 cup Alfredo pasta sauce

1 package (12 ounces) uncooked spinach noodles

1. Place flour, salt and pepper in large bowl; stir to combine. Add chicken; toss to coat. Heat butter and oil in large skillet over medium-high heat. Add chicken; cook 3 minutes per side or until browned. Remove chicken to **CROCK-POT**® slow cooker in single layer.

2. Add Alfredo pasta sauce to **CROCK-POT**® slow cooker. Cover; cook on LOW 1 to 1½ hours.

3. Meanwhile, cook noodles according to package directions. Drain; place in large shallow bowl. Spoon chicken and sauce over noodles.

Makes 6 servings

Chili and Cheese "Baked" Potato Supper

4 russet potatoes (about 2 pounds), unpeeled

2 cups prepared meatless chili

½ cup (2 ounces) shredded Cheddar cheese

¼ cup sour cream (optional)

2 green onions, sliced

1. Prick potatoes in several places with fork. Wrap potatoes in foil. Place in **CROCK-POT®** slow cooker. Cover; cook on LOW 8 to 10 hours or on HIGH 4 to 5 hours.

2. Carefully unwrap potatoes and place on serving dish. Place chili in medium microwavable dish; microwave on HIGH 3 to 5 minutes. Split potatoes and spoon chili on top. Sprinkle with cheese, sour cream, if desired, and green onions.

Makes 4 servings

Apricot and Brie Dip

½ cup dried apricots, finely chopped

⅓ cup plus 1 tablespoon apricot preserves, divided

¼ cup apple juice

1 round wheel Brie cheese (2 pounds), rind removed and cut into cubes

Bread or crackers

Combine dried apricots, ⅓ cup apricot preserves and apple juice in **CROCK-POT®** slow cooker; stir to blend. Cover; cook on HIGH 40 minutes. Stir in cheese. Cover; cook on HIGH 30 to 40 minutes or until cheese is melted. Stir in remaining 1 tablespoon preserves. Turn **CROCK-POT®** slow cooker to LOW. Serve warm with bread or crackers.

Makes 3 cups

Spicy Turkey with Citrus au Jus

1 bone-in turkey breast, rinsed and patted dry (about 4 pounds)

¼ cup (½ stick) butter, softened

Grated peel of 1 medium lemon

1 teaspoon chili powder

¼ teaspoon black pepper, plus additional for seasoning

⅛ to ¼ teaspoon red pepper flakes

1 tablespoon lemon juice

Salt

1. Coat inside of **CROCK-POT**® slow cooker with nonstick cooking spray. Add turkey breast.

2. Mix butter, lemon peel, chili powder, ¼ teaspoon black pepper and red pepper flakes in small bowl until well blended. Spread mixture over top and sides of turkey. Cover; cook on LOW 4 to 5 hours or on HIGH 2½ to 3 hours.

3. Turn off heat. Remove turkey to large cutting board. Cover loosely with foil; let stand 10 to 15 minutes before slicing. Let cooking liquid stand 5 minutes. Skim off and discard fat. Stir lemon juice into cooking liquid. Season with salt and additional black pepper. Serve turkey with sauce.

Makes 6 to 8 servings

Chili con Queso

- **1** package (16 ounces) pasteurized process cheese product, cubed
- **1** can (10 ounces) diced tomatoes with mild green chiles
- **1** cup sliced green onions
- **2** teaspoons ground coriander
- **2** teaspoons ground cumin
- **¾** teaspoon hot pepper sauce
- **Green onion strips (optional)**
- **Jalapeño pepper slices (optional)***
- **Tortilla chips**

*Jalapeño peppers can sting and irritate the skin, so wear rubber gloves when handling peppers and do not touch your eyes.

1. Combine cheese product, tomatoes, sliced green onions, coriander, cumin and hot pepper sauce in **CROCK-POT®** slow cooker; stir to blend.

2. Cover; cook on LOW 2 to 3 hours. Garnish with green onion strips and jalapeño pepper slices, if desired. Serve with tortilla chips.

Makes 3 cups

Serving Suggestion: Serve Chili con Queso with tortilla chips. For something different, cut pita bread into triangles and toast them in a preheated 400°F oven for 5 minutes or until crisp.

Braised Beets with Cranberries

2½ pounds medium beets, peeled and
    cut into wedges
1 cup cranberry juice
½ cup sweetened dried cranberries
2 tablespoons quick-cooking tapioca
2 tablespoons butter, cubed
2 tablespoons honey
½ teaspoon salt
⅓ cup crumbled blue cheese (optional)
    Orange peel, thinly sliced (optional)

1. Combine beets, cranberry juice, cranberries, tapioca, butter, honey and salt in **CROCK-POT®** slow cooker; stir to blend. Cover; cook on LOW 7 to 8 hours.

2. Remove beets to large serving bowl using slotted spoon. Pour half of cooking liquid over beets. Garnish with blue cheese and orange peel.

Makes 6 to 8 servings

Cheese Soup

2 cans (10¾ ounces *each*) condensed
    cream of celery soup, undiluted
4 cups (16 ounces) shredded Cheddar
    cheese
1 teaspoon paprika, plus additional
    for garnish

1 teaspoon Worcestershire sauce
1¼ cups half-and-half
    Salt and black pepper
    Snipped fresh chives (optional)

1. Combine soup, cheese, 1 teaspoon paprika and Worcestershire sauce in **CROCK-POT®** slow cooker; stir to blend. Cover; cook on LOW 2 to 3 hours.

2. Add half-and-half; stir until blended. Cover; cook on LOW 20 minutes. Season with salt and pepper. Sprinkle with additional paprika and chives.

Makes 4 servings

Tip: Turn simple soup into a super supper by serving it in individual bread bowls. Cut a small slice from the tops of small, round loaves of a hearty bread (such as Italian or sourdough) and remove the insides, leaving a 1½-inch shell. Pour in soup and serve.

Curried Lentils with Fruit

5 cups water

1½ cups dried brown lentils, rinsed and sorted

1 Granny Smith apple, chopped, plus additional for garnish

¼ cup golden raisins

¼ cup lemon yogurt

1 teaspoon salt

1 teaspoon curry powder

1. Combine water, lentils, 1 apple and raisins in **CROCK-POT®** slow cooker. Cover; cook on LOW 8 to 9 hours or until lentils are tender. (Lentils should absorb most or all of the water. Slightly tilt **CROCK-POT®** slow cooker to check.)

2. Remove lentil mixture to large bowl; stir in yogurt, salt and curry powder until blended. Garnish with additional apple.

Makes 6 servings

Cheesy Polenta

6 cups vegetable broth

1½ cups uncooked medium-grind instant polenta

½ cup grated Parmesan cheese, plus additional for serving

4 tablespoons (½ stick) butter, cubed

Fried sage leaves (optional)

1. Coat inside of **CROCK-POT**® slow cooker with nonstick cooking spray. Heat broth in large saucepan over high heat. Remove to **CROCK-POT**® slow cooker; whisk in polenta.

2. Cover; cook on LOW 2 to 2½ hours or until polenta is tender and creamy. Stir in ½ cup cheese and butter. Serve with additional cheese. Garnish with sage.

Makes 6 servings

Tip: Spread any leftover polenta in a baking dish and refrigerate until cold. Cut cold polenta into sticks or slices. You can then fry or grill the polenta until lightly browned.

Chicken with Italian Sausage

10 ounces bulk mild or hot Italian sausage

6 boneless, skinless chicken thighs, trimmed

1 can (about 15 ounces) white beans, rinsed and drained

1 can (about 15 ounces) red beans, rinsed and drained

1 cup chicken broth

1 onion, chopped

1 teaspoon black pepper

½ teaspoon salt

Chopped fresh Italian parsley

1. Brown sausage in large skillet over medium-high heat, stirring to break up meat. Remove to **CROCK-POT®** slow cooker using slotted spoon.

2. Add chicken, beans, broth, onion, pepper and salt to **CROCK-POT®** slow cooker. Cover; cook on LOW 5 to 6 hours.

3. Serve chicken with sausage and beans. Garnish with parsley.

Makes 6 servings

Winter Squash and Apples

1 butternut squash (about 2 pounds), cut into 2-inch pieces

2 apples, sliced

1 medium onion, quartered and sliced

1 teaspoon salt, plus additional for seasoning

½ teaspoon black pepper, plus additional for seasoning

1½ tablespoons butter

Combine squash, apples and onion in **CROCK-POT®** slow cooker. Sprinkle with 1 teaspoon salt and ½ teaspoon pepper; stir to blend. Cover; cook on LOW 6 to 7 hours. Stir in butter; season with additional salt and pepper.

Makes 4 to 6 servings

Mixed Herb and Butter Rubbed Chicken

3 tablespoons butter, softened

1 tablespoon grated lemon peel

2 teaspoons chopped fresh rosemary

1 teaspoon chopped fresh thyme

¾ teaspoon salt

¼ teaspoon black pepper

1 whole chicken (4½ to 5 pounds)

1. Coat inside of **CROCK-POT**® slow cooker with nonstick cooking spray. Combine butter, lemon peel, rosemary, thyme, salt and pepper in small bowl; stir to blend. Loosen skin over breast meat and drumsticks; pat chicken dry with paper towels. Rub butter mixture over and under the chicken skin. Place chicken in **CROCK-POT**® slow cooker.

2. Cover; cook on LOW 5 to 6 hours, basting every 30 minutes with cooking liquid. Remove chicken to large cutting board. Cover loosely with foil; let stand 15 minutes before cutting into pieces.

Makes 4 to 6 servings

Manchego Eggplant

1 cup all-purpose flour

4 large eggplants, peeled and sliced horizontally into ¾-inch-thick pieces

2 tablespoons olive oil

1 jar (24 to 26 ounces) roasted garlic-flavor pasta sauce

2 tablespoons Italian seasoning

1 cup (4 ounces) grated manchego cheese

1 jar (24 to 26 ounces) roasted eggplant-flavor marinara pasta sauce

1. Place flour in shallow medium bowl. Add eggplants; toss to coat. Heat oil in large skillet over medium-high heat. Lightly brown eggplants in batches 3 to 4 minutes on each side.

2. Pour thin layer of garlic pasta sauce into bottom of **CROCK-POT**® slow cooker. Top with eggplant slices, Italian seasoning, cheese and marinara pasta sauce. Repeat layers until all ingredients have been used. Cover; cook on HIGH 2 hours.

Makes 12 servings

Pesto Rice and Beans

1 can (about 15 ounces) Great Northern beans, rinsed and drained

1 can (about 14 ounces) vegetable broth

¾ cup uncooked converted long grain rice

1½ cups frozen cut green beans, thawed and drained

½ cup prepared pesto

Grated Parmesan cheese (optional)

1. Combine Great Northern beans, broth and rice in **CROCK-POT**® slow cooker. Cover; cook on LOW 2 hours.

2. Stir in green beans. Cover; cook on LOW 1 hour or until rice and beans are tender.

3. Turn off heat. Transfer **CROCK-POT**® stoneware to heatproof surface. Stir in pesto and cheese, if desired. Let stand, covered, 5 minutes or until cheese is melted. Serve immediately.

Makes 8 servings

Creamy Chicken

3 boneless, skinless chicken breasts *or* 6 boneless, skinless chicken thighs

2 cans (10½ ounces *each*) condensed cream of chicken soup, undiluted

1 can (about 14 ounces) chicken broth

1 can (4 ounces) sliced mushrooms, drained

½ medium onion, diced

Salt and black pepper

Place all ingredients except salt and pepper in **CROCK-POT**® slow cooker. Cover; cook on LOW 6 to 8 hours. Season with salt and pepper.

Makes 3 servings

Broccoli and Cheese Strata

2 cups chopped broccoli florets

4 slices firm white bread, ½ inch thick

1 tablespoon butter

1 cup (4 ounces) shredded Cheddar cheese

1½ cups milk

2 eggs

2 egg whites

½ teaspoon salt

½ teaspoon hot pepper sauce

⅛ teaspoon black pepper

1 cup water

1. Spray 1-quart casserole or soufflé dish that fits inside of 2½- to 3-quart **CROCK-POT®** slow cooker with nonstick cooking spray. Fill large saucepan with water; bring to a boil. Add broccoli; cook 5 minutes or until tender. Drain.

2. Spread one side of each bread slice with butter. Arrange 2 bread slices, buttered sides up, in prepared casserole. Layer with cheese, broccoli and remaining 2 bread slices, buttered sides down. Whisk milk, eggs, egg whites, salt, hot pepper sauce and black pepper in medium bowl; slowly pour over bread.

3. Place small wire rack in **CROCK-POT®** slow cooker. Pour in 1 cup water. Place casserole on rack. Cover; cook on HIGH 3 hours.

Makes 6 servings

Fresh Herbed Turkey Breast

¼ cup fresh sage, minced

¼ cup fresh tarragon, minced

2 tablespoons butter, softened

1 clove garlic, minced

1 teaspoon black pepper

½ teaspoon salt

1 split turkey breast (about 4 pounds)

1 tablespoon plus 1½ teaspoons cornstarch

1. Combine sage, tarragon, butter, garlic, pepper and salt in small bowl. Rub butter mixture all over turkey breast.

2. Place turkey breast in **CROCK-POT®** slow cooker. Cover; cook on LOW 8 to 10 hours or on HIGH 4 to 5 hours or until turkey is no longer pink in center.

3. Remove turkey breast to serving platter; cover loosely with foil to keep warm. Slowly whisk cornstarch into cooking liquid; cook on HIGH 10 minutes or until thickened and smooth. Slice turkey breast. Serve with sauce.

Makes 8 servings

Cauliflower Mash

2 heads cauliflower (8 cups florets)
1 tablespoon butter
1 tablespoon milk
   Salt
   Sprigs fresh Italian parsley (optional)

1. Place cauliflower in **CROCK-POT**® slow cooker; add enough water to fill **CROCK-POT**® slow cooker about 2 inches. Cover; cook on LOW 5 to 6 hours. Drain well.

2. Place cooked cauliflower in food processor or blender; process until almost smooth. Add butter; process until smooth. Add milk as needed to reach desired consistency. Season with salt. Garnish with parsley.

Makes 6 servings

Southwestern Mac and Cheese

1 package (8 ounces) uncooked elbow macaroni
1 can (about 14 ounces) diced tomatoes with green peppers and onions
1 can (10 ounces) diced tomatoes with mild green chiles
1½ cups salsa
3 cups (12 ounces) shredded Mexican cheese blend, divided

1. Coat inside of **CROCK-POT**® slow cooker with nonstick cooking spray. Layer macaroni, tomatoes, salsa and 2 cups cheese in **CROCK-POT**® slow cooker. Cover; cook on LOW 3¾ hours.

2. Sprinkle remaining 1 cup cheese over macaroni. Cover; cook on LOW 15 minutes or until cheese is melted.

Makes 6 servings

Artichoke and Nacho Cheese Dip

2 cans (10¾ ounces *each*) condensed nacho cheese soup, undiluted

1 can (14 ounces) quartered artichoke hearts, drained and coarsely chopped

1 cup (4 ounces) shredded pepper jack cheese

1 can (5 ounces) evaporated milk

2 tablespoons snipped fresh chives, divided

½ teaspoon paprika

Crackers or chips

Combine soup, artichokes, cheese, evaporated milk, 1 tablespoon chives and paprika in **CROCK-POT**® slow cooker; stir to blend. Cover; cook on LOW 2 hours. Stir; sprinkle with remaining 1 tablespoon chives. Serve with crackers.

Makes about 1 quart

Chicken and Butternut Squash

6 boneless, skinless chicken thighs (1½ pounds *total*)

1 butternut squash (1½ to 2 pounds), cubed

2 tablespoons balsamic vinegar

4 cloves garlic, minced

6 fresh sage leaves

Salt and black pepper

Combine chicken, squash, vinegar, garlic, sage, salt and pepper in **CROCK-POT**® slow cooker. Cover; cook on LOW 4 to 6 hours.

Makes 6 servings

Mile-High Enchilada Pie

6 (6-inch) corn tortillas

1 jar (12 ounces) salsa

1 can (about 15 ounces) kidney beans, rinsed and drained

1 cup shredded cooked chicken

1 cup (4 ounces) shredded Monterey Jack cheese with jalapeño peppers

Chopped fresh cilantro and sliced red bell pepper (optional)

1. Prepare foil handles by tearing off three 18×2-inch strips heavy foil or use regular foil folded to double thickness. Crisscross foil strips in spoke design; place in **CROCK-POT®** slow cooker to make lifting tortilla stack easier. Place 1 tortilla on top of foil handles. Top with small amount of salsa, beans, chicken and cheese. Continue layering in order using remaining ingredients, ending with tortilla and cheese. Cover; cook on LOW 6 to 8 hours or on HIGH 3 to 4 hours.

2. Pull pie out by foil handles. Garnish with cilantro and bell pepper.

Makes 4 to 6 servings

Figs Poached in Red Wine

2 cups dry red wine

1 cup packed brown sugar

12 dried Calimyrna or Mediterranean figs (about 6 ounces)

2 (3-inch) whole cinnamon sticks

1 teaspoon finely grated orange peel, plus additional for garnish

¼ cup whipping cream (optional)

1. Combine wine, brown sugar, figs, cinnamon sticks and 1 teaspoon orange peel in **CROCK-POT®** slow cooker. Cover; cook on LOW 5 to 6 hours or on HIGH 4 to 5 hours.

2. Remove and discard cinnamon sticks. To serve, spoon syrup into serving dish; top with figs and cream, if desired. Garnish with additional orange peel.

Makes 4 servings

Chunky Ranch Potatoes

3 pounds unpeeled red potatoes, quartered

1 cup water

½ cup prepared ranch dressing

½ cup grated Parmesan or Cheddar cheese

¼ cup minced fresh chives

1. Place potatoes in **CROCK-POT®** slow cooker. Add water. Cover; cook on LOW 7 to 9 hours or on HIGH 4 to 6 hours.

2. Stir in ranch dressing, cheese and chives. Break up potatoes into large pieces.

Makes 8 servings

Collard Greens

4 bunches collard greens, stemmed, washed and torn into bite-size pieces

2 cups water

½ medium red bell pepper, cut into strips

⅓ medium green bell pepper, cut into strips

¼ cup olive oil

¼ teaspoon salt

¼ teaspoon black pepper

Combine collard greens, water, bell peppers, oil, salt and black pepper in **CROCK-POT®** slow cooker; stir to blend. Cover; cook on LOW 3 to 4 hours or on HIGH 2 hours or until heated through.

Makes 10 servings

Warm Salsa and Goat Cheese Dip

1¼ cups salsa

2 ounces goat cheese crumbles

2 tablespoons coarsely chopped fresh cilantro

Tortilla chips

1. Heat salsa in medium saucepan over medium-high heat. Bring to a boil. Remove from heat; cool slightly.

2. Coat inside of **CROCK-POT®** "No Dial" slow cooker with nonstick cooking spray. Fill with heated salsa. Sprinkle with goat cheese and cilantro. (Do not stir.) Serve with tortilla chips.

Makes 1¼ cups

Chili Verde

1 tablespoon vegetable oil
1 to 2 pounds boneless pork chops
2 cups sliced carrots
1 jar (24 ounces) mild green salsa
1 cup chopped onion

1. Heat oil in large skillet over medium-low heat. Add pork; cook 3 to 5 minutes or until browned on both sides.

2. Place carrots in bottom of **CROCK-POT®** slow cooker; top with pork. Pour salsa and onion over pork. Cover; cook on HIGH 6 to 8 hours.

Makes 4 to 8 servings

Serving Suggestion: The pork can also be shredded and served in tortillas.

Cheesy Corn and Peppers

2 pounds frozen corn
2 poblano peppers, chopped
2 tablespoons butter, cubed
1 teaspoon salt
½ teaspoon ground cumin

¼ teaspoon black pepper
3 ounces cream cheese, cubed
1 cup (4 ounces) shredded sharp Cheddar cheese

1. Coat inside of **CROCK-POT®** slow cooker with nonstick cooking spray. Combine corn, poblano peppers, butter, salt, cumin and black pepper in **CROCK-POT®** slow cooker; stir to blend. Cover; cook on HIGH 2 hours.

2. Stir in cheeses. Cover; cook on HIGH 15 minutes or until cheeses are melted.

Makes 8 servings

BARBECUE FAVORITES

Texas-Style Barbecued Brisket

- 3 tablespoons Worcestershire sauce
- 1 tablespoon chili powder
- 1 teaspoon celery salt
- 1 teaspoon black pepper
- 1 teaspoon liquid smoke
- 2 cloves garlic, minced

- 1 beef brisket (3 to 4 pounds), trimmed*
- 2 whole bay leaves
- 1¾ cups barbecue sauce, plus additional for serving

*Unless you have a 5-, 6- or 7-quart **CROCK-POT®** slow cooker, cut any roast larger than 2½ pounds in half so it cooks completely.

1. Combine Worcestershire sauce, chili powder, celery salt, pepper, liquid smoke and garlic in small bowl; stir to blend. Spread mixture on all sides of beef. Place beef in large resealable food storage bag; seal bag. Refrigerate 24 hours.

2. Place beef, marinade and bay leaves in **CROCK-POT®** slow cooker. Cover; cook on LOW 7 hours.

3. Remove beef to large cutting board. Pour cooking liquid into 2-cup measure; let stand 5 minutes. Skim off and discard fat. Remove and discard bay leaves. Stir 1 cup cooking liquid into 1¾ cups barbecue sauce in medium bowl. Discard any cooking liquid remaining in **CROCK-POT®** slow cooker.

4. Return beef and barbecue sauce mixture to **CROCK-POT®** slow cooker. Cover; cook on LOW 1 hour or until meat is fork-tender. Remove beef to cutting board. Cut across grain into ¼-inch-thick slices. Serve with additional barbecue sauce.

Makes 10 to 12 servings

Chili Barbecue Beans

- 1 cup dried Great Northern beans, rinsed and sorted
- 1 cup dried red beans or dried kidney beans, rinsed and sorted
- 1 cup dried baby lima beans, rinsed and sorted
- 3 cups water
- 8 slices bacon, crisp-cooked and crumbled *or* 8 ounces smoked sausage, sliced
- ¼ cup packed brown sugar
- 2 tablespoons minced onion
- 2 cubes beef bouillon
- 1 teaspoon dry mustard
- 1 teaspoon chili powder
- 1 teaspoon minced garlic
- ½ teaspoon black pepper
- ¼ teaspoon red pepper flakes
- 2 whole bay leaves
- 1 to 1½ cups barbecue sauce

1. Place beans in large bowl and add enough cold water to cover by at least 2 inches. Soak 6 to 8 hours or overnight.* Drain beans; discard water.

2. Combine soaked beans, 3 cups water, bacon, brown sugar, onion, bouillon cubes, dry mustard, chili powder, garlic, black pepper, red pepper flakes and bay leaves in **CROCK-POT®** slow cooker; stir to blend. Cover; cook on LOW 8 to 10 hours.

3. Stir in barbecue sauce. Cover; cook on LOW 1 hour or until heated through. Remove and discard bay leaves.

To quick soak beans, place beans in large saucepan. Cover with water. Bring to a boil over high heat. Boil 2 minutes. Remove from heat; let soak, covered, 1 hour.

Makes 8 to 10 servings

Barbecue Beef Sliders

- **1** tablespoon packed brown sugar
- **1** teaspoon ground cumin
- **1** teaspoon chili powder
- **1** teaspoon paprika
- **½** teaspoon salt
- **¼** teaspoon ground red pepper
- **3** pounds beef short ribs

- **½** cup plus **2** tablespoons barbecue sauce, divided
- **¼** cup water
- **12** slider rolls
- **¾** cup prepared coleslaw
- **12** bread and butter pickle chips

1. Coat inside of **CROCK-POT®** slow cooker with nonstick cooking spray. Combine brown sugar, cumin, chili powder, paprika, salt and ground red pepper in small bowl. Rub ribs with spice mixture. Remove to **CROCK-POT®** slow cooker. Pour in ½ cup barbecue sauce and ¼ cup water.

2. Cover; cook on LOW 7 to 8 hours or on HIGH 4 to 4½ hours or until ribs are very tender and meat shreds easily. Remove ribs to large cutting board. Discard bones; remove meat to large bowl. Shred meat using two forks, discarding any large pieces of fat or sinew. Stir in remaining 2 tablespoons barbecue sauce and 2 tablespoons liquid from **CROCK-POT®** slow cooker.

3. Arrange bottom half of rolls on platter or work surface. Top each with ¼ cup beef mixture, 1 tablespoon coleslaw and 1 pickle chip. Place roll tops on each.

Makes 6 servings

Hoisin Barbecue Chicken Thighs

⅔ cup hoisin sauce

⅓ cup barbecue sauce

3 tablespoons quick-cooking tapioca

1 tablespoon sugar

1 tablespoon soy sauce

¼ teaspoon red pepper flakes

12 skinless, bone-in chicken thighs (3½ to 4 pounds)

1½ pounds uncooked ramen noodles or other pasta

Sliced green onions (optional)

1. Combine hoisin sauce, barbecue sauce, tapioca, sugar, soy sauce and red pepper flakes in **CROCK-POT**® slow cooker; stir to blend. Add chicken, flesh side down. Cover; cook on LOW 8 to 9 hours.

2. Meanwhile, cook ramen noodles according to package directions. Serve chicken over noodles. Garnish with green onions.

Makes 6 to 8 servings

Barbecue Turkey Legs

6 turkey drumsticks
2 teaspoons salt
2 teaspoons black pepper
½ cup white vinegar
½ cup ketchup
½ cup molasses

¼ cup Worcestershire sauce
1 tablespoon onion powder
1 tablespoon garlic powder
1 teaspoon hickory liquid smoke
⅛ teaspoon chipotle chili powder

1. Season drumsticks with salt and pepper. Place in **CROCK-POT®** slow cooker.

2. Combine vinegar, ketchup, molasses, Worcestershire sauce, onion powder, garlic powder, liquid smoke and chili powder in medium bowl; stir to blend. Add to **CROCK-POT®** slow cooker; turn drumsticks to coat. Cover; cook on LOW 7 to 8 hours or on HIGH 3 to 4 hours.

Makes 6 servings

Pulled Pork Sliders with Cola Barbecue Sauce

1 teaspoon vegetable oil

1 boneless pork shoulder roast (3 pounds)*

1 cup cola

¼ cup tomato paste

2 tablespoons packed brown sugar

2 teaspoons Worcestershire sauce

2 teaspoons spicy brown mustard

Hot pepper sauce

Salt

16 dinner rolls or potato rolls

Sliced pickles (optional)

*Unless you have a 5-, 6- or 7-quart **CROCK-POT**® slow cooker, cut any roast larger than 2½ pounds in half so it cooks completely.

1. Heat oil in large skillet over medium-high heat. Add pork; cook until browned on all sides. Remove to **CROCK-POT**® slow cooker. Pour cola over pork. Cover; cook on LOW 7½ to 8 hours or on HIGH 3½ to 4 hours.

2. Turn off heat. Remove pork to large cutting board; shred with two forks. Let cooking liquid stand 5 minutes. Skim off and discard fat. Whisk tomato paste, brown sugar, Worcestershire sauce and mustard into cooking liquid. Cover; cook on HIGH 15 minutes or until thickened.

3. Stir shredded pork back into **CROCK-POT**® slow cooker. Season with hot pepper sauce and salt. Serve on rolls. Top with pickles, if desired.

Makes 16 sliders

Simple Barbecue Chicken

1 bottle (20 ounces) ketchup

⅔ cup packed brown sugar

⅔ cup cider vinegar

2 tablespoons chili powder

2 tablespoons tomato paste

1 tablespoon onion powder

2 teaspoons garlic powder

2 teaspoons liquid smoke (optional)

1 teaspoon hot pepper sauce (optional)

8 boneless, skinless chicken breasts (6 ounces *each*)

8 whole wheat rolls

1. Combine ketchup, brown sugar, vinegar, chili powder, tomato paste, onion powder, garlic powder, liquid smoke and hot pepper sauce, if desired, in **CROCK-POT**® slow cooker.

2. Add chicken. Cover; cook on LOW 4 to 6 hours or on HIGH 2 to 3 hours or until chicken is cooked through. Serve with rolls.

Makes 8 servings

Pulled Chicken Sandwiches: Shred the chicken and serve on whole wheat rolls or hamburger buns. Top with mixed greens or coleslaw.

Korean Barbecue Beef

4 to 4½ pounds beef short ribs

¼ cup chopped green onions

¼ cup tamari or soy sauce

¼ cup beef broth or water

1 tablespoon packed brown sugar

2 teaspoons minced fresh ginger

2 teaspoons minced garlic

½ teaspoon black pepper

2 teaspoons dark sesame oil

Hot cooked rice

2 teaspoons sesame seeds, toasted*

*To toast sesame seeds, spread in small skillet. Shake skillet over medium-low heat 2 minutes or until seeds begin to pop and turn golden brown.

1. Place ribs in **CROCK-POT®** slow cooker. Combine green onions, tamari, broth, brown sugar, ginger, garlic and pepper in medium bowl; pour over ribs. Cover; cook on LOW 7 to 8 hours or until ribs are fork-tender.

2. Remove ribs from cooking liquid. Cool slightly. Trim excess fat and discard. Cut rib meat into bite-size pieces, discarding bones.

3. Let cooking liquid stand 5 minutes to allow fat to rise. Skim off fat and discard. Stir sesame oil into cooking liquid.

4. Return beef to cooking liquid in **CROCK-POT®** slow cooker. Cover; cook on LOW 15 to 30 minutes or until heated through. Serve over rice; sprinkle with sesame seeds.

Makes 6 servings

BBQ Pulled Chicken Sandwiches

1¼ to 1½ pounds boneless, skinless chicken
    thighs

¾ cup barbecue sauce, divided

1 package (14 ounces) frozen bell pepper
    and onion strips cut for stir-fry

¼ to ½ teaspoon hot pepper sauce

6 Kaiser rolls, split in half and toasted

Dill pickle spears (optional)

1. Combine chicken and ¼ cup barbecue sauce in **CROCK-POT**® slow cooker; stir to blend. Add bell pepper and onion strips; mix well. Cover; cook on LOW 5 to 6 hours or on HIGH 2 to 3 hours.

2. Remove chicken to medium bowl; shred with two forks. Drain pepper mixture; add to bowl with chicken. Add remaining ½ cup barbecue sauce and hot pepper sauce; mix well. Serve on rolls with pickles, if desired.

Makes 6 servings

Turkey Meatballs in Cranberry-Barbecue Sauce

1 can (16 ounces) jellied cranberry sauce

½ cup barbecue sauce

1 egg white

1 pound ground turkey

1 green onion, sliced

2 teaspoons grated orange peel

1 teaspoon reduced-sodium soy sauce

¼ teaspoon black pepper

⅛ teaspoon ground red pepper (optional)

1. Combine cranberry sauce and barbecue sauce in **CROCK-POT®** slow cooker. Cover; cook on HIGH 20 to 30 minutes or until cranberry sauce melts and mixture is heated through.

2. Meanwhile, place egg white in large bowl; beat lightly. Add turkey, green onion, orange peel, soy sauce, black pepper and ground red pepper, if desired; mix until well blended. Shape into 24 meatballs.

3. Spray large skillet with nonstick cooking spray. Add meatballs; cook over medium heat 8 to 10 minutes or until meatballs are browned. Add to **CROCK-POT®** slow cooker; stir gently to coat.

4. Turn **CROCK-POT®** slow cooker to LOW. Cover; cook on LOW 3 hours.

Makes 12 servings

Asian Barbecue Skewers

2 pounds boneless, skinless chicken thighs

½ cup soy sauce

⅓ cup packed brown sugar

2 tablespoons sesame oil

3 cloves garlic, minced

½ cup thinly sliced green onions (optional)

1 tablespoon toasted sesame seeds (optional)*

*To toast sesame seeds, spread in small skillet. Shake skillet over medium-low heat 2 minutes or until seeds begin to pop and turn golden brown.

1. Cut each chicken thigh into four pieces, about 1½ inches thick. Thread chicken onto 7-inch-long wooden skewers, folding thinner pieces, if necessary. Place skewers into **CROCK-POT**® slow cooker, layering as flat as possible.

2. Combine soy sauce, brown sugar, oil and garlic in small bowl. Reserve ⅓ cup sauce; set aside. Pour remaining sauce over skewers. Cover; cook on LOW 2 hours. Turn skewers over. Cover; cook on LOW 1 hour.

3. Remove skewers to serving platter. Discard cooking liquid. Pour reserved sauce over skewers. Sprinkle with green onions and sesame seeds, if desired.

Makes 4 to 6 servings

Fall-off-the-Bone BBQ Ribs

½ cup paprika

¼ cup sugar

¼ cup onion powder

1½ teaspoons salt

1½ teaspoons black pepper

2½ pounds pork baby back ribs, silver skin removed and cut into 3 to 4 sections

1 can (20 ounces) beer or beef broth

1 quart barbecue sauce

½ cup honey

Sesame seeds and fresh chopped chives (optional)

1. Combine paprika, sugar, onion powder, salt and pepper in small bowl; stir to blend. Season ribs with dry rub mixture. Heat large skillet over medium-high heat. Add ribs; cook 3 minutes on each side or until ribs are browned.

2. Remove to **CROCK-POT**® slow cooker. Pour beer over ribs. Cover; cook on HIGH 2 hours. Combine barbecue sauce and honey in medium bowl; add to **CROCK-POT**® slow cooker. Cover; cook on HIGH 1½ hours. Sprinkle with sesame seeds and chives, if desired. Serve with extra sauce.

Makes 6 to 8 servings

Barbecued Beef Sandwiches

2 cups ketchup

1 onion, chopped

¼ cup cider vinegar

¼ cup dark molasses

2 tablespoons Worcestershire sauce

2 cloves garlic, minced

½ teaspoon salt

½ teaspoon ground mustard

½ teaspoon black pepper

¼ teaspoon garlic powder

¼ teaspoon red pepper flakes

1 boneless beef chuck shoulder roast (about 3 pounds), trimmed*

12 sesame seed buns

*Unless you have a 5-, 6- or 7-quart **CROCK-POT®** slow cooker, cut any roast larger than 2½ pounds in half so it cooks completely.

1. Combine ketchup, onion, vinegar, molasses, Worcestershire sauce, garlic, salt, mustard, black pepper, garlic powder and red pepper flakes in **CROCK-POT®** slow cooker; stir to blend. Place beef in **CROCK-POT®** slow cooker. Cover; cook on LOW 8 to 10 hours or on HIGH 4 to 5 hours.

2. Turn off heat. Remove beef to large cutting board; shred with two forks. Let cooking liquid stand 5 minutes. Skim off fat and discard.

3. Turn **CROCK-POT®** slow cooker to HIGH. Add shredded beef; stir to coat. Cover; cook on HIGH 15 to 30 minutes or until heated through. Spoon filling into buns; top with additional sauce, if desired.

Makes 12 servings

Raspberry BBQ Chicken Wings

3 pounds (10 to 12) chicken wings, tips removed and split at joints

¾ cup seedless raspberry jam

½ cup sweet and tangy prepared barbecue sauce

1 tablespoon raspberry red wine vinegar

1 teaspoon chili powder

1. Coat inside of **CROCK-POT®** slow cooker with nonstick cooking spray. Preheat broiler. Spray large baking sheet with nonstick cooking spray. Arrange wings on prepared baking sheet. Broil 6 to 8 minutes until browned, turning once. Remove to **CROCK-POT®** slow cooker.

2. Combine jam, barbecue sauce, vinegar and chili powder in medium bowl; stir to blend. Pour sauce over wings in **CROCK-POT®** slow cooker; stir to coat. Cover; cook on LOW 3½ to 4 hours. Remove wings to large serving platter; cover to keep warm.

3. Turn **CROCK-POT®** slow cooker to HIGH. Cook, uncovered, on HIGH 10 to 15 minutes or until sauce is thickened. Spoon sauce over wings.

Makes 5 to 6 servings

Root Beer BBQ Pulled Pork

1 can (12 ounces) root beer

1 bottle (18 ounces) sweet barbecue sauce, divided

1 package (1 ounce) dry onion soup mix

1 boneless pork shoulder roast (6 to 8 pounds)*

Salt and black pepper

Hamburger buns

*Unless you have a 5-, 6- or 7-quart **CROCK-POT**® slow cooker, cut any roast larger than 2½ pounds in half so it cooks completely.

1. Coat inside of **CROCK-POT**® slow cooker with nonstick cooking spray. Combine root beer and ½ bottle barbecue sauce in medium bowl. Rub dry soup mix over pork. Combine barbecue mixture and pork in **CROCK-POT**® slow cooker. Cover; cook on LOW 8 to 10 hours.

2. Remove pork to large cutting board; shred with two forks. Reserve 1 cup barbecue mixture in **CROCK-POT**® slow cooker; discard remaining mixture. Turn **CROCK-POT**® slow cooker to HIGH. Stir shredded pork, remaining ½ bottle barbecue sauce, salt and pepper into **CROCK-POT**® slow cooker. Cover; cook on HIGH 20 minutes or until heated through. Serve on buns.

Makes 8 servings

GRAIN-PACKED PLATES

Farro Risotto with Mushrooms and Spinach

2 tablespoons olive oil, divided

1 onion, chopped

12 ounces cremini mushrooms, stems trimmed and quartered

¼ teaspoon black pepper

2 cloves garlic, minced

1 cup uncooked pearled farro

1 sprig fresh thyme

4 cups reduced-sodium vegetable broth

8 ounces baby spinach

½ cup grated Parmesan cheese

1. Heat 1 tablespoon oil in large skillet over medium heat. Add onion; cook 8 minutes or until tender. Remove to **CROCK-POT**® slow cooker. Add remaining 1 tablespoon oil to same skillet; heat over medium-high heat. Add mushrooms and pepper; cook 6 to 8 minutes or until mushrooms have released their liquid and are browned. Add garlic; cook 1 minute. Stir in farro and thyme; cook 1 minute. Remove to **CROCK-POT**® slow cooker.

2. Stir broth into **CROCK-POT**® slow cooker. Cover; cook on HIGH 3½ hours or until farro is tender and broth is absorbed. Remove thyme sprig. Stir in spinach and cheese just before serving.

Makes 4 servings

Vegetarian Sausage Rice

- 2 cups chopped green bell peppers
- 1 can (about 15 ounces) dark kidney beans, rinsed and drained
- 1 can (about 14 ounces) diced tomatoes with bell peppers and onions
- 1 cup chopped onion
- 1 cup sliced celery
- 1 cup water, divided
- ½ cup uncooked converted long grain rice
- 1¼ teaspoons salt
- 1 teaspoon hot pepper sauce, plus additional for garnish
- ½ teaspoon dried thyme
- ½ teaspoon red pepper flakes
- 3 whole bay leaves
- 1 package (8 ounces) frozen meatless breakfast patties, thawed
- 2 tablespoons extra virgin olive oil
- ½ cup chopped fresh parsley

1. Combine bell peppers, beans, tomatoes, onion, celery, ½ cup water, rice, salt, 1 teaspoon hot pepper sauce, thyme, red pepper flakes and bay leaves in **CROCK-POT**® slow cooker. Cover; cook on LOW 4 to 5 hours. Remove and discard bay leaves.

2. Dice meatless patties. Heat oil in large nonstick skillet over medium-high heat. Add patties; cook 2 minutes or until lightly browned, scraping bottom of skillet occasionally.

3. Remove patties to **CROCK-POT**® slow cooker. *Do not stir.* Add remaining ½ cup water to skillet. Bring to a boil over high heat; cook 1 minute, scraping up browned bits from bottom of skillet. Stir liquid and parsley into **CROCK-POT**® slow cooker. Serve immediately with additional hot pepper sauce, if desired.

Makes 8 cups

Lentil Stew over Couscous

3 cups dried lentils (1 pound), sorted and rinsed

3 cups water

1 can (about 14 ounces) reduced-sodium vegetable broth

1 can (about 14 ounces) diced tomatoes

1 large onion, chopped

1 green bell pepper, chopped

4 stalks celery, chopped

1 medium carrot, halved lengthwise and sliced

2 cloves garlic, chopped

1 teaspoon dried marjoram

¼ teaspoon black pepper

1 tablespoon olive oil

1 tablespoon cider vinegar

4½ to 5 cups hot cooked couscous

1. Combine lentils, water, broth, tomatoes, onion, bell pepper, celery, carrot, garlic, marjoram and black pepper in **CROCK-POT®** slow cooker; stir to blend. Cover; cook on LOW 8 to 9 hours or until vegetables are tender.

2. Stir in oil and vinegar. Serve over couscous.

Makes 12 servings

Tip: Lentil stew keeps well in the refrigerator for up to 1 week. Stew can also be frozen in an airtight container for up to 3 months.

Barley and Vegetable Risotto

2 teaspoons olive oil

1 small onion, diced

8 ounces sliced mushrooms

¾ cup uncooked pearl barley

1 large red bell pepper, diced

4½ cups reduced-sodium vegetable broth

2 cups packed baby spinach

¼ cup grated Parmesan cheese

¼ teaspoon black pepper

1. Heat oil in large skillet over medium-high heat. Add onion; cook and stir 2 minutes or until lightly browned. Add mushrooms; cook and stir 5 minutes or until mushrooms have released their liquid and are just beginning to brown. Remove to **CROCK-POT**® slow cooker.

2. Add barley and bell pepper to **CROCK-POT**® slow cooker; pour in broth. Cover; cook on LOW 4 to 5 hours or on HIGH 2½ to 3 hours or until barley is tender and liquid is absorbed.

3. Stir in spinach. Turn off heat. Let stand 5 minutes. Gently stir in cheese and black pepper just before serving.

Makes 6 servings

Italian Eggplant with Millet and Pepper Stuffing

¼ cup uncooked millet

2 small eggplants (about ¾ pound *total*)

¼ cup chopped red bell pepper, divided

¼ cup chopped green bell pepper, divided

1 teaspoon olive oil

1 clove garlic, minced

1½ cups reduced-sodium vegetable broth

½ teaspoon ground cumin

½ teaspoon dried oregano

⅛ teaspoon red pepper flakes

1. Cook and stir millet in large heavy skillet over medium heat 5 minutes or until golden. Remove to small bowl.

2. Cut eggplants lengthwise into halves. Scoop out flesh, leaving about ¼-inch-thick shell. Reserve shells; chop eggplant flesh. Combine 1 tablespoon red bell pepper and 1 tablespoon green bell pepper in small bowl; set aside.

3. Heat oil in same skillet over medium heat. Add chopped eggplant, remaining red and green bell pepper and garlic; cook and stir about 8 minutes or until eggplant is tender.

4. Combine eggplant mixture, millet, broth, cumin, oregano and red pepper flakes in **CROCK-POT®** slow cooker. Cover and cook on LOW 4½ hours or until all liquid has been absorbed and millet is tender.

5. Fill eggplant shells with eggplant-millet mixture. Sprinkle with reserved chopped bell peppers, pressing in lightly. Carefully place filled shells in **CROCK-POT®** slow cooker. Cover; cook on HIGH 1½ to 2 hours.

Makes 4 servings

Garlic and Herb Polenta

3 tablespoons butter, divided

8 cups water

2 cups yellow cornmeal

2 teaspoons finely minced garlic

2 teaspoons salt

3 tablespoons chopped fresh herbs such as parsley, chives, thyme or chervil (or a combination)

Coat inside of **CROCK-POT®** slow cooker with 1 tablespoon butter. Add water, cornmeal, garlic, salt and remaining 2 tablespoons butter; stir to blend. Cover; cook on LOW 4 hours or on HIGH 3 hours, stirring occasionally. Stir in chopped herbs just before serving.

Makes 6 servings

Tip: Polenta may also be poured into a greased 13×9-inch pan and allowed to cool until set. Cut into squares (or slice as desired) to serve. For even more great flavor, chill polenta slices until firm, then grill or fry until golden brown.

Mushroom Barley Stew

1 tablespoon olive oil

1 medium onion, finely chopped

1 cup chopped carrots (about 2 carrots)

1 clove garlic, minced

1 cup uncooked pearl barley

1 cup dried wild mushrooms, broken into pieces

1 teaspoon salt

½ teaspoon dried thyme

½ teaspoon black pepper

5 cups vegetable broth

1. Heat oil in medium skillet over medium-high heat. Add onion, carrots and garlic; cook and stir 5 minutes or until tender. Remove to **CROCK-POT**® slow cooker.

2. Add barley, mushrooms, salt, thyme and pepper. Stir in broth. Cover; cook on LOW 6 to 7 hours. Adjust seasonings.

Makes 4 to 6 servings

Tip: To turn this thick, robust stew into a soup, add 2 to 3 additional cups of broth. Cook the same length of time.

Mexican Corn Bread Pudding

1 can (about 14¾ ounces) cream-style corn

¾ cup yellow cornmeal

1 can (4 ounces) diced mild green chiles

2 eggs

2 tablespoons sugar

2 tablespoons vegetable oil

2 teaspoons baking powder

¾ teaspoon salt

½ cup (2 ounces) shredded Cheddar cheese

1. Coat inside of 2-quart **CROCK-POT**® slow cooker with nonstick cooking spray. Combine corn, cornmeal, chiles, eggs, sugar, oil, baking powder and salt in medium bowl; stir to blend. Pour into **CROCK-POT**® slow cooker.

2. Cover; cook on LOW 2 to 2½ hours or until center is set. Turn off heat. Sprinkle cheese over top. Cover; let stand 5 minutes or until cheese is melted.

Makes 8 servings

Mexican Hot Pot

1 tablespoon canola oil

1 medium onion, chopped

3 cloves garlic, minced

2 teaspoons red pepper flakes

2 teaspoons dried oregano

1 teaspoon ground cumin

1 can (28 ounces) whole tomatoes, drained and chopped

2 cups corn

1 can (about 15 ounces) chickpeas, rinsed and drained

1 can (about 15 ounces) pinto beans, rinsed and drained

1 cup water

6 cups shredded iceberg lettuce

1. Heat oil in large nonstick skillet over medium-high heat. Add onion and garlic; cook and stir 5 minutes. Add red pepper flakes, oregano and cumin; mix well. Remove to **CROCK-POT**® slow cooker.

2. Stir in tomatoes, corn, chickpeas, beans and water. Cover; cook on LOW 7 to 8 hours or on HIGH 2 to 3 hours. Top each serving with 1 cup shredded lettuce.

Makes 6 servings

Barley Salad

2 onions, chopped

2 sweet potatoes, diced

1 cup uncooked pearl barley

1 teaspoon salt

½ teaspoon ground cinnamon

¼ teaspoon ground red pepper (optional)

1½ cups water

2 apples, peeled and chopped

1 cup dried cranberries

1 cup chopped pecans

Spread onions and potatoes on bottom of **CROCK-POT**® slow cooker. Add barley, salt, cinnamon and ground red pepper, if desired. Pour in water. Cook on LOW 4 hours or on HIGH 2 hours. Stir in apples, cranberries and pecans. Serve warm or at room temperature.

Makes 16 servings

Barley with Currants and Pine Nuts

1 tablespoon butter

1 small onion, finely chopped

2 cups vegetable broth

½ cup uncooked pearl barley

½ teaspoon salt

¼ teaspoon black pepper

⅓ cup currants

¼ cup pine nuts

Melt butter in small skillet over medium-high heat. Add onion; cook and stir 2 minutes or until lightly browned. Remove to **CROCK-POT**® slow cooker. Add broth, barley, salt and pepper to **CROCK-POT**® slow cooker. Stir in currants. Cover; cook on LOW 3 hours. Stir in pine nuts just before serving.

Makes 4 servings

Quinoa and Vegetable Medley

2   medium sweet potatoes, cut into ½-inch-thick slices

1   medium eggplant, cut into ½-inch cubes

1   large green bell pepper, sliced

1   medium tomato, cut into wedges

1   small onion, cut into wedges

½   teaspoon salt

¼   teaspoon ground red pepper

¼   teaspoon black pepper

1   cup uncooked quinoa

2   cups reduced-sodium vegetable broth or water

2   cloves garlic, minced

½   teaspoon dried thyme

¼   teaspoon dried marjoram

1. Coat inside of **CROCK-POT**® slow cooker with nonstick cooking spray. Combine potatoes, eggplant, bell pepper, tomato, onion, salt, ground red pepper and black pepper in **CROCK-POT**® slow cooker; stir to blend.

2. Place quinoa in strainer; rinse well. Add quinoa to vegetable mixture in **CROCK-POT**® slow cooker. Stir in broth, garlic, thyme and marjoram. Cover; cook on LOW 5 hours or on HIGH 2½ hours or until quinoa is tender and broth is absorbed.

Makes 6 servings

Wild Rice and Dried Cherry Risotto

1 cup dry-roasted salted peanuts

6 teaspoons sesame oil, divided

1 cup chopped onion

4 cups hot water

6 ounces uncooked wild rice

1 cup diced carrots

1 cup chopped green or red bell pepper

½ cup dried cherries

⅛ to ¼ teaspoon red pepper flakes

¼ cup teriyaki or soy sauce

1 teaspoon salt

1. Coat inside of **CROCK-POT**® slow cooker with nonstick cooking spray. Heat large skillet over medium-high heat. Add peanuts; cook and stir 2 to 3 minutes or until nuts begin to brown. Remove to plate; set aside.

2. Heat 2 teaspoons oil in same skillet. Add onion; cook and stir 6 minutes or until browned. Remove to **CROCK-POT**® slow cooker.

3. Stir in water, rice, carrots, bell pepper, cherries and red pepper flakes. Cover; cook on HIGH 3 hours.

4. Turn off heat. Let stand 15 minutes, uncovered, until rice absorbs liquid. Stir in teriyaki sauce, peanuts, remaining 4 teaspoons oil and salt.

Makes 8 to 10 servings

Cran-Orange Acorn Squash

5 tablespoons instant brown rice

3 tablespoons minced onion

3 tablespoons diced celery

3 tablespoons dried cranberries

Pinch ground sage

3 small acorn or carnival squash, cut in half

1 teaspoon butter, cubed

3 tablespoons orange juice

½ cup warm water

1. Combine rice, onion, celery, cranberries and sage in small bowl; stir to blend. Stuff each squash half with rice mixture; dot with butter. Pour ½ tablespoon orange juice into each squash half over stuffing.

2. Stand squash in **CROCK-POT**® slow cooker. Pour water into **CROCK-POT**® slow cooker. Cover; cook on LOW 2½ hours or until squash is tender.

Makes 6 servings

Asian Golden Barley with Cashews

2 tablespoons olive oil

1 cup uncooked pearl barley

3 cups vegetable broth

1 cup chopped celery

1 medium green bell pepper, chopped

1 medium yellow onion, chopped

1 clove garlic, minced

¼ teaspoon black pepper

Chopped cashew nuts

1. Heat large skillet over medium heat. Add oil and barley; cook and stir 10 minutes or until barley is slightly browned. Remove to **CROCK-POT®** slow cooker.

2. Add broth, celery, bell pepper, onion, garlic and black pepper; stir to blend. Cover; cook on LOW 4 to 5 hours or on HIGH 2 to 3 hours or until liquid is absorbed. Top with cashews.

Makes 4 servings

Red Beans and Rice

2 cans (about 15 ounces *each*) red beans, undrained

1 can (about 14 ounces) diced tomatoes

½ cup chopped celery

½ cup chopped green bell pepper

½ cup chopped green onions

2 cloves garlic, minced

1 to 2 teaspoons hot pepper sauce

1 teaspoon Worcestershire sauce

1 whole bay leaf

3 cups hot cooked rice

1. Combine beans, tomatoes, celery, bell pepper, green onions, garlic, hot pepper sauce, Worcestershire sauce and bay leaf in **CROCK-POT®** slow cooker; stir to blend. Cover; cook on LOW 4 to 6 hours or on HIGH 2 to 3 hours.

2. Mash bean mixture slightly in **CROCK-POT®** slow cooker until mixture thickens. Cover; cook on HIGH ½ to 1 hour. Remove and discard bay leaf. Serve bean mixture over rice.

Makes 6 servings

Greek Rice

2 tablespoons butter

1¾ cups uncooked converted long grain rice

2 cans (about 14 ounces *each*) vegetable broth

1 teaspoon Greek seasoning

1 teaspoon ground oregano

1 cup pitted kalamata olives, drained and chopped

¾ cup chopped roasted red peppers

Crumbled feta cheese (optional)

Chopped fresh Italian parsley (optional)

1. Melt butter in large nonstick skillet over medium-high heat. Add rice; cook and stir 4 minutes or until golden brown. Remove to **CROCK-POT**® slow cooker. Stir in broth, Greek seasoning and oregano.

2. Cover; cook on LOW 4 hours or until liquid is absorbed and rice is tender. Stir in olives and roasted red peppers. Cover; cook on LOW 5 minutes. Garnish with cheese and parsley, if desired.

Makes 6 to 8 servings

Mushroom and Romano Risotto

3 tablespoons extra virgin olive oil

8 ounces sliced mushrooms

½ cup chopped shallots

½ cup chopped onion

3 cloves garlic, minced

1½ cups uncooked Arborio rice

½ cup Madeira wine

4½ cups vegetable broth

½ cup Romano cheese

3 tablespoons butter

3 tablespoons chopped fresh Italian parsley

¼ teaspoon black pepper

1. Heat oil in large skillet over medium-high heat. Add mushrooms; cook and stir 6 to 7 minutes or until mushrooms begin to brown. Stir in shallots, onion and garlic; cook and stir 2 to 3 minutes or until vegetables begin to soften. Add rice; cook and stir 1 minute. Add Madeira; cook and stir 1 minute or until almost absorbed.

2. Remove mixture to **CROCK-POT**® slow cooker. Add broth. Cover; cook on HIGH 2 hours or until liquid is absorbed and rice is tender.

3. Turn off heat. Stir in cheese, butter, parsley and pepper.

Makes 4 servings

Polenta Lasagna

4 cups boiling water	**2** tablespoons chopped fresh basil
1½ cups whole grain yellow cornmeal	**1** tablespoon chopped fresh oregano
4 teaspoons finely chopped fresh marjoram	**⅛** teaspoon black pepper
1 teaspoon olive oil	**2** medium red bell peppers, chopped
1 pound mushrooms, sliced	**¼** cup water
1 cup chopped leeks	**¼** cup freshly grated Parmesan cheese, divided
1 clove garlic, minced	
½ cup (2 ounces) shredded mozzarella cheese	

1. Coat inside of **CROCK-POT®** slow cooker with nonstick cooking spray. Combine 4 cups boiling water and cornmeal in **CROCK-POT®** slow cooker; stir to blend. Stir in marjoram. Cover; cook on LOW 3 to 4 hours or on HIGH 1 to 2 hours, stirring occasionally. Cover; chill 1 hour or until firm.

2. Heat oil in medium nonstick skillet over medium heat. Add mushrooms, leeks and garlic; cook and stir 5 minutes or until leeks are crisp-tender. Stir in mozzarella cheese, basil, oregano and black pepper. Place bell peppers and ¼ cup water in food processor or blender; process until smooth.

3. Cut cold polenta in half and place one half on bottom of **CROCK-POT®** slow cooker. Top with half of bell pepper mixture, half of vegetable mixture and 2 tablespoons Parmesan cheese. Place remaining polenta over Parmesan cheese; layer with remaining bell pepper and vegetable mixtures and Parmesan cheese. Cover; cook on LOW 3 hours or until cheese is melted and polenta is golden brown.

Makes 6 servings

Creamy Barley Risotto

3 cups vegetable broth

1 cup uncooked pearl barley

1 large leek (white and light green parts only), thinly sliced, separated into rings

1 cup frozen baby peas

1 tablespoon lemon juice

1 teaspoon grated lemon peel, plus additional for garnish

2 tablespoons butter, cut into 4 pieces

Salt and black pepper

Shaved Parmesan cheese (optional)

Chopped fresh Italian parsley (optional)

1. Coat inside of **CROCK-POT**® slow cooker with nonstick cooking spray. Combine broth, barley and leek in **CROCK-POT**® slow cooker. Cover; cook on LOW 4 to 5 hours or on HIGH 2 to 2½ hours or until most liquid is absorbed.

2. Stir in peas, lemon juice and 1 teaspoon lemon peel. Cover; cook on HIGH 10 minutes or until heated through. Stir in butter until melted. Season with salt and pepper. Garnish with cheese, parsley and additional lemon peel.

Makes 4 servings

Mushroom Wild Rice

1½ cups reduced-sodium chicken broth

1 cup uncooked wild rice

½ cup diced onion

½ cup sliced mushrooms

½ cup diced red or green bell pepper

1 tablespoon olive oil

¼ teaspoon salt

¼ teaspoon black pepper

Combine broth, rice, onion, mushrooms, bell pepper, oil, salt and black pepper in **CROCK-POT**® slow cooker. Cover; cook on HIGH 2½ hours or until rice is tender and liquid is absorbed.

Makes 8 servings

COOKING WITH BEER

Fall Beef and Beer Casserole

2 tablespoons oil

1½ pounds cubed beef stew meat

2 tablespoons all-purpose flour

1 cup beef broth

2 cups brown ale or beer

1 cup water

1 onion, sliced

2 carrots, sliced

1 leek, sliced

2 stalks celery, sliced

1 cup mushrooms, sliced

1 turnip, peeled and cubed

Salt and black pepper

1. Heat oil in large skillet over medium-high heat. Add beef; cook 6 to 8 minutes or until browned on all sides. Remove to **CROCK-POT**® slow cooker.

2. Sprinkle flour over contents of skillet; cook and stir 2 minutes. Gradually stir in broth, ale and water. Bring to a boil; pour over beef.

3. Add onion, carrots, leek, celery, mushrooms, turnip, salt and pepper to **CROCK-POT**® slow cooker; stir to blend. Cover; cook on LOW 8 to 10 hours or on HIGH 4 to 6 hours.

Makes 4 to 6 servings

Best Beef Brisket Sandwich Ever

1 beef brisket (about 3 pounds)*

2 cups apple cider, divided

1 head garlic, cloves separated, crushed and peeled

⅓ cup chopped fresh thyme *or* 2 tablespoons dried thyme

2 tablespoons whole black peppercorns

1 tablespoon mustard seeds

1 tablespoon Cajun seasoning

1 teaspoon ground allspice

1 teaspoon ground cumin

1 teaspoon celery seeds

2 to 4 whole cloves

1 can (12 ounces) dark beer

10 to 12 sourdough sandwich rolls, sliced in half

10 to 12 slices Swiss cheese (optional)

*Unless you have a 5-, 6- or 7-quart **CROCK-POT®** slow cooker, cut any roast larger than 2½ pounds in half so it cooks completely.

1. Combine brisket, ½ cup cider, garlic, thyme, peppercorns, mustard seeds, Cajun seasoning, allspice, cumin, celery seeds and cloves in large resealable food storage bag. Seal bag; turn to coat. Marinate in refrigerator overnight.

2. Place brisket and marinade in **CROCK-POT®** slow cooker. Add remaining 1½ cups cider and beer. Cover; cook on LOW 10 hours or until brisket is tender.

3. Slice brisket and place on sandwich rolls. Strain sauce; drizzle over meat. Top with cheese, if desired.

Makes 10 to 12 servings

Seafood Bouillabaisse

½ bulb fennel, chopped

1 medium onion, chopped

2 cloves garlic, minced

1 can (28 ounces) tomato purée

2 cans (12 ounces *each*) beer

2 cups water

8 ounces clam juice

1 whole bay leaf

½ teaspoon salt

¼ teaspoon black pepper

½ pound red snapper, cut into 1-inch pieces

8 mussels, scrubbed and debearded

8 cherrystone clams

8 large raw shrimp, unpeeled and rinsed (with tails on)

4 lemon wedges

1. Spray large skillet with nonstick cooking spray; heat over medium-high heat. Add fennel, onion and garlic; cook and stir 5 minutes or until onion is soft and translucent. Remove to **CROCK-POT**® slow cooker. Add tomato purée, beer, water, clam juice, bay leaf, salt and pepper to **CROCK-POT**® slow cooker. Cover; cook on LOW 6 to 8 hours or on HIGH 3 to 4 hours.

2. Add fish, mussels, clams and shrimp to **CROCK-POT**® slow cooker. Cover; cook on LOW 15 minutes or until fish begins to flake when tested with fork. Discard any mussels and clams that do not open.

3. Remove and discard bay leaf. Ladle broth into wide soup bowls; top with fish, mussels, clams and shrimp. Squeeze lemon over each serving.

Makes 4 servings

Beef Cabbage Rolls with Beer

12 ounces ground beef

12 ounces ground pork

1 medium onion, chopped

1 can (15 ounces) tomato sauce, divided

1 teaspoon salt

1 teaspoon dried thyme

¼ teaspoon black pepper

1 large head green cabbage

1 bottle (12 ounces) beer

Salt and black pepper

Chopped fresh parsley (optional)

1. Combine beef, pork, onion, 1 cup tomato sauce, salt, thyme and pepper in large bowl; mix well.

2. Pour ¼ cup tomato sauce into **CROCK-POT**® slow cooker.

3. Cut out core from cabbage and carefully remove leaves. Place golf ball-sized mound of meat mixture in center of large cabbage leaf, edges curling upward. Starting with thickest side, fold leaf over meat mixture, burrito-style. Place, fold side down, in **CROCK-POT**® slow cooker. Repeat with remaining meat and cabbage leaves, stacking as necessary.

4. Pour beer over cabbage rolls. Pour remaining tomato sauce on top of rolls.

5. Cover; cook on LOW 5 hours. Halfway through cooking time, push cabbage rolls under liquid to submerge. Season with salt and pepper. Sprinkle with parsley, if desired.

Makes about 12 rolls

Slow Cooker Beer Bolognese

3 slices bacon, chopped

1 large onion, chopped

1 stalk celery, chopped

1 carrot, chopped

2 cloves garlic, minced

3 teaspoons olive oil, divided

8 ounces mushrooms, sliced

¾ pound ground beef

¾ pound ground pork

1 can (28 ounces) tomato purée

1 bottle (12 ounces) dark beer

1 cup beef broth

1 tablespoon tomato paste

1 teaspoon salt

¼ teaspoon black pepper

¼ teaspoon red pepper flakes

Hot cooked pasta

Shaved Parmesan cheese and chopped fresh parsley

1. Heat large skillet over medium heat. Add bacon; cook and stir until crisp. Remove to paper towel-lined plate using slotted spoon.

2. Add onion, celery and carrot to same skillet; cook and stir 5 minutes or until vegetables begin to brown. Add garlic; cook and stir 1 to 2 minutes. Remove to **CROCK-POT**® slow cooker. Add 1 teaspoon oil to skillet. Add mushrooms; cook and stir until mushrooms begin to brown. Remove to **CROCK-POT**® slow cooker.

3. Heat remaining 2 teaspoons oil in skillet. Brown beef and pork over medium-high heat, stirring to break up meat. Drain fat. Remove to **CROCK-POT**® slow cooker. Add bacon, tomato purée, beer, broth, tomato paste, salt, black pepper and red pepper flakes; stir to blend Cover; cook on LOW 8 to 10 hours. Serve over pasta. Top with cheese and parsley.

Makes 6 to 8 servings

Hearty Pork and Bacon Chili

2½ pounds pork shoulder, cut into 1-inch pieces

3½ teaspoons salt, divided

1¼ teaspoons black pepper, divided

1 tablespoon vegetable oil

4 slices thick-cut bacon, diced

2 medium onions, chopped

1 red bell pepper, chopped

¼ cup chili powder

2 tablespoons tomato paste

1 tablespoon minced garlic

1 tablespoon ground cumin

1 tablespoon smoked paprika

1 bottle (12 ounces) pale ale

2 cans (about 14 ounces *each*) diced tomatoes

2 cups water

¾ cup dried kidney beans, rinsed and sorted

¾ cup dried black beans, rinsed and sorted

3 tablespoons cornmeal

Feta cheese and chopped fresh cilantro (optional)

1. Season pork with 1 teaspoon salt and 1 teaspoon black pepper. Heat oil in large skillet over medium-high heat. Cook pork in batches 6 minutes or until browned on all sides. Remove to **CROCK-POT**® slow cooker using slotted spoon.

2. Heat same skillet over medium heat. Add bacon; cook and stir until crisp. Remove to **CROCK-POT**® slow cooker using slotted spoon.

3. Pour off all but 2 tablespoons fat from skillet. Return skillet to medium heat. Add onions and bell pepper; cook and stir 6 minutes or just until softened. Stir in chili powder, tomato paste, garlic, cumin, paprika, remaining 2½ teaspoons salt and ¼ teaspoon black pepper; cook and stir 1 minute. Stir in ale. Bring to a simmer, scraping up any browned bits from bottom of skillet. Pour over pork in **CROCK-POT**® slow cooker. Stir in tomatoes, water, beans and cornmeal.

4. Cover; cook on LOW 10 hours. Turn off heat. Let stand 10 minutes. Skim fat from surface and discard. Garnish with cheese and cilantro.

Makes 8 to 10 servings

Beer Chicken

2 tablespoons olive oil

1 cut-up whole chicken (3 to 5 pounds)

10 new potatoes, halved

1 can (12 ounces) beer

2 medium carrots, sliced

1 cup chopped celery

1 medium onion, chopped

1 tablespoon chopped fresh rosemary

1. Heat oil in large skillet over medium heat. Add chicken; cook 5 to 7 minutes on each side or until browned. Remove to **CROCK-POT®** slow cooker.

2. Add potatoes, beer, carrots, celery, onion and rosemary to **CROCK-POT®** slow cooker. Cover; cook on HIGH 5 hours.

Makes 4 to 6 servings

Ale'd Pork and Sauerkraut

1 jar (32 ounces) sauerkraut, undrained

1½ tablespoons sugar

1 can (12 ounces) ale or dark beer

1 boneless pork shoulder or pork butt roast (3½ pounds)*

½ teaspoon salt

½ teaspoon paprika

¼ teaspoon garlic powder

¼ teaspoon black pepper

*Unless you have a 5-, 6- or 7-quart **CROCK-POT®** slow cooker, cut any roast larger than 2½ pounds in half so it cooks completely.

1. Place sauerkraut in **CROCK-POT®** slow cooker. Sprinkle with sugar; add ale. Place pork, fat side up, on top of sauerkraut mixture; sprinkle evenly with salt, paprika, garlic powder and black pepper. Cover; cook on HIGH 6 hours.

2. Remove pork to large serving platter. Remove sauerkraut using slotted spoon; arrange around pork. Spoon cooking liquid over sauerkraut as desired.

Makes 6 to 8 servings

Veal Pot Roast

2 tablespoons olive oil

1 veal shoulder roast (2½ pounds)
    Salt and black pepper

2 cloves garlic, slivered

¾ pound pearl onions, peeled (see Tip)

½ cup sliced fennel

1 package (3½ ounces) shiitake
    mushrooms, sliced

6 plum tomatoes, quartered

2 cups chicken broth

1 cup light beer

1 teaspoon minced fresh herbs
    (rosemary leaves, thyme and sage)

¼ teaspoon red pepper flakes

¼ teaspoon grated lemon peel
    Hot cooked rice (optional)

1. Heat oil in large skillet over medium-high heat. Season veal with salt and black pepper. Add to skillet; cook until browned on all sides. Remove to **CROCK-POT**® slow cooker. Push garlic slivers into veal.

2. Add onions, fennel, mushrooms and tomatoes to **CROCK-POT**® slow cooker. Pour broth and beer over veal. Sprinkle with herbs, red pepper flakes and lemon peel.

3. Cover; cook on LOW 8 to 10 hours or until tender. Remove veal from **CROCK-POT**® slow cooker; let rest 10 minutes. Slice veal. Serve with vegetables, sauce and rice, if desired.

Makes 4 to 6 servings

Tip: To peel pearl onions, place in a large pot of boiling water and cook 1 minute. Drain well and run under cold water to cool slightly. Rub lightly, if necessary. The skins should come off easily.

Spicy Italian Beef

1 boneless beef chuck roast
   (3 to 4 pounds)*

1 jar (12 ounces) pepperoncini peppers**

1 can (about 14 ounces) beef broth

1 can (12 ounces) beer

1 onion, minced

2 tablespoons Italian seasoning

1 loaf French bread, cut into thick slices

8 to 10 slices provolone cheese (optional)

*Unless you have a 5-, 6-, or 7-quart **CROCK-POT**®
slow cooker, cut any roast larger than 2½ pounds
in half so it cooks completely.

**Pepperoncini peppers are pickled peppers sold in
jars with brine. They are available in the condiment
aisle of large supermarkets.

1. Place beef in **CROCK-POT**® slow cooker.

2. Drain pepperoncini peppers. Pull off stem ends and discard. Add pepperoncini peppers, broth, beer, onion and Italian seasoning to **CROCK-POT**® slow cooker. *Do not stir.* Cover; cook on LOW 8 to 10 hours.

3. Remove beef to large cutting board; shred with two forks. Return beef to cooking liquid; mix well. Serve on French bread. Top with cheese, if desired.

Makes 8 to 10 servings

Wisconsin Beer and Cheese Soup

2 to 3 slices pumpernickel or rye bread,
 cut into ½-inch cubes

1 can (about 14 ounces) vegetable broth

1 cup beer

¼ cup finely chopped onion

2 cloves garlic, minced

¾ teaspoon dried thyme

1½ cups (6 ounces) American cheese,
 shredded or diced

1 to 1½ cups (4 to 6 ounces) shredded
 sharp Cheddar cheese

1 cup milk

½ teaspoon paprika

1. Preheat oven to 425°F. Place bread on small baking sheet. Bake 10 to 12 minutes or until crisp; set aside.

2. Combine broth, beer, onion, garlic and thyme in **CROCK-POT®** slow cooker. Cover; cook on LOW 4 hours.

3. Turn **CROCK-POT®** slow cooker to HIGH. Stir in cheeses, milk and paprika. Cover; cook on HIGH 45 minutes to 1 hour or until soup is heated through and cheeses are melted. Stir soup well to blend cheeses. Ladle soup into mugs or bowls; top with croutons.

Makes 4 servings

Tip: Choose a light-tasting beer when making this soup. Hearty ales have a stronger flavor that might not please your family's taste buds.

Chicken Curry with Beer

⅓ cup vegetable oil

1 cut-up whole chicken (4 pounds)

1 cup chicken broth

1 cup beer

1 cup tomato sauce

1 large onion, chopped

1 tablespoon minced ginger

2½ teaspoons curry powder

1 teaspoon salt

1 teaspoon garam masala

2 cloves garlic, minced

½ teaspoon chili powder

⅛ teaspoon ground red pepper

4 cups hot cooked basmati rice

1. Heat oil in large skillet over medium-high heat. Add chicken in batches; cook until browned on all sides.

2. Remove to **CROCK-POT**® slow cooker. Add remaining ingredients except rice.

3. Cover; cook on LOW 8 hours. Serve chicken with sauce over rice.

Makes 4 servings

Slow Cooker Brisket of Beef

1 whole beef brisket (about 5 pounds)*

2 teaspoons minced garlic

½ teaspoon black pepper

2 large onions, cut into ¼-inch slices and separated into rings

1 bottle (12 ounces) chili sauce

12 ounces dark ale, beef broth or water

2 tablespoons Worcestershire sauce

1 tablespoon packed brown sugar

*Unless you have a 5-, 6- or 7-quart **CROCK-POT**® slow cooker, cut any roast larger than 2½ pounds in half so it cooks completely.

1. Place brisket, fat side down, in **CROCK-POT**® slow cooker. Spread garlic evenly over brisket; sprinkle with pepper. Arrange onions over brisket. Combine chili sauce, ale, Worcestershire sauce and brown sugar in medium bowl; pour over brisket and onions. Cover; cook on LOW 8 hours.

2. Turn brisket over; stir onions into sauce and spoon over brisket. Cover; cook on LOW 1 to 2 hours or until brisket is fork-tender. Remove brisket to large cutting board. Cover loosely with foil; let stand 10 minutes.

3. Turn off heat. Stir cooking liquid; let stand 5 minutes. Skim off fat. Carve brisket across the grain into thin slices. Spoon cooking liquid over brisket.

Makes 10 to 12 servings

Tip: Cooking liquid may be thinned to desired consistency with water or thickened by simmering, uncovered, in saucepan over medium-high heat.

Beef Chuck Chili

½ cup plus 2 tablespoons olive oil, divided

1 boneless beef chuck roast
   (5 pounds), trimmed*

3 cups finely chopped onions

2 green bell peppers, chopped

4 poblano peppers, seeded and finely
   chopped**

2 serrano peppers, seeded and minced**

3 jalapeño peppers, seeded and minced**

2 tablespoons minced garlic

1 can (28 ounces) crushed tomatoes,
   undrained

½ cup Mexican lager

¼ cup hot pepper sauce

1 tablespoon ground cumin

   Corn bread

*Unless you have a 5-, 6- or 7-quart **CROCK-POT**®
slow cooker, cut any roast larger than 2½ pounds
in half so it cooks completely.

**Poblano, serrano and jalapeño peppers can sting
and irritate the skin. Wear rubber gloves when
handling peppers and do not touch your eyes.

1. Heat ½ cup oil in large skillet over medium-high heat. Add beef; brown on both sides. Remove to **CROCK-POT**® slow cooker.

2. Heat remaining 2 tablespoons oil in same skillet over low heat. Add onions, peppers and garlic; cook and stir 7 minutes or until onions are tender. Remove to **CROCK-POT**® slow cooker. Stir in tomatoes. Cover; cook on LOW 4 to 5 hours.

3. Remove beef to large cutting board; shred with two forks. Add lager, hot pepper sauce and cumin to cooking liquid. Return beef to cooking liquid; mix well. Serve over corn bread.

Makes 8 to 10 servings

SENSATIONAL SANDWICHES

Pork Tenderloin Sliders

2 teaspoons chili powder

¾ teaspoon ground cumin

½ teaspoon salt

½ teaspoon black pepper

2 tablespoons olive oil, divided

2 pork tenderloins (about 1 pound *each*)

2 cups chicken broth

12 green onions, ends trimmed

½ cup mayonnaise

1 canned chipotle pepper in adobo sauce, minced

2 teaspoons lime juice

12 dinner rolls, sliced in half

12 slices Monterey Jack cheese

1. Coat inside of **CROCK-POT**® slow cooker with nonstick cooking spray. Combine chili powder, cumin, salt and black pepper in small bowl. Rub 1 tablespoon oil evenly over each pork tenderloin. Sprinkle cumin mixture evenly over tenderloins, turning to coat. Heat large skillet over medium heat. Cook tenderloins 7 to 10 minutes or until browned on all sides. Remove to **CROCK-POT**® slow cooker; add broth and green onions. Cover; cook on LOW 6 to 8 hours.

2. Combine mayonnaise, chipotle pepper and lime juice is small bowl. Cover and refrigerate.

3. Remove pork and green onions from **CROCK-POT**® slow cooker. Coarsely chop green onions. Thinly slice pork. Spread chipotle mayonnaise evenly on bottom halves of rolls. Top with green onions, pork slices, cheese and roll tops. Serve immediately.

Makes 12 sandwiches

Campfired-Up Sloppy Joes

1½ pounds ground beef

½ cup chopped sweet onion

1 medium red bell pepper, chopped

1 large clove garlic, crushed

½ cup ketchup

½ cup barbecue sauce

2 tablespoons cider vinegar

1 tablespoon Worcestershire sauce

1 tablespoon packed brown sugar

1 teaspoon chili powder

1 can (about 8 ounces) baked beans

6 Kaiser rolls, sliced in half and warmed

Shredded sharp Cheddar cheese (optional)

1. Brown ground beef, onion, bell pepper and garlic in large skillet over medium-high heat 6 to 8 minutes, stirring to break up meat. Remove to **CROCK-POT**® slow cooker using slotted spoon.

2. Combine ketchup, barbecue sauce, vinegar, Worcestershire sauce, brown sugar and chili powder in small bowl; stir to blend. Pour over beef mixture in **CROCK-POT**® slow cooker.

3. Add beans. Stir well to combine. Cover; cook on HIGH 3 hours.

4. Serve beef mixture on rolls. Sprinkle with Cheddar cheese, if desired.

Makes 6 servings

Serving Suggestion: Serve with a side of coleslaw.

Hot and Juicy Reuben Sandwiches

1 corned beef brisket, trimmed (about 1½ pounds)

2 cups sauerkraut, drained

½ cup beef broth

1 small onion, sliced

1 clove garlic, minced

¼ teaspoon caraway seeds

4 to 6 whole black peppercorns

8 slices pumpernickel or rye bread

4 slices Swiss cheese

Prepared mustard

1. Combine corned beef, sauerkraut, broth, onion, garlic, caraway seeds and peppercorns in **CROCK-POT®** slow cooker. Cover; cook on LOW 7 to 9 hours.

2. Remove beef to large cutting board. Cut beef across grain into slices. Divide among 4 bread slices. Top beef with drained sauerkraut mixture and 1 slice cheese. Spread mustard on remaining 4 bread slices; place on sandwiches.

Makes 4 servings

Big Al's Hot and Sweet Sausage Sandwiches

4 to 5 pounds hot Italian sausage links

1 jar (24 to 26 ounces) pasta sauce

1 large Vidalia onion (or other sweet onion), sliced

1 green bell pepper, sliced

1 red bell pepper, sliced

¼ cup packed dark brown sugar

Italian rolls, split

Provolone cheese, sliced (optional)

1. Combine sausages, pasta sauce, onion, bell peppers and brown sugar in **CROCK-POT®** slow cooker. Cover; cook on LOW 8 to 10 hours or on HIGH 4 to 6 hours.

2. Place sausages in rolls. Top with vegetable mixture. Add provolone cheese, if desired.

Makes 8 to 10 servings

Chicken and Brie Sliders

1 red bell pepper, chopped

1 to 2 carrots, sliced

½ cup sliced celery

1 onion, chopped

1 clove garlic, minced

¼ teaspoon dried oregano

¼ teaspoon red pepper flakes

¼ cup all-purpose flour

1 teaspoon salt

½ teaspoon black pepper

6 boneless, skinless chicken thighs
   or breasts

1 tablespoon vegetable oil

1 can (about 14 ounces) chicken broth

6 sub rolls, sliced in half and toasted *or*
   2 thin baguettes (about 12 ounces
   each), sliced in half and toasted

1 large wedge brie cheese, cut into
   12 pieces

1. Place bell pepper, carrots, celery, onion, garlic, oregano and red pepper flakes in **CROCK-POT**® slow cooker.

2. Combine flour, salt and black pepper in large resealable food storage bag. Add chicken, 2 pieces at a time; shake to coat with flour mixture. Heat oil in large skillet over medium-high heat. Brown chicken on both sides.

3. Place chicken over vegetables in **CROCK-POT**® slow cooker; add broth. Cover; cook on LOW 5 to 6 hours.

4. Remove 1 piece of chicken from **CROCK-POT**® slow cooker; slice thinly and arrange on 1 sub roll. Spoon 1 to 2 tablespoons broth mixture over chicken and top with 2 slices cheese. Repeat with remaining chicken, bread and cheese. Slice each sandwich into 3 equal pieces.

Makes 18 sliders

Cuban Pork Sandwiches

1 pork loin roast (about 2 pounds)

½ cup orange juice

2 tablespoons lime juice

1 tablespoon minced garlic

1½ teaspoons salt

½ teaspoon red pepper flakes

2 tablespoons yellow mustard

8 crusty bread rolls, sliced in half (6 inches *each*)

8 slices Swiss cheese

8 thin ham slices

4 small dill pickles, thinly sliced lengthwise

1. Coat inside of **CROCK-POT**® slow cooker with nonstick cooking spray. Add pork loin.

2. Combine orange juice, lime juice, garlic, salt and red pepper flakes in small bowl. Pour over pork. Cover; cook on LOW 7 to 8 hours or on HIGH 3½ to 4 hours. Remove pork to large cutting board. Cover loosely with foil; let stand 10 to 15 minutes before slicing.

3. To serve, spread mustard on both sides of rolls. Divide pork slices among bottom halves of rolls. Top with Swiss cheese, ham and pickle slices and roll tops.

4. Coat large skillet with nonstick cooking spray; heat over medium heat. Working in batches, arrange sandwiches in skillet. Cover with foil and top with dinner plate to press down sandwiches. (If necessary, weigh down with 2 to 3 cans to compress sandwiches lightly.) Heat about 8 minutes or until cheese is slightly melted.*

*Or use table top grill to compress and heat sandwiches.

Makes 8 servings

Green Chile Pulled Pork Sandwiches

1 boneless pork shoulder roast
   (3½ to 4 pounds)*

1 teaspoon salt

½ teaspoon black pepper

1 can (about 14 ounces) diced tomatoes
   with mild green chiles

1 cup chopped onion

½ cup water

2 tablespoons lime juice

1 teaspoon ground cumin

1 teaspoon minced garlic

2 canned chipotle peppers in adobo sauce,
   minced

8 hard rolls or hoagie buns, split

½ cup sour cream

2 avocados, sliced

3 tablespoons chopped fresh cilantro
   (optional)

*Unless you have a 5-, 6- or 7-quart **CROCK-POT**®
slow cooker, cut any roast larger than 2½ pounds
in half so it cooks completely.

1. Season pork with salt and black pepper. Place pork in **CROCK-POT**® slow cooker.

2. Combine tomatoes, onion, water, lime juice, cumin, garlic and chipotle peppers in medium bowl; stir to blend. Pour over pork in **CROCK-POT**® slow cooker. Cover; cook on LOW 7 to 8 hours or until pork is tender.

3. Turn off heat. Remove pork to large cutting board; cool slightly. Remove any fat from surface of meat and discard. Shred pork with two forks. Return to cooking liquid; stir to combine. Spoon pork into rolls. Top with sour cream, avocado and cilantro, if desired.

Makes 8 servings

Meatball Grinders

1 can (about 14 ounces) diced tomatoes

1 can (8 ounces) tomato sauce

¼ cup chopped onion

2 tablespoons tomato paste

1 teaspoon Italian seasoning

1 pound ground chicken

½ cup fresh whole wheat or white bread crumbs (1 slice bread)

1 egg white, lightly beaten

3 tablespoons finely chopped fresh Italian parsley

2 cloves garlic, minced

¼ teaspoon salt

⅛ teaspoon black pepper

4 small hard rolls, split

2 tablespoons grated Parmesan cheese

1. Combine tomatoes, tomato sauce, onion, tomato paste and Italian seasoning in **CROCK-POT**® slow cooker; stir to blend. Cover; cook on LOW 3 to 4 hours.

2. Halfway through cooking time, prepare meatballs. Combine chicken, bread crumbs, egg white, parsley, garlic, salt and pepper in medium bowl. Shape mixture into 12 to 16 meatballs. Spray medium nonstick skillet with nonstick cooking spray; heat over medium heat. Add meatballs; cook 8 to 10 minutes or until well browned on all sides. Remove to **CROCK-POT**® slow cooker.

3. Cover; cook on LOW 1 to 2 hours or until meatballs are no longer pink in centers and are heated through. Place 3 to 4 meatballs in each roll. Spoon sauce over meatballs. Sprinkle with cheese.

Makes 4 servings

Philly Cheese Steaks

2 pounds beef round steak, sliced

4 onions, sliced

2 green bell peppers, sliced

2 tablespoons butter, melted

1 tablespoon garlic-pepper seasoning

Salt

½ cup water

2 teaspoons beef bouillon granules

8 crusty Italian or French rolls, split*

8 slices Cheddar cheese, cut in half

*Toast rolls under broiler or on griddle, if desired.

1. Combine steak, onions, bell peppers, butter, garlic-pepper seasoning and salt in **CROCK-POT®** slow cooker; stir to blend.

2. Whisk together water and bouillon in small bowl; pour into **CROCK-POT®** slow cooker. Cover; cook on LOW 6 to 8 hours.

3. Remove beef, onions and bell peppers from **CROCK-POT®** slow cooker and pile into rolls. Top with cheese and place under broiler until cheese is melted.

Makes 8 servings

Burgundy Beef Po' Boys with Dipping Sauce

2 cups chopped onions

1 boneless beef chuck shoulder or bottom round roast (about 3 pounds), trimmed*

¼ cup dry red wine

3 tablespoons balsamic vinegar

1 tablespoon beef bouillon granules

1 tablespoon Worcestershire sauce

¾ teaspoon dried thyme

½ teaspoon garlic powder

Italian rolls, split and warmed

*Unless you have a 5-, 6- or 7-quart **CROCK-POT®** slow cooker, cut any roast larger than 2½ pounds in half so it cooks completely.

1. Place onions in bottom of **CROCK-POT®** slow cooker. Top with beef, wine, vinegar, bouillon granules, Worcestershire sauce, thyme and garlic powder. Cover; cook on HIGH 8 to 10 hours.

2. Remove beef to large cutting board; shred with two forks. Turn off heat. Let cooking liquid stand 5 minutes. Skim off any fat and discard. Spoon beef into rolls. Serve with cooking liquid as dipping sauce.

Makes 6 to 8 servings

Easy Beef Sandwiches

1 large onion, sliced

1 boneless beef bottom round roast (about 3 to 5 pounds)*

1 cup water

1 package (about 1 ounce) au jus gravy mix

French rolls, sliced in half

Provolone cheese

*Unless you have a 5-, 6- or 7-quart **CROCK-POT**® slow cooker, cut any roast larger than 2½ pounds in half so it cooks completely.

1. Place onion slices in bottom of **CROCK-POT**® slow cooker; top with roast. Combine water and dry gravy mix in small bowl; pour over roast. Cover; cook on LOW 7 to 9 hours.

2. Remove roast to large cutting board; shred with two forks. Turn off heat. Let cooking liquid stand 5 to 10 minutes. Skim off and discard fat. Spoon beef onto rolls; top with cheese. Serve cooking liquid on the side for dipping.

Makes 6 to 8 servings

Shredded Pork Roast

1 boneless pork shoulder, well trimmed (3½ to 4 pounds)*

1 medium onion, finely chopped

⅔ cup ketchup

⅓ cup water

2 tablespoons chili powder

2 tablespoons packed brown sugar

1 tablespoon ground cumin

2 teaspoons garlic powder

1 teaspoon salt

1 teaspoon Worcestershire sauce

½ teaspoon black pepper

Hoagie rolls, split

Carrots and celery sticks (optional)

*Unless you have a 5-, 6- or 7-quart **CROCK-POT**® slow cooker, cut any roast larger than 2½ pounds in half so it cooks completely.

1. Coat inside of **CROCK-POT**® slow cooker with nonstick cooking spray. Place pork in **CROCK-POT**® slow cooker. Combine onion, ketchup, water, chili powder, brown sugar, cumin, garlic powder, salt, Worcestershire sauce and pepper in medium bowl; stir to blend. Pour over pork; turn to coat. Cover; cook on LOW 8 to 10 hours or on HIGH 4½ to 5 hours or until pork is very tender.

2. Remove pork to large bowl and shred with two forks, discarding fat. Pour ¾ cup cooking liquid into bowl; toss to coat. Spoon pork into rolls. Serve with carrots and celery, if desired.

Makes 8 to 10 servings

Mini Swiss Steak Sandwiches

2 tablespoons all-purpose flour

¼ teaspoon salt

¼ teaspoon black pepper

1¾ pounds boneless beef chuck steak, about 1 inch thick

2 tablespoons vegetable oil

1 medium onion, sliced

1 green bell pepper, sliced

1 clove garlic, sliced

1 cup stewed tomatoes

¾ cup condensed beef broth, undiluted

2 teaspoons Worcestershire sauce

1 whole bay leaf

2 tablespoons cornstarch

2 packages (12 ounces *each*) sweet Hawaiian-style dinner rolls

1. Coat inside of **CROCK-POT**® slow cooker with nonstick cooking spray. Combine flour, salt and black pepper in large resealable food storage bag. Add steak. Seal bag; shake to coat.

2. Heat oil in large skillet over high heat. Brown steak on both sides. Remove to **CROCK-POT**® slow cooker.

3. Add onion and bell pepper to skillet; cook and stir over medium-high heat 3 minutes or until softened. Add garlic; cook and stir 30 seconds. Pour mixture over steak.

4. Add tomatoes, broth, Worcestershire sauce and bay leaf to **CROCK-POT**® slow cooker. Cover; cook on HIGH 3½ hours or until steak is tender. Remove steak to cutting board. Remove and discard bay leaf.

5. Stir 2 tablespoons cooking liquid into cornstarch in small bowl until smooth. Whisk into cooking liquid in **CROCK-POT**® slow cooker. Cover; cook on HIGH 10 minutes or until thickened.

6. Thinly slice steak against the grain to shred. Return steak to **CROCK-POT**® slow cooker; stir to coat. Serve steak mixture on rolls.

Makes 16 to 18 servings

SAVORY SIDES

Braised Sweet and Sour Cabbage and Apples

- **2** tablespoons butter
- **6** cups coarsely shredded red cabbage
- **1** large sweet apple, peeled, cored and cut into bite-size pieces
- **½** cup raisins
- **½** cup apple cider

- **3** tablespoons cider vinegar, divided
- **2** tablespoons packed dark brown sugar
- **½** teaspoon salt
- **¼** teaspoon black pepper
- **3** whole cloves

1. Melt butter in very large skillet or saucepan over medium heat. Add cabbage; cook and stir 3 minutes or until glossy. Remove to **CROCK-POT**® slow cooker.

2. Add apple, raisins, apple cider, 2 tablespoons vinegar, brown sugar, salt, pepper and cloves. Cover; cook on LOW 2½ to 3 hours.

3. To serve, remove cloves. Stir in remaining 1 tablespoon vinegar.

Makes 4 to 6 servings

Mashed Rutabagas and Potatoes

2 pounds rutabagas, peeled and cut into ½-inch pieces

1 pound potatoes, peeled and cut into ½-inch pieces

½ cup milk

½ teaspoon ground nutmeg

2 tablespoons chopped fresh Italian parsley

Sprigs fresh Italian parsley (optional)

1. Place rutabagas and potatoes in **CROCK-POT®** slow cooker; add enough water to cover vegetables. Cover; cook on LOW 6 hours or on HIGH 3 hours. Remove vegetables to large bowl using slotted spoon. Discard cooking liquid.

2. Mash vegetables with potato masher. Add milk, nutmeg and chopped parsley; stir until smooth. Garnish with parsley sprigs.

Makes 8 servings

Scalloped Tomatoes and Corn

1 can (15 ounces) cream-style corn

1 can (about 14 ounces) diced tomatoes

¾ cup saltine or soda cracker crumbs

1 egg, lightly beaten

2 teaspoons sugar

¾ teaspoon black pepper

Chopped fresh tomatoes

Chopped fresh Italian parsley

Combine corn, diced tomatoes, cracker crumbs, egg, sugar and pepper in **CROCK-POT®** slow cooker; stir to blend. Cover; cook on LOW 4 to 6 hours. Sprinkle with fresh tomatoes and parsley just before serving.

Makes 4 to 6 servings

Spring Vegetable Ragoût

1 tablespoon olive oil

2 leeks, thinly sliced

3 cloves garlic, minced

3 cups small cherry tomatoes, halved

1 package (10 ounces) frozen corn

1 cup vegetable broth

½ pound yellow squash, halved lengthwise and cut into ½-inch pieces (about 1¼ cups)

1 small bag (6 ounces) frozen edamame (soybeans), shelled

1 small bag (4 ounces) shredded carrots

1 teaspoon dried tarragon

1 teaspoon dried basil

1 teaspoon dried oregano

Salt and black pepper

Minced fresh Italian parsley (optional)

1. Heat oil in large skillet over medium heat. Add leeks and garlic; cook and stir just until fragrant.

2. Stir leeks and garlic mixture, tomatoes, corn, broth, squash, edamame, carrots, tarragon, basil and oregano into **CROCK-POT®** slow cooker. Cover; cook on LOW 6 to 8 hours or on HIGH 3 to 4 hours or until vegetables are tender. Season with salt and pepper. Garnish with parsley.

Makes 6 servings

Fennel Braised with Tomato

2 bulbs fennel

1 tablespoon olive oil

1 onion, sliced

1 clove garlic, sliced

4 tomatoes, chopped

⅔ cup reduced-sodium vegetable broth
  or water

3 tablespoons dry white wine or vegetable
  broth

1 tablespoon chopped fresh marjoram
  or 1 teaspoon dried marjoram

¼ teaspoon salt

¼ teaspoon black pepper

1. Trim stems and bottoms from fennel bulbs, reserving green leafy tops for garnish. Cut each bulb lengthwise into four wedges.

2. Heat oil in large skillet over medium heat. Add fennel, onion and garlic; cook and stir 5 minutes or until onion is soft and translucent.

3. Combine all ingredients in **CROCK-POT**® slow cooker. Cover; cook on LOW 2 to 3 hours or on HIGH 1 to 1½ hours or until vegetables are tender. Garnish with reserved fennel leaves.

Makes 6 servings

Mediterranean Red Potatoes

3 medium unpeeled red potatoes, cubed

⅔ cup fresh or frozen pearl onions

¾ teaspoon Italian seasoning

¼ teaspoon black pepper

1 small tomato, seeded and chopped

2 ounces feta cheese, crumbled

2 tablespoons chopped black olives

1. Combine potatoes and onions in 1½-quart soufflé dish that fits inside of **CROCK-POT®** slow cooker. Spray with nonstick cooking spray; toss to coat. Add Italian seasoning and pepper; mix well. Cover dish tightly with foil.

2. Make foil handles using three 18×3-inch strips of heavy-duty foil or use regular foil folded to double thickness. Crisscross foil in spoke design; place across bottom and up side of stoneware. Place soufflé dish in center of strips in **CROCK-POT®** slow cooker. Pull foil strips up and over dish.

3. Pour hot water into **CROCK-POT®** slow cooker to about 1½ inches from top of soufflé dish. Cover; cook on LOW 7 to 8 hours.

4. Use foil handles to lift dish out of **CROCK-POT®** slow cooker. Stir tomato, cheese and olives into potato mixture.

Makes 4 servings

Asian Kale and Chickpeas

1 tablespoon sesame oil

1 medium onion, thinly sliced

2 teaspoons grated fresh ginger

2 cloves garlic, minced

2 jalapeño peppers, chopped*

8 cups chopped kale

1 cup reduced-sodium vegetable broth

2 cans (about 15 ounces *each*) unsalted chickpeas, rinsed and drained

1 tablespoon lime juice

1 teaspoon grated lime peel

2 cups hot cooked rice (optional)

*Jalapeño peppers can sting and irritate the skin, so wear rubber gloves when handling peppers and do not touch your eyes.

1. Coat inside of **CROCK-POT**® slow cooker with nonstick cooking spray. Heat oil in large skillet over medium-high heat. Add onion, ginger, garlic and jalapeño peppers; cook 1 minute. Add kale; cook and stir 2 minutes or until slightly wilted. Remove to **CROCK-POT**® slow cooker. Stir in broth and chickpeas.

2. Cover; cook on LOW 3 hours. Turn off heat. Stir in lime juice and lime peel. Serve with rice, if desired.

Makes 4 servings

Orange-Spiced Sweet Potatoes

2 pounds sweet potatoes, diced

½ cup packed dark brown sugar

½ cup (1 stick) butter, cubed

1 teaspoon ground cinnamon

1 teaspoon vanilla

½ teaspoon salt

½ teaspoon ground nutmeg

½ teaspoon grated orange peel

  Juice of 1 medium orange

  Chopped toasted pecans*

*To toast pecans, spread in single layer in small skillet. Cook and stir over medium heat 1 to 2 minutes or until nuts are lightly browned.

Combine potatoes, brown sugar, butter, cinnamon, vanilla, salt, nutmeg, orange peel and juice in **CROCK-POT®** slow cooker; stir to blend. Cover; cook on LOW 4 hours or on HIGH 2 hours. Sprinkle with pecans.

Makes 8 servings

Red Hot Applesauce

10 to 12 apples, peeled, cored and chopped

¾ cup hot cinnamon candies

½ cup apple juice or water

  Lemon peel twist (optional)

  Sprig fresh mint (optional)

Combine apples, candies and apple juice in **CROCK-POT®** slow cooker. Cover; cook on LOW 7 to 8 hours or on HIGH 4 hours or until desired consistency. Garnish with lemon peel and mint.

Makes 6 servings

Simmered Napa Cabbage with Dried Apricots

4 cups napa cabbage or green cabbage, cored, cleaned and thinly sliced

1 cup chopped dried apricots

¼ cup clover honey

2 tablespoons orange juice

½ cup dry red wine

Salt and black pepper

Grated orange peel (optional)

1. Combine cabbage and apricots in **CROCK-POT**® slow cooker; stir to blend.

2. Combine honey and orange juice in small bowl; stir until smooth. Drizzle over cabbage. Add wine. Cover; cook on LOW 5 to 6 hours or on HIGH 2 to 3 hours.

3. Season with salt and pepper. Garnish with orange peel.

Makes 4 servings

Swiss Cheese Scalloped Potatoes

2 pounds baking potatoes, thinly sliced

½ cup finely chopped yellow onion

¼ teaspoon salt

¼ teaspoon ground nutmeg

2 tablespoons butter, cut into small pieces

½ cup milk

2 tablespoons all-purpose flour

¾ cup (3 ounces) shredded Swiss cheese

¼ cup finely chopped green onions

1. Layer half of potatoes, ¼ cup onion, ⅛ teaspoon salt, ⅛ teaspoon nutmeg and 1 tablespoon butter in **CROCK-POT**® slow cooker. Repeat layers. Cover; cook on LOW 7 hours or on HIGH 4 hours.

2. Remove potatoes with slotted spoon to serving dish; keep warm.

3. Stir milk into flour in small bowl until smooth; whisk into cooking liquid. Stir in cheese. Cover; cook on HIGH 10 minutes or until slightly thickened. Stir; pour cheese mixture over potatoes. Sprinkle with green onions.

Makes 5 to 6 servings

Lemon Cauliflower

1 tablespoon butter

3 cloves garlic, minced

½ cup water

2 tablespoons lemon juice

6 cups (about 1 ½ pounds) cauliflower florets

4 tablespoons chopped fresh Italian parsley, divided

½ teaspoon grated lemon peel

¼ cup grated Parmesan cheese

Lemon wedges (optional)

1. Heat butter in small saucepan over medium heat. Add garlic; cook and stir 2 to 3 minutes or until soft. Stir in water and lemon juice.

2. Combine garlic mixture, cauliflower, 1 tablespoon parsley and lemon peel in **CROCK-POT**® slow cooker; stir to blend. Cover; cook on LOW 4 hours.

3. Sprinkle with remaining 3 tablespoons parsley and cheese before serving. Garnish with lemon wedges.

Makes 6 servings

Mexican-Style Spinach

3 packages (10 ounces *each*) frozen chopped spinach

1 tablespoon canola oil

1 onion, chopped

1 clove garlic, minced

2 Anaheim chiles, roasted, peeled and minced*

3 fresh tomatillos, roasted, husks removed and chopped**

6 tablespoons sour cream (optional)

*To roast chiles, heat large heavy skillet over medium-high heat. Add chiles; cook and turn until blackened all over. Place chiles in brown paper bag 2 to 5 minutes. Remove chiles from bag; scrape off charred skin. Cut off top and pull out core. Slice lengthwise; scrape off veins and any remaining seeds with a knife.

**To roast tomatillos, heat large heavy skillet over medium heat. Add tomatillos with papery husks; cook 10 minutes or until husks are brown and interior flesh is soft. Remove and discard husks when cool enough to handle.

1. Place spinach in **CROCK-POT**® slow cooker. Heat oil in large skillet over medium heat. Add onion and garlic; cook and stir 5 minutes or until onion is tender. Add chiles and tomatillos; cook 3 to 4 minutes. Remove onion mixture to **CROCK-POT**® slow cooker.

2. Cover; cook on LOW 4 to 6 hours. Serve with sour cream, if desired.

Makes 6 servings

Coconut-Lime Sweet Potatoes with Walnuts

2½ pounds sweet potatoes, cut into 1-inch pieces

8 ounces shredded carrots

¾ cup shredded coconut, toasted and divided*

3 tablespoons sugar

1 tablespoon butter, melted

½ teaspoon salt

3 tablespoons walnuts, toasted and coarsely chopped**

2 teaspoons grated lime peel

*To toast coconut, spread evenly on ungreased baking sheet. Toast in preheated 350°F oven 5 to 7 minutes or until light golden brown, stirring occasionally.

**To toast walnuts, spread in single layer in small skillet. Cook and stir over medium heat 1 to 2 minutes or until nuts are lightly browned.

1. Combine potatoes, carrots, ½ cup coconut, sugar, butter and salt in **CROCK-POT®** slow cooker. Cover; cook on LOW 5 to 6 hours. Remove to large bowl.

2. Mash potatoes with potato masher. Stir in walnuts and lime peel. Sprinkle with remaining ¼ cup coconut.

Makes 8 servings

Lemon and Tangerine Glazed Carrots

6 cups sliced carrots

1½ cups apple juice

6 tablespoons (¾ stick) butter

¼ cup packed brown sugar

2 tablespoons grated lemon peel

2 tablespoons grated tangerine peel

½ teaspoon salt

Chopped fresh Italian parsley (optional)

Combine carrots, apple juice, butter, brown sugar, lemon peel, tangerine peel and salt in **CROCK-POT®** slow cooker; stir to blend. Cover; cook on LOW 4 to 5 hours or on HIGH 1 to 3 hours. Garnish with parsley.

Makes 10 to 12 servings

Blue Cheese Potatoes

2 pounds red potatoes, peeled and cut into ½-inch pieces

1¼ cups chopped green onions, divided

2 tablespoons olive oil, divided

1 teaspoon dried basil

½ teaspoon salt

¼ teaspoon black pepper

½ cup crumbled blue cheese

1. Layer potatoes, 1 cup green onions, 1 tablespoon oil, basil, salt and pepper in **CROCK-POT®** slow cooker. Cover; cook on LOW 7 hours or on HIGH 4 hours.

2. Gently stir in cheese and remaining 1 tablespoon oil. Cover; cook on HIGH 5 minutes. Remove potatoes to large serving platter; top with remaining ¼ cup green onions.

Makes 5 servings

Red Cabbage and Apples

1 small head red cabbage, cored and thinly sliced

3 medium apples, peeled and grated

¾ cup sugar

½ cup red wine vinegar

1 teaspoon ground cloves

1 cup bacon, crisp-cooked and crumbled (optional)

Fresh apple slices (optional)

Combine cabbage, grated apples, sugar, vinegar and cloves in **CROCK-POT®** slow cooker; stir to blend. Cover; cook on HIGH 6 hours, stirring after 3 hours. Sprinkle with bacon, if desired, and garnish with apple slices.

Makes 4 to 6 servings

Escalloped Corn

2 tablespoons butter	½ teaspoon salt
½ cup chopped onion	½ teaspoon dried thyme
3 tablespoons all-purpose flour	¼ teaspoon black pepper
1 cup milk	⅛ teaspoon ground nutmeg
4 cups frozen corn, divided	Sprigs fresh thyme (optional)

1. Melt butter in medium saucepan over medium heat. Add onion; cook and stir 5 minutes or until tender. Add flour; cook and stir 1 minute. Stir in milk. Bring to a boil; cook and stir 1 minute or until thickened.

2. Add 2 cups corn to food processor or blender; process until coarsely chopped. Combine milk mixture, chopped and remaining whole corn, salt, dried thyme, pepper and nutmeg in **CROCK-POT®** slow cooker; stir to blend.

3. Cover; cook on LOW 3½ to 4 hours or until mixture is bubbly around edge. Garnish with fresh thyme.

Makes 6 servings

Cheesy Cauliflower

3 pounds cauliflower florets

¼ cup water

5 tablespoons unsalted butter

1 cup finely chopped onion

6 tablespoons all-purpose flour

¼ teaspoon dry mustard

2 cups milk

2 cups (8 ounces) shredded sharp Cheddar cheese

Salt and black pepper

1. Coat inside of **CROCK-POT**® slow cooker with nonstick cooking spray. Add cauliflower and water.

2. Melt butter in medium saucepan over medium-high heat. Add onion; cook 4 to 5 minutes or until slightly softened. Add flour and dry mustard; cook and stir 3 minutes or until well combined. Whisk in milk until smooth. Bring to a boil; cook 1 to 2 minutes or until thickened. Stir in cheese, salt and pepper; cook and stir until cheese is melted. Pour cheese mixture over top of cauliflower in **CROCK-POT**® slow cooker. Cover; cook on LOW 4 to 4½ hours.

Makes 8 to 10 servings

French Carrot Medley

2 cups fresh or frozen sliced carrots

¾ cup unsweetened orange juice

1 can (4 ounces) sliced mushrooms, undrained

4 stalks celery, sliced

2 tablespoons chopped onion

½ teaspoon dried dill weed

Salt and black pepper (optional)

¼ cup cold water

2 teaspoons cornstarch

1. Combine all ingredients except water and cornstarch in **CROCK-POT**® slow cooker. Cover; cook on LOW 3 to 4 hours or on HIGH 2 hours.

2. Stir water into cornstarch in small bowl until smooth; whisk into cooking liquid. Cover; cook on HIGH 15 minutes or until sauce has thickened. Spoon sauce over vegetable mixture before serving.

Makes 6 servings

Buttery Vegetable Gratin

- 3 leeks (white and light green parts only), halved lengthwise and cut into 1-inch pieces
- 1 large red bell pepper, cut into ¾-inch-thick slices
- 5 tablespoons butter, softened, divided
- ¼ cup grated Parmesan cheese
- 1 teaspoon chopped fresh thyme
- ¾ teaspoon salt
- ⅜ teaspoon black pepper
- 2 large zucchini (about 1½ pounds *total*), cut into ¾-inch-thick slices
- 2 large yellow squash (about 1½ pounds *total*), cut into ¾-inch-thick slices
- 1½ cups fresh bread crumbs

1. Coat inside of **CROCK-POT**® slow cooker with nonstick cooking spray. Place leeks and bell pepper in bottom of **CROCK-POT**®slow cooker. Dot with 1 tablespoon butter, 1 tablespoon cheese, ½ teaspoon thyme, ¼ teaspoon salt and ⅛ teaspoon black pepper.

2. Arrange zucchini in single layer over leeks, overlapping as necessary. Dot with 1 tablespoon butter, 1 tablespoon cheese, remaining ½ teaspoon thyme, ¼ teaspoon salt and ⅛ teaspoon black pepper.

3. Arrange yellow squash over zucchini, overlapping as necessary. Dot with 1 tablespoon butter, remaining 2 tablespoons cheese, ¼ teaspoon salt and ⅛ teaspoon black pepper. Cover; cook on LOW 4 to 5 hours or until vegetables are soft.

4. Meanwhile, melt remaining 2 tablespoons butter in large skillet over medium-high heat. Add bread crumbs; cook and stir 6 minutes or until crisp and golden brown. Remove to medium bowl; set aside to cool. Sprinkle over vegetable gratin just before serving.

Makes 12 servings

Southwestern Corn and Beans

1 tablespoon olive oil

1 large onion, chopped

1 or 2 jalapeño peppers, diced*

1 clove garlic, minced

2 cans (about 15 ounces *each*) red kidney beans, rinsed and drained

1 bag (16 ounces) frozen corn

1 can (about 14 ounces) diced tomatoes

1 green bell pepper, cut into 1-inch pieces

2 teaspoons chili powder

½ teaspoon salt

½ teaspoon ground cumin

½ teaspoon black pepper

Sour cream or plain yogurt (optional)

Sliced black olives (optional)

*Jalapeño peppers can sting and irritate the skin, so wear rubber gloves when handling peppers and do not touch your eyes.

1. Heat oil in medium skillet over medium heat. Add onion, jalapeño peppers and garlic; cook and stir 5 minutes. Combine onion mixture, beans, corn, tomatoes, bell pepper, chili powder, salt, cumin and black pepper in **CROCK-POT**® slow cooker; stir to blend. Cover; cook on LOW 7 to 8 hours or on HIGH 2 to 3 hours.

2. Serve with sour cream and black olives, if desired.

Makes 6 servings

Serving Suggestion: Spoon this colorful vegetarian dish into hollowed-out bell peppers or bread bowls.

Cheesy Mashed Potato Casserole

4 pounds Yukon Gold potatoes, cut into 1-inch pieces

2 cups vegetable broth

3 tablespoons butter, cubed

2 cups (8 ounces) shredded sharp Cheddar cheese, plus additional for garnish

½ cup milk, heated

⅓ cup sour cream

½ teaspoon salt

¼ teaspoon black pepper

Chopped fresh Italian parsley (optional)

1. Coat inside of **CROCK-POT**® slow cooker with nonstick cooking spray. Add potatoes and broth; dot with butter. Cover; cook on LOW 4½ to 5 hours.

2. Mash potatoes with potato masher; stir in 2 cups cheese, milk, sour cream, salt and pepper until cheese is melted. Garnish with additional cheese and parsley.

Makes 10 to 12 servings

Creamy Red Pepper Polenta

6 cups boiling water

2 cups yellow cornmeal

1 small red bell pepper, finely chopped

¼ cup (½ stick) butter, melted

2 teaspoons salt

¼ teaspoon paprika, plus additional for garnish

⅛ teaspoon ground red pepper

⅛ teaspoon ground cumin

Combine water, cornmeal, bell pepper, butter, salt, ¼ teaspoon paprika, ground red pepper and cumin in **CROCK-POT**® slow cooker; stir to blend. Cover; cook on LOW 3 to 4 hours or on HIGH 1 to 2 hours, stirring occasionally. Garnish with additional paprika.

Makes 4 to 6 servings

Orange-Spiced Glazed Carrots

1 package (32 ounces) baby carrots
½ cup packed brown sugar
½ cup orange juice
3 tablespoons butter
¾ teaspoon ground cinnamon

¼ teaspoon ground nutmeg
¼ cup cold water
2 tablespoons cornstarch
Orange peel (optional)

1. Combine carrots, brown sugar, orange juice, butter, cinnamon and nutmeg in **CROCK-POT**® slow cooker. Cover; cook on LOW 3½ to 4 hours or until carrots are crisp-tender.

2. Spoon carrots into large serving bowl; keep warm. Turn **CROCK-POT**® slow cooker to HIGH.

3. Stir water into cornstarch in small bowl until smooth; whisk into cooking liquid. Cover; cook on HIGH 15 minutes or until thickened. Spoon over carrots. Garnish with orange peel.

Makes 6 servings

Garden Potatoes

1¼ pounds baking potatoes, sliced
1 small green or red bell pepper, thinly sliced
¼ cup finely chopped yellow onion
2 tablespoons butter, divided
½ teaspoon salt

½ teaspoon dried thyme
Black pepper
1 small yellow squash, thinly sliced
1 cup (4 ounces) shredded sharp Cheddar cheese
Chopped fresh chives

1. Combine potatoes, bell pepper, onion, 1 tablespoon butter, salt, thyme and black pepper in **CROCK-POT**® slow cooker; stir to blend. Evenly layer squash over potato mixture; add remaining 1 tablespoon butter. Cover; cook on LOW 7 hours or on HIGH 4 hours.

2. Remove potato mixture to serving bowl. Sprinkle with cheese; let stand 2 to 3 minutes or until cheese is melted. Sprinkle with chives.

Makes 5 servings

Lemon Dilled Parsnips and Turnips

4 turnips, peeled and cut into ½-inch pieces
3 parsnips, cut into ½-inch pieces
2 cups chicken broth
¼ cup chopped green onions
¼ cup dried dill weed
¼ cup lemon juice
1 teaspoon minced garlic
¼ cup cold water
¼ cup cornstarch

1. Combine turnips, parsnips, broth, green onions, dill, lemon juice and garlic in **CROCK-POT®** slow cooker; stir to blend. Cover; cook on LOW 3 to 4 hours or on HIGH 1 to 3 hours.

2. Stir water into cornstarch in small bowl until smooth; whisk into **CROCK-POT®** slow cooker. Cover; cook on HIGH 15 minutes or until thickened.

Makes 10 servings

Slow-Good Apples and Carrots

6 carrots, sliced into ½-inch slices
4 apples, peeled, cored and sliced
¼ cup plus 1 tablespoon all-purpose flour
1 tablespoon packed brown sugar
½ teaspoon ground nutmeg
1 tablespoon butter, cubed
½ cup orange juice

Layer carrots and apples in **CROCK-POT®** slow cooker. Combine flour, brown sugar and nutmeg in small bowl; sprinkle over carrots and apples. Dot with butter; pour in orange juice. Cover; cook on LOW 3½ to 4 hours or until carrots are crisp-tender.

Makes 6 servings

SWEET TREATS

Triple Chocolate Fantasy

2 pounds white almond bark, broken into pieces

1 bar (4 ounces) sweetened chocolate, broken into pieces*

1 package (12 ounces) semisweet chocolate chips

2 cups coarsely chopped pecans, toasted**

*Use your favorite high-quality chocolate candy bar.

**To toast pecans, spread in single layer in heavy skillet. Cook and stir over medium heat 1 to 2 minutes or until nuts are lightly browned.

1. Line mini muffin pan with paper baking cups. Place bark, sweetened chocolate and chocolate chips in **CROCK-POT**® slow cooker. Cover; cook on HIGH 1 hour. *Do not stir.*

2. Turn **CROCK-POT**® slow cooker to LOW. Cover; cook on LOW 1 hour, stirring every 15 minutes. Stir in pecans.

3. Drop mixture by tablespoonfuls into prepared baking cups; cool completely. Store in tightly covered container.

Makes 36 pieces

Variations: In addition to or instead of the pecans, try adding raisins, crushed peppermint candy, candy-coated baking bits, crushed toffee, peanuts or pistachio nuts, chopped gum drops, chopped dried fruit, candied cherries, chopped marshmallows or sweetened coconut to the chocolate mixture.

Pineapple Daiquiri Sundae Topping

1 pineapple, peeled, cored and cut into ½-inch chunks

½ cup sugar

½ cup dark rum

3 tablespoons lime juice

Peel of 2 limes, cut into long strips

1 tablespoon cornstarch

Ice cream, pound cake or shortcake

Fresh raspberries (optional)

1. Combine pineapple, sugar, rum, lime juice, lime peel and cornstarch in 1½-quart **CROCK-POT®** "No Dial" slow cooker; stir to blend. Cover; heat 3 to 4 hours.

2. Serve hot over ice cream, pound cake or shortcake. Garnish with raspberries.

Makes 4 to 6 servings

Decadent Chocolate Delight

1 package (about 15 ounces) chocolate cake mix

1 container (8 ounces) sour cream

1 cup semisweet chocolate chips

1 cup water

4 eggs

½ cup vegetable oil

1 package (4-serving size) instant chocolate pudding and pie filling mix

Vanilla ice cream (optional)

1. Coat inside of **CROCK-POT®** slow cooker with nonstick cooking spray.

2. Beat cake mix, sour cream, chocolate chips, water, eggs, oil and pie filling mix in medium bowl with electric mixer 5 minutes or until well blended. Remove to **CROCK-POT®** slow cooker.

3. Cover; cook on LOW 3 to 4 hours or on HIGH 1½ to 1¾ hours. Serve warm with ice cream, if desired.

Makes 12 servings

Cran-Cherry Bread Pudding

1½ cups light cream

3 egg yolks, beaten

⅓ cup sugar

¼ teaspoon salt

1½ teaspoons cherry extract

⅔ cup dried sweetened cranberries

⅔ cup golden raisins

½ cup whole candied red cherries, halved

½ cup dry sherry

9 cups unseasoned stuffing mix

1 cup white chocolate baking chips

Whipped cream (optional)

1. Prepare foil handles by tearing off three 18×2-inch strips heavy foil or use regular foil folded to double thickness. Crisscross foil strips in spoke design; place in **CROCK-POT**® slow cooker. Coat 2-quart baking dish that fits inside of **CROCK-POT**® slow cooker with nonstick cooking spray.

2. Combine cream, egg yolks, sugar and salt in medium heavy saucepan. Heat over medium heat until mixture coats back of spoon. Remove from heat. Set saucepan in bowl of ice water; stir to cool. Stir in cherry extract. Remove to large bowl; press plastic wrap onto surface of custard. Refrigerate.

3. Combine cranberries, raisins and cherries in small bowl. Heat sherry in small saucepan until warm. Pour over fruit; let stand 10 minutes.

4. Fold stuffing mix and baking chips into custard. Drain fruit, reserving sherry; stir into custard. Pour into prepared dish. Top with reserved sherry; cover tightly with foil. Place on foil handles in **CROCK-POT**® slow cooker. Add water to come 1 inch up side of dish.

5. Cover; cook on LOW 3½ to 5½ hours or until pudding springs back when touched. Remove dish using foil handles. Uncover; let stand 10 minutes. Serve warm with whipped cream, if desired.

Makes 12 servings

Bittersweet Chocolate-Espresso Crème Brûlée

½ **cup chopped bittersweet chocolate**

5 **egg yolks**

1½ **cups whipping cream**

½ **cup granulated sugar**

¼ **cup espresso**

¼ **cup Demerara or raw sugar**

1. Arrange five 6-ounce ramekins or custard cups inside of **CROCK-POT®** slow cooker. Pour enough water to come halfway up sides of ramekins (taking care to keep water out of ramekins). Divide chocolate among ramekins.

2. Whisk egg yolks in small bowl; set aside. Heat small saucepan over medium heat. Add cream, granulated sugar and espresso; cook and stir until mixture begins to boil. Pour hot cream in thin, steady stream into egg yolks, whisking constantly. Pour through fine mesh strainer into clean bowl.

3. Ladle into prepared ramekins over chocolate. Cover; cook on HIGH 1 to 2 hours or until custard is set around edges but still soft in centers. Carefully remove ramekins; cool to room temperature. Cover; refrigerate until ready to serve.

4. Preheat broiler. Place ramekins on baking sheet; sprinkle Demerara sugar over custards. Broil 4 inches from heat 1 minute or until sugar begins to bubble and turns golden brown. Serve immediately.

Makes 5 servings

Chocolate Orange Fondue

½ cup whipping cream

1½ tablespoons butter

6 ounces 60 to 70% bittersweet chocolate, coarsely chopped

⅓ cup orange liqueur

¾ teaspoon vanilla

   Marshmallows, strawberries and cubes pound cake

1. Bring cream and butter to a boil in medium saucepan over medium heat. Remove from heat. Stir in chocolate, liqueur and vanilla until chocolate is melted. Place over medium-low heat; cook and stir 2 minutes until smooth.

2. Coat inside of **CROCK-POT**® "No-Dial" slow cooker with nonstick cooking spray. Fill with warm fondue. Serve with marshmallows, strawberries and pound cake.

Makes 1½ cups

Pineapple Rice Pudding

1 can (20 ounces) crushed pineapple in juice, undrained

1 can (13½ ounces) unsweetened coconut milk

1 can (12 ounces) evaporated milk

¾ cup uncooked Arborio rice

2 eggs, lightly beaten

¼ cup granulated sugar

¼ cup packed brown sugar

½ teaspoon ground cinnamon

¼ teaspoon salt

¼ teaspoon ground nutmeg

   Toasted coconut and pineapple slices (optional)*

   Pineapple slices (optional)

*To toast coconut, spread in single layer in small heavy-bottomed skillet. Cook and stir over medium heat 1 to 2 minutes or until lightly browned. Remove from skillet immediately.

1. Combine crushed pineapple with juice, coconut milk, evaporated milk, rice, eggs, granulated sugar, brown sugar, cinnamon, salt and nutmeg in **CROCK-POT**® slow cooker; stir to blend. Cover; cook on HIGH 3 to 4 hours or until thickened and rice is tender.

2. Stir to blend. Serve warm or chilled. Garnish with toasted coconut and pineapple slices.

Makes 8 servings

Fudge and Cream Pudding Cake

2 tablespoons butter

1 cup all-purpose flour

½ cup packed light brown sugar

5 tablespoons unsweetened cocoa powder, divided

2 teaspoons baking powder

½ teaspoon ground cinnamon

⅛ teaspoon salt

1 cup whipping cream

1 tablespoon vegetable oil

1 teaspoon vanilla

1½ cups hot water

½ cup packed dark brown sugar

Whipped cream (optional)

1. Prepare foil handles by tearing off three 18×2-inch strips heavy foil or use regular foil folded to double thickness. Crisscross foil strips in spoke design; place in **CROCK-POT**® slow cooker. Coat inside of 5-quart **CROCK-POT**® slow cooker with butter.

2. Combine flour, light brown sugar, 3 tablespoons cocoa, baking powder, cinnamon and salt in medium bowl. Add cream, oil and vanilla; stir to blend. Pour batter into **CROCK-POT**® slow cooker.

3. Combine hot water, dark brown sugar and remaining 2 tablespoons cocoa in medium bowl; stir well. Pour sauce over cake batter. *Do not stir.* Cover; cook on HIGH 2 hours. Turn off heat. Let stand 10 minutes. Remove with foil handles to wire rack. Cut into wedges to serve. Serve with whipped cream, if desired.

Makes 8 to 10 servings

Pumpkin Bread Pudding

- 2 cups whole milk
- ½ cup (1 stick) plus 2 tablespoons butter, divided
- 1 cup packed brown sugar, divided
- 1 cup canned solid-pack pumpkin
- 3 eggs
- 1 tablespoon ground cinnamon

- 2 teaspoons vanilla
- ½ teaspoon ground nutmeg
- ¼ teaspoon salt
- 16 slices cinnamon raisin bread, torn into small pieces (8 cups *total*)
- ½ cup whipping cream
- 2 tablespoons bourbon (optional)

1. Coat inside of **CROCK-POT**® slow cooker with nonstick cooking spray. Combine milk and 2 tablespoons butter in medium microwavable bowl. Microwave on HIGH 2½ to 3 minutes or until very warm.

2. Whisk ½ cup brown sugar, pumpkin, eggs, cinnamon, vanilla, nutmeg and salt in large bowl until well blended. Whisk in milk mixture until blended. Add bread pieces; toss to coat. Spoon into **CROCK-POT**® slow cooker.

3. Cover; cook on HIGH 2 hours or until knife inserted into center comes out clean. Turn off heat. Uncover; let stand 15 minutes.

4. Combine remaining ½ cup butter, remaining ½ cup brown sugar and cream in small saucepan; bring to a boil over high heat, stirring frequently. Remove from heat. Stir in bourbon, if desired. Spoon bread pudding into individual bowls; top with sauce.

Makes 8 servings

Rustic Peach-Oat Crumble

8 cups frozen sliced peaches, thawed and juice reserved

¾ cup packed brown sugar, divided

1½ tablespoons cornstarch

1 tablespoon lemon juice (optional)

1½ teaspoons vanilla

½ teaspoon almond extract

1 cup quick oats

¼ cup all-purpose flour

¼ cup granulated sugar

1 teaspoon ground cinnamon

¼ teaspoon salt

½ cup (1 stick) cold butter, cubed

1. Coat inside of 5-quart **CROCK-POT**® slow cooker with nonstick cooking spray. Combine peaches with juice, ½ cup brown sugar, cornstarch, lemon juice, if desired, vanilla and almond extract in large bowl; toss to coat. Spoon into **CROCK-POT**® slow cooker.

2. Combine oats, flour, remaining ¼ cup brown sugar, granulated sugar, cinnamon and salt in medium bowl. Cut in butter with pastry blender or two knives until mixture resembles coarse crumbs. Sprinkle over peaches. Cover; cook on HIGH 1½ hours or until bubbly at edge. Remove stoneware to wire rack; let cool 20 minutes.

Makes about 8 servings

Rocky Road Brownie Bottoms

½ cup packed brown sugar

½ cup water

2 tablespoons unsweetened cocoa powder

2½ cups packaged brownie mix

1 package (4-serving size) instant chocolate pudding and pie filling mix

½ cup milk chocolate chips

2 eggs, beaten

3 tablespoons butter, melted

2 cups mini marshmallows

1 cup chopped pecans or walnuts, toasted*

½ cup chocolate syrup

*To toast pecans, spread in single layer on small baking sheet. Bake in preheated 350°F oven 5 to 7 minutes or until fragrant, stirring frequently.

1. Prepare foil handles by tearing off three 18×2-inch strips heavy foil or use regular foil folded to double thickness. Crisscross foil strips in spoke design; place in **CROCK-POT®** slow cooker. Coat inside of **CROCK-POT®** slow cooker with nonstick cooking spray.

2. Combine brown sugar, water and cocoa in small saucepan over medium heat; bring to a boil over medium-high heat. Meanwhile, combine brownie mix, pudding mix, chocolate chips, eggs and butter in medium bowl; stir until well blended. Spread batter in **CROCK-POT®** slow cooker; pour boiling sugar mixture over batter.

3. Cover; cook on HIGH 1½ hours. Turn off heat. Top brownies with marshmallows, pecans and chocolate syrup. Let stand 15 minutes. Use foil handles to lift brownie to serving platter.

Makes 6 servings

Spiked Sponge Cake

1 package (about 18 ounces) yellow cake mix

1 cup water

4 eggs

½ cup vegetable oil

1 tablespoon grated orange peel

1 package (6 ounces) golden raisins and cherries or other chopped dried fruit (about 1 cup)

1 cup chopped pecans

½ cup sugar

½ cup (1 stick) butter

¼ cup bourbon or apple juice

1. Coat inside of 5-quart **CROCK-POT®** slow cooker with nonstick cooking spray.

2. Combine cake mix, water, eggs and oil in large bowl; stir to blend. (Batter will be lumpy). Stir in orange peel. Pour two thirds of batter into **CROCK-POT®** slow cooker. Sprinkle dried fruit evenly over batter. Top evenly with remaining batter. Cover; cook on HIGH 1½ to 1¾ hours or until toothpick inserted into center comes out clean.

3. Immediately remove stoneware and cool 10 minutes on wire rack. Run flat rubber spatula around edge of cake, lifting bottom slightly. Invert onto large serving plate.

4. Heat large skillet over medium-high heat. Add pecans; cook and stir 2 to 3 minutes or until pecans are golden brown. Add sugar, butter and bourbon; bring to a boil, stirring constantly. Cook 1 to 2 minutes or until sugar dissolves. Pour over cake.

Makes 8 to 10 servings

Tip: Allow breads, cakes and puddings to cool at least 5 minutes before scooping or removing them from the **CROCK-POT®** slow cooker.

Hot Fudge Cake

2 cups all-purpose flour

1½ cups packed brown sugar, divided

¼ cup plus 3 tablespoons unsweetened cocoa powder, divided, plus additional for dusting

2 teaspoons baking powder

1 teaspoon salt

1 cup milk

¼ cup (½ stick) butter, melted

1 teaspoon vanilla

3½ cups boiling water

1. Coat inside of 5-quart **CROCK-POT**® slow cooker with nonstick cooking spray. Prepare foil handles by tearing off three 18×2-inch strips heavy foil or use regular foil folded to double thickness. Crisscross foil strips in spoke design; place in **CROCK-POT**® slow cooker.

2. Mix flour, 1 cup brown sugar, 3 tablespoons cocoa, baking powder and salt in medium bowl. Add milk, butter and vanilla; stir until well blended. Pour into **CROCK-POT**® slow cooker. Blend remaining ½ cup brown sugar and ¼ cup cocoa in small bowl. Sprinkle evenly over mixture in **CROCK-POT**® slow cooker. Pour in boiling water. *Do not stir.*

3. Cover; cook on HIGH 1 to 1½ hours or until toothpick inserted into center comes out clean. Turn off heat. Let stand 10 minutes. Use foil handles to lift cake from **CROCK-POT**® slow cooker onto large serving platter. Cut into wedges to serve. Dust with additional cocoa.

Makes 6 to 8 servings

Bananas Foster

12 bananas, cut into quarters

1 cup flaked coconut

1 cup dark corn syrup

⅔ cup butter, melted

¼ cup lemon juice

2 teaspoons grated lemon peel

2 teaspoons rum

1 teaspoon ground cinnamon

½ teaspoon salt

12 slices prepared pound cake

1 quart vanilla ice cream

1. Combine bananas and coconut in **CROCK-POT**® slow cooker. Combine corn syrup, butter, lemon juice, lemon peel, rum, cinnamon and salt in medium bowl; stir to blend. Pour over bananas.

2. Cover; cook on LOW 1 to 2 hours. To serve, arrange bananas on pound cake slices. Top with ice cream and warm sauce.

Makes 12 servings

Mexican Chocolate Bread Pudding

1½ cups whipping cream

4 ounces unsweetened chocolate, coarsely chopped

½ cup currants

2 eggs, beaten

½ cup sugar

1 teaspoon vanilla

¾ teaspoon ground cinnamon, plus additional for topping

½ teaspoon ground allspice

⅛ teaspoon salt

3 cups Hawaiian-style sweet bread, challah or rich egg bread, cut into ½-inch cubes

Whipped cream (optional)

1. Heat cream in large saucepan. Add chocolate; stir until melted.

2. Combine currants, eggs, sugar, vanilla, ¾ teaspoon cinnamon, allspice and salt in medium bowl; stir to blend. Add to chocolate mixture; stir to blend. Pour into **CROCK-POT**® slow cooker.

3. Gently fold in bread cubes using plastic spatula. Cover; cook on HIGH 3 to 4 hours or until knife inserted near center comes out clean.

4. Serve warm or chilled. Top with whipped cream sprinkled with additional cinnamon, if desired.

Makes 6 to 8 servings

Mixed Berry Cobbler

- **1** package (16 ounces) frozen mixed berries
- **½** cup granulated sugar
- **2** tablespoons quick-cooking tapioca
- **2** teaspoons grated lemon peel
- **1½** cups all-purpose flour
- **½** cup packed brown sugar
- **2¼** teaspoons baking powder
- **¼** teaspoon ground nutmeg
- **½** cup milk
- **⅓** cup butter, melted
- Vanilla ice cream (optional)

1. Coat inside of **CROCK-POT**® slow cooker with nonstick cooking spray. Stir berries, granulated sugar, tapioca and lemon peel in medium bowl. Remove to **CROCK-POT**® slow cooker.

2. Combine flour, brown sugar, baking powder and nutmeg in medium bowl. Add milk and butter; stir just until blended. Drop spoonfuls of dough on top of berry mixture. Cover; cook on LOW 4 hours. Turn off heat. Uncover; let stand 30 minutes. Serve with ice cream, if desired.

Makes 8 servings

Tip: Cobblers are year-round favorites. Experiment with seasonal fresh fruits, such as pears, plums, peaches, rhubarb, blueberries, raspberries, strawberries, blackberries or gooseberries.

S'mores Fondue

- **1** pound milk chocolate, chopped
- **2** jars (7 ounces *each*) marshmallow creme
- **⅔** cup half-and-half
- **2** teaspoons vanilla
- **1** cup mini marshmallows
- Banana slices, apple slices, strawberries and/or graham crackers

1. Combine chocolate, marshmallow creme, half-and-half and vanilla in **CROCK-POT**® slow cooker. Cover; cook on LOW 1½ to 3 hours, stirring after 1 hour.

2. Sprinkle top of fondue with mini marshmallows. Serve with banana and apple slices, strawberries and graham crackers.

Makes about 4 cups

Peanut Fudge Pudding Cake

1 cup all-purpose flour	**1** teaspoon vanilla
1 cup sugar, divided	**¼** cup unsweetened cocoa powder
1½ teaspoons baking powder	**1** cup boiling water
⅔ cup milk	Chopped peanuts (optional)
½ cup peanut butter	Vanilla ice cream (optional)
2 tablespoons vegetable oil	

1. Coat inside of 5-quart **CROCK-POT®** slow cooker with nonstick cooking spray. Combine flour, ½ cup sugar and baking powder in medium bowl. Stir in milk, peanut butter, oil and vanilla until well blended. Pour batter into **CROCK-POT®** slow cooker.

2. Combine remaining ½ cup sugar and cocoa in small bowl. Stir in boiling water. Pour into **CROCK-POT®** slow cooker. *Do not stir.*

3. Cover; cook on HIGH 1¼ to 1½ hours or until toothpick inserted into center comes out clean. Turn off heat. Let stand 10 minutes. Scoop into serving dishes. Serve warm with peanuts and ice cream, if desired.

Makes 4 servings

Apple Crumble Pot

4 Granny Smith apples (about 2 pounds), cored and *each* cut into 8 wedges

1 cup packed dark brown sugar, divided

½ cup dried cranberries

1 cup plus 2 tablespoons biscuit baking mix, divided

2 tablespoons butter, cubed

1½ teaspoons ground cinnamon, plus additional for topping

1 teaspoon vanilla

¼ teaspoon ground allspice

½ cup rolled oats

3 tablespoons cold butter, cubed

½ cup chopped pecans

Whipped cream (optional)

1. Coat inside of **CROCK-POT**® slow cooker with nonstick cooking spray. Combine apples, ⅔ cup brown sugar, cranberries, 2 tablespoons baking mix, 2 tablespoons butter, 1½ teaspoons cinnamon, vanilla and allspice in **CROCK-POT**® slow cooker; toss gently to coat.

2. Combine remaining 1 cup baking mix, oats and remaining ⅓ cup brown sugar in large bowl. Cut in 3 tablespoons cold butter with pastry blender or two knives until mixture resembles coarse crumbs. Sprinkle evenly over filling in **CROCK-POT**® slow cooker. Top with pecans. Cover; cook on HIGH 2¼ hours or until apples are tender. *Do not overcook.*

3. Turn off heat. Let stand, uncovered, 15 to 30 minutes before serving. Top with whipped cream sprinkled with additional cinnamon, if desired.

Makes 6 to 8 servings

Brownie Bottoms

½ cup packed brown sugar

½ cup water

2 tablespoons unsweetened cocoa powder

2½ cups packaged brownie mix

1 package (4-serving size) instant chocolate pudding and filling mix

½ cup milk chocolate chips

2 eggs, beaten

3 tablespoons butter, melted

Whipped cream or ice cream (optional)

1. Coat inside of **CROCK-POT®** slow cooker with nonstick cooking spray. Combine brown sugar, water and cocoa in small saucepan over medium heat; bring to a boil over medium-high heat.

2. Meanwhile, combine brownie mix, pudding mix, chocolate chips, eggs and butter in medium bowl; stir until well blended. Spread batter in **CROCK-POT®** slow cooker; pour boiling sugar mixture over batter.

3. Cover; cook on HIGH 1½ hours. Turn off heat. Let stand 30 minutes. Serve with whipped cream, if desired.

Makes 6 servings

Dulce de Leche

1 can (14 ounces) sweetened condensed milk

1. Pour milk into 9×5-inch loaf pan. Cover tightly with foil. Place loaf pan in **CROCK-POT®** slow cooker. Pour enough water to reach halfway up sides of loaf pan. Cover; cook on LOW 5 to 6 hours or until golden and thickened.

2. Coat inside of **CROCK-POT®** "No-Dial" slow cooker slow cooker with nonstick cooking spray. Fill with warm dip.

Makes about 1½ cups

Italian Cheesecake

6 graham crackers, crushed to fine crumbs

2 tablespoons packed brown sugar

2 tablespoons butter, melted

2 packages (8 ounces *each*) cream cheese

1½ cups granulated sugar

1 container (15 ounces) ricotta cheese

2 cups sour cream

1 teaspoon vanilla

4 eggs

3 tablespoons all-purpose flour

3 tablespoons cornstarch

3 graham crackers, broken into 1-inch pieces (optional)

Fresh strawberries (optional)

Fresh mint (optional)

1. Prepare foil handles by tearing off three 18×2-inch strips heavy foil or use regular foil folded to double thickness. Crisscross foil strips in spoke design; place in **CROCK-POT**® slow cooker. Coat inside of 5-quart **CROCK-POT**® slow cooker with nonstick cooking spray.

2. Combine crushed graham crackers and brown sugar in medium bowl. Stir in melted butter until crumbs hold shape when pinched. Pat firmly into **CROCK-POT**® slow cooker. Refrigerate until needed.

3. Beat cream cheese and granulated sugar in large bowl with electric mixer at medium speed until smooth. Add ricotta, sour cream and vanilla; beat until blended. Add eggs, one at a time, beating well after each addition. Beat in flour and cornstarch. Pour filling into prepared crust. Cover; cook on LOW 3 to 4 hours or until cheesecake is nearly set.

4. Turn off heat. Remove lid; cover top of stoneware with clean kitchen towel. Replace lid; cool 1 hour. Remove stoneware from base; cool completely. Remove cheesecake to serving plate using foil as handle. Cover; refrigerate until ready to serve. Garnish with graham cracker pieces, strawberries and mint.

Makes 16 servings

Apple-Pecan Bread Pudding

8 cups cubed bread

3 cups Granny Smith apples, cubed

1 cup chopped pecans

8 eggs

1 can (12 ounces) evaporated milk

1 cup packed brown sugar

½ cup apple cider or apple juice

2 teaspoons ground cinnamon

1 teaspoon ground nutmeg

1 teaspoon vanilla

½ teaspoon salt

½ teaspoon ground allspice

Ice cream (optional)

Caramel sauce (optional)

1. Coat inside of **CROCK-POT**® slow cooker with nonstick cooking spray. Add bread cubes, apples and pecans.

2. Combine eggs, evaporated milk, brown sugar, apple cider, cinnamon, nutmeg, vanilla, salt and allspice in large bowl; whisk to blend. Pour into **CROCK-POT**® slow cooker. Cover; cook on LOW 3 hours. Serve with ice cream topped with caramel sauce, if desired.

Makes 8 servings

Pumpkin Custard

<table>
<tr><td>1</td><td>cup canned solid-pack pumpkin</td><td>½</td><td>teaspoon grated lemon peel</td></tr>
<tr><td>½</td><td>cup packed brown sugar</td><td>½</td><td>teaspoon ground cinnamon, plus additional for garnish</td></tr>
<tr><td>2</td><td>eggs, beaten</td><td></td><td></td></tr>
<tr><td>½</td><td>teaspoon ground ginger</td><td>1</td><td>can (12 ounces) evaporated milk</td></tr>
</table>

1. Combine pumpkin, brown sugar, eggs, ginger, lemon peel and ½ teaspoon cinnamon in large bowl. Stir in evaporated milk. Divide mixture among six ramekins or custard cups. Cover each cup tightly with foil.

2. Place ramekins in **CROCK-POT**® slow cooker. Pour water into **CROCK-POT**® slow cooker to come about ½ inch from top of ramekins. Cover; cook on LOW 4 hours.

3. Use tongs or slotted spoon to remove ramekins from **CROCK-POT**® slow cooker. Sprinkle with additional cinnamon. Serve warm.

Makes 6 servings

Variation: To make Pumpkin Custard in a single dish, pour custard into 1½-quart soufflé dish instead of ramekins. Cover with foil; place in **CROCK-POT**® slow cooker. (Place soufflé dish on two or three 18×2-inch strips of foil in **CROCK-POT**® slow cooker to make removal easier, if desired.) Add water to come 1½ inches from the top of the soufflé dish. Cover; cook as directed above.

Chocolate Hazelnut Pudding Cake

1 box (about 18 ounces) golden yellow
     cake mix

1 cup water

4 eggs

½ cup sour cream

½ cup vegetable oil

1 cup mini semisweet chocolate chips

½ cup chopped hazelnuts

    Whipped cream or ice cream (optional)

1. Coat inside of 6-quart **CROCK-POT**® slow cooker with nonstick cooking spray. Combine cake mix, water, eggs, sour cream and oil in large bowl; stir until smooth. Pour batter into **CROCK-POT**® slow cooker. Cover; cook on HIGH 2 hours or until batter is nearly set.

2. Sprinkle with chocolate chips and hazelnuts. Cover; cook on HIGH 30 minutes or until toothpick inserted into center comes out clean or cake begins to pull away from side of **CROCK-POT**® slow cooker. Turn off heat. Let stand until cooled slightly. Slice or spoon out while warm. Serve with whipped cream, if desired.

Makes 10 servings

Cherry Delight

1 can (21 ounces) cherry pie filling

1 package (about 18 ounces) yellow
     cake mix

½ cup (1 stick) butter, melted

⅓ cup chopped walnuts

Place pie filling in **CROCK-POT**® slow cooker. Combine cake mix and butter in medium bowl. Spread evenly over pie filling. Sprinkle with walnuts. Cover; cook on LOW 3 to 4 hours or on HIGH 1½ to 2 hours.

Makes 8 to 10 servings

Caribbean Sweet Potato and Bean Stew
(page 160)

METRIC CONVERSION CHART

VOLUME MEASUREMENTS (dry)

$1/8$ teaspoon = 0.5 mL
$1/4$ teaspoon = 1 mL
$1/2$ teaspoon = 2 mL
$3/4$ teaspoon = 4 mL
1 teaspoon = 5 mL
1 tablespoon = 15 mL
2 tablespoons = 30 mL
$1/4$ cup = 60 mL
$1/3$ cup = 75 mL
$1/2$ cup = 125 mL
$2/3$ cup = 150 mL
$3/4$ cup = 175 mL
1 cup = 250 mL
2 cups = 1 pint = 500 mL
3 cups = 750 mL
4 cups = 1 quart = 1 L

VOLUME MEASUREMENTS (fluid)

1 fluid ounce (2 tablespoons) = 30 mL
4 fluid ounces ($1/2$ cup) = 125 mL
8 fluid ounces (1 cup) = 250 mL
12 fluid ounces ($1 1/2$ cups) = 375 mL
16 fluid ounces (2 cups) = 500 mL

WEIGHTS (mass)

$1/2$ ounce = 15 g
1 ounce = 30 g
3 ounces = 90 g
4 ounces = 120 g
8 ounces = 225 g
10 ounces = 285 g
12 ounces = 360 g
16 ounces = 1 pound = 450 g

DIMENSIONS

$1/16$ inch = 2 mm
$1/8$ inch = 3 mm
$1/4$ inch = 6 mm
$1/2$ inch = 1.5 cm
$3/4$ inch = 2 cm
1 inch = 2.5 cm

OVEN TEMPERATURES

250°F = 120°C
275°F = 140°C
300°F = 150°C
325°F = 160°C
350°F = 180°C
375°F = 190°C
400°F = 200°C
425°F = 220°C
450°F = 230°C

BAKING PAN SIZES

Utensil	Size in Inches/Quarts	Metric Volume	Size in Centimeters
Baking or Cake Pan (square or rectangular)	8×8×2	2 L	20×20×5
	9×9×2	2.5 L	23×23×5
	12×8×2	3 L	30×20×5
	13×9×2	3.5 L	33×23×5
Loaf Pan	8×4×3	1.5 L	20×10×7
	9×5×3	2 L	23×13×7
Round Layer Cake Pan	8×1½	1.2 L	20×4
	9×1½	1.5 L	23×4
Pie Plate	8×1¼	750 mL	20×3
	9×1¼	1 L	23×3
Baking Dish or Casserole	1 quart	1 L	—
	1½ quart	1.5 L	—
	2 quart	2 L	—